Freeman's
Arrival

Freeman's
Arrival

Est. 2015

Edited by

John Freeman

Grove Press UK

First published in the United States of America in 2015 by Grove/Atlantic Inc.

First published in Great Britain in 2015 by Grove Press UK, an imprint of Grove/Atlantic Inc.

1 3 5 7 9   8 6 4 2

A CIP record for this book is available from the British Library.

Grove Press, UK
Ormond House
26–27 Boswell Street
London
WC1N 3JZ

www.groveatlantic.com

ISBN 978 1 61185 541 8
Ebook ISBN 978 1 61185 962 1

Printed in Great Britain by Bell and Bain Ltd, Glasgow

Published in collaboration with the MFA in Creative Writing at The New School

THE NEW SCHOOL
CREATIVE WRITING

Cover and interior design by Michael Salu

Contents

Introduction
John Freeman............................. vii

Six Shorts
    Louise Erdrich 1
    Kamila Shamsie...................... 7
    Sjón 10
    Colum McCann 15
    David Mitchell........................ 19
    Daniel Galera........................ 22

Drive My Car
Haruki Murakami........................ 27

In Search of Space Lost
Aleksandar Hemon 65

When This Happens
Ghassan Zaqtan 79

Mellow
Etgar Keret................................. 83

SAPPHO DRIVES UPSTATE (FR. 2)
Anne Carson 91

Garments
Tahmima Anam 93

Arizona
Helen Simpson 109

Windfall
Ishion Hutchinson 127

Black and Blue
Garnette Cadogan 129

The Dog
Laura van den Berg 145

The Last Road North
Barry Lopez & Ben Huff..........insert

On a Morning
Fatin Abbas 155

The Nod
Michael Salu 205

The Mogul Gardens Near Mah, 1962
Honor Moore 215

The Fork
Dave Eggers 219

On Learning Norwegian
Lydia Davis............................. 225

Contributor Notes..................... 283

Introduction

JOHN FREEMAN

Twenty-five years ago, I took a flight from Philadelphia to Syracuse with my mother on a regional airline that has since gone out of business. Not long into our journey, we encountered a thunderstorm. The plane was a tiny turboprop number, where you stoop to enter, luggage compartments no bigger than a bread box. Before the weather hit, it had felt cozy, like flying in a child's toy. Then the aircraft began to dip and dive, at first gently, then, as the storm worsened, abruptly, even violently. I was a teenager, mortality but a rumor, so while my mother laughed nervously and gripped the armrest, I did what I would never do today: I leaned across her seat and looked out the window with excitement.

The sky was a deep, midnight blue, so vast it felt like the plane, our lives, were simply ideas inside the head of a much larger being. Veins of lightning lit up the night every few seconds, forking and connecting. I had seen pictures of brain scans, and I was struck by the visual similarity between an August lightning storm and how the mind works through series of electrical pulses: messages bouncing from one cell to the next, carrying dreams and shadows, bits of information to be reassembled into something that can be called thought. *Oh, John*, my mother said, *I really don't like this*.

Eventually, my mother's fear took over and I became very afraid. We held hands for the rest of the trip, which must have been short, but now feels endless. We had dressed for the flight, as you did then, and I sweated through my seersucker suit. It suddenly felt ominous, vain and foolish to have dandied up for something so obviously full of risk. I even pictured scraps of our clothes scattered over a mountainside in the Adirondacks.

Eventually, thankfully, we left the storm, our hands glued to one another, and landed in a light drizzle in Syracuse. I will never forget how exhilarating it was to be welcomed back into gravity's gentler embrace. Standing on the slick corrugated metal gangway. The air creamy and ionized. The familiar mulchy scents of upstate New York. A huge smile of relief on my mother's face when her feet touched the tarmac. I had never seen her frightened.

Every time I read, I look to re-create the feeling of arriving that day. Very little in the world that is interesting happens without risk, movement, and wonder. Yet to live constantly in this state—or even for the duration of a flight—is untenable. We need habits for comfort, and safety for sanity. For the lucky among us, though, who can make this choice rather than have it made for us, a departing flight to the edges perpetually sits on the tarmac, propellers turning, luggage loaded. It lives in the pages of books. The Greek word for porter, John Berger reminds, is "metaphor." Stories and essays, even the right kind of poem, will take us somewhere else, put us down somewhere new.

The journal you hold in your hands is an experiment in re-creating the elemental feel of that journey. It would be traditional at this point for me to explain why *Freeman's* needs to exist: to gripe or complain, to slight fellow travelers, to declare an aesthetic manifesto, or to apologize for bringing more. I won't do that. Any true reader always wants more—more life, more experiences, more risk than one's own life can contain. The hard thing, perhaps, is where to find it in one place. My hope is that, two times a year, *Freeman's* can bring that to you in this form: a collection of writing grouped loosely around a theme. A collection of writing that will carry you.

Several writers in this first issue are visitors, rather than travelers, in far-flung places, and discover the difference in this distinction. David Mitchell feels what he perceives to be a ghost, lingering over his bed in a small house in Hiroshima Prefecture, Japan. Colum McCann describes returning home to an Ireland where the streets are rearranged, his normal orienting points scrambled. Kamila Shamsie takes friends to an inn in rural Pakistan and runs into a reminder that even though she is a citizen, her passage is granted and adjudicated by others. This feeling finds echoes in Honor Moore's poem about arriving in Pakistan fifty years ago, in a different time.

Arriving involves coping strategies, negotiating postures, and several pieces here conjure what that feels like. Born in Jamaica, Garnette Cadogan began life walking one way; upon moving to New Orleans, and then to New York City, he has to relearn that simple act, because his skin color means something else in America. In "The Nod," Michael Salu gives this signifying dance a science-fictional twist. Meanwhile, in his essay "In Search of Lost Space," Aleksandar Hemon chronicles the ways his parents, Bosnian emigrants to Canada, made their new country and the plot of land they occupy their own.

Comedy lurks in all arrivals; coping crutches can backfire, often hilariously. In her story, "Arizona," Helen Simpson conjures two women discussing the reliefs and indignities of menopause during an acupuncture sessions. An aging man in Dave Eggers' story "The Fork" brings a utensil to his daughter's wedding and then forgets why. Etgar Keret partakes of a nervous driver's marijuana and gives his first major public reading so deeply under the influence he's not sure what he says. In a version of Sappho's Fragment 2, Anne Carson imagines what the poet would have made of a trip to upstate New York. And in her essay "On Learning Norwegian," Lydia Davis wants to read an untranslated new novel by the Norwegian writer Dag Solstad, so she ventures off on her own into the text, using nothing but her wits and scraps of childhood German to guide her up its foreign terrain.

There are many landscapes described here, stretching from Bangladesh to Japan, but several pieces return to the familiar territory of love and marriage. The factory worker heroine of Tahmima Anam's story "Garments" seeks refuge in a husband, and then discovers the many perils that dependency entails. In "Drive My Car," Haruki Murakami writes of a grieving actor and his newly hired driver, a woman with whom he takes an illuminating ride into his past. Finally, in Laura van den Berg's "Dog," a woman waiting for her husband to sail his midlife crisis boat around the world decides he will never arrive at a shore where their marriage is safe.

The endlessly postponed arrival creates a special mixture of dread and longing. In her first published piece of fiction, Fatin Abbas paints a thrilling portrait of a village pitched between north and south in a Sudan forever tilting toward war, then toward peace. Traveling to Paris by train, Daniel Galera describes an incident that shakes him to the very core and that makes all movement seem a precursor to something darker. And in a long poem, the Palestinian poet Ghassan Zaqtan describes the improbability of returning to a homeland that, with time, comes to seem destined (and designed) not to exist.

In an older world, boundaries would have been less important. We could, as Ishion Hutchinson does in a poem about a Utah landscape, simply appreciate the mixture of what is before us. Perhaps, too, in some cases we see boundaries where there are none. In his introduction to Ben Huff's stunning photographs of a road in Alaska that goes nowhere, Barry Lopez ruminates on how we create a concept of nature so that we can separate ourselves from what is out there. In a humorous piece about growing up in Iceland, the novelist Sjón describes his flirtation with a reincarnation set in 1970s Reyjavik.

Perhaps the world is more benign than we give it credit for being. In a memoir of returning home to Turtle Island, Louise Erdrich visits a cemetery lit up festively for the dead's departure and simultaneous arrival. "There are photographs attached to the stones in waterproof cases or even expensively carved by waterjet into polished granite," she writes. "Those faces are always smiling, unaware of what is coming." But we are; it is our burden and our gift, for it points us into the present and forward to the future, looking, as all these stories do, for that moment of contact.

Freeman's
Arrival

Six Shorts

When I reached the Turtle Mountains and descended the long curve of hill into the center of town, I decided to continue a mile or so past an all-night gas station that functions as a desperation pharmacy for drug users and a meeting place for many of the reservation insomniacs. I went on because the August dark had fallen at last on the plains, filling the air with a dry softness. There was no cloud in the sky, the moon hadn't risen yet, and just about now the glowing lanterns in the cemetery would be visible. These lights dot the graves old and recent, casting a wobbling greenish radiance. People of the reservation community place the lights, which are solar garden ornaments purchased in the yard sections of large discount stores, there in the ground just over their loved ones. I do not know when this started, but the impulse to light the way for our relatives and keep vigil for them on their journey goes back as far as anyone can remember. The numbers of lights grow every year as the dead increase. They seem to move or sway as modest spirits might, though that is probably an illusion cast by the shadows of the unmown grass. This late in summer, there are a few fireflies as well, stationed in the moist bushes, but they blink on and off and move erratically, and are more reminiscent perhaps of the spirits of unborn children, commemorated by the antiabortion Virgin at the front of the church—that is, the fireflies are very different from the spirits who'd had lives and bills to pay or school at least and are anchored in the dirt by solar lanterns.

The other spirits have the freedom to flit where they might, and, not having been socialized into human life, do not care anything for us. On the other hand, the dead of this graveyard and the others—the old Catholic one at the top of the hill that contains the first priests and most of my ancestors, and the traditional graveyard nobody will point out the way to—those dead are thought to look after the people of the town and bush and to exert a powerful influence.

I turned a corner and made a complete loop down onto the road that leads past several constructions by Patrick Bouvray and up toward the old Queen of Peace convent, where I like to stay.

As I passed the small wooden replicas of a church and a turtle, I remembered visiting Patrick in hope that I might persuade him to play the fiddle on my wedding day. Patrick, an old man with a long judicious face, wore the same sort of green Sears work shirts my grandfather wore, and had been sitting it seemed for many years among bicycle tires under the concrete awning in the courtyard of the retirement home. There were small cans of paint tucked against the cinder-block wall, rags, brushes, tools, pieces of an old refrigerator, and scrap wood of various shapes and thickness. Someone else had called on Patrick's fiddle that night, but all the same I stayed on talking because I became very interested in his latest pieces, which were parked in a proud little row. Out of the reservation detritus, Patrick had made a series of wooden automobiles. They were painted in the leftover colors people gave him—an odd coral, a vibrant lavender blue,

2

deep green. The delightful small-scale ambulance he'd made was painted an appropriate white. These conveyances were about the size for preschool children to drive, though I could more easily picture dogs behind the wheels. Patrick opened the back doors of the ambulance, doors scavenged from an old kitchen cupboard. Inside was a miniature blanketed and sheeted gurney with a convincing IV drip set up next to it. The dog would be a rez-dog beagle-Lab-shih tzu-Doberman-coyote with its limp paw bandaged. There would have to be a hole cut in the gurney for its sweeping tail. Dogs do not commit suicide, exactly, though they are known to starve themselves out of longing. This dog would have become too weak to function, I thought, and needed treatment for dehydration. I had closed the doors and thanked Patrick, who ignored me.

Now, pulling up before the convent, I parked and turned my car off. The mosquitoes would just have risen out of the tall wet reeds behind the building. Not wanting yet to brave them, I continued to sit in the car. After the strain of constant motion, I allowed my eyes to adjust to the still scene before me. Much as a person reeling from loss after loss stares at one solid thing that will not move, I watched the convent, a plainly built brick box. One of Patrick's wooden cars, the green one, had featured a tiny grille which probably once belonged in a compact refrigerator. The grille was screwed to the front end of the car and a tiny souvenir license plate labeled "Patrick" was wired onto it. My grandfather's first name was Patrick also. He is buried in the graveyard containing the solar lights, and he had once owned a real Model T of the type Patrick Bouvray had made. My grandfather had in fact owned a series of automobiles and was proud of each of them. His cars were often the centerpiece or focal points of family photographs and so they had been documented one after the next. He had, in addition, written about these cars to

3

my mother and father. His letters were elaborate, exquisitely polite, and full of news of the family and of course the cars, but he never mentioned sightings of the Virgin Mary, perhaps because although he practiced Catholicism he had also been brought into the religion of our ancestors, the Midewiwin. So I would not find any hint about her there. I would have to see what I could find all on my own while referring to the newspaper clippings I had collected.

Although I have returned time and again for all of my life to my home reservation to visit relatives or teach at the community college, I have only recently begun to catalog my papers regarding this place. I've kept far too much paper in my life; however, I began to realize, as I made piles to burn, keep, shred, recycle, or read, that in the last pile a pattern emerged, a design which resulted in an inappropriate number of relatives flickering away on that grassy hill. As I sat before the evenly spaced bricks in the wall of the Queen of Peace I had the absurd thought that mathematics could be part of this. Events thought random have been recently theorized to be part of some infinite or infinitesimal design. I know that my dormouse storage of old paper was a nervous habit and nowhere near grand on any scale. Yet each of us may contribute an inkling of knowledge to a vastness of understanding which when we stretch our minds to consider it sickens or engulfs us. I have trouble with long division, so the idea that I might apply a mathematical construction to the sightings and the tragedies was on the face of it foolish. I knew of someone, however, who had never thought me foolish and who did math to occupy himself—a surprising hobby not just because he happens to live on a reservation. He spends his evenings drinking Blatz beer and making notations. Once he solves a problem on the walls of his little house he usually paints carefully over his neatly penciled calculations and when he is finished gives the leftover

4

paint to Patrick. My mathematical friend's name, too, is Patrick, but he shortens it to Pat. He is married to my aunt, LaRose. Their walls have gone from yellow to green to lavender in the past six months, and now are white. Between the colors, of course, there is the math. I visited last spring and as I sat looking at those walls, only beginning to be decorated with purposeful marks, I asked Pat what problem he'd solved between each application of the paint. He looked meaningfully at LaRose and told me that within one layer he had calculated the odds against me sitting in that very place and at that very time—they were so improbably vast when considering the age of the universe and that of all life on earth including our own descent from apes and our outward migrations or even our sudden appearance (traditionally speaking) untold millennia ago on this continent that it could be said my sitting there across from him drinking a weak cup of coffee from his plastic coffeemaker was impossible. We were not there. It was not happening. The slightly burnt taste of coffee, LaRose's filtered cigarette, the ovenbird we both could hear in the thick patch of chokecherry, oak scrub, wild sage, and alfalfa, the sound of his reedy voice, my daughter coloring at the next table, none of this was taking place. The peace I felt at that moment surprised me. A satisfaction at not having existed in the first place. Simultaneously, I was overcome with horror at the implications for my daughter, and I rapped superstitiously on the wooden table.

Still, the memory of that sudden glimpse into fathomless nonexistence could not fail to raise the question now of whether I was truly once again sitting before the Queen of Peace convent on a dark August evening waiting for the mosquitoes to feel the chill creep into the air and kill their lust. I cracked the window. Heard the horde's thin whine. I closed the window quickly, and waited. Behind me, my young daughter sleepily stirred in her car seat, and then fell silent. At last I left the car, looping several canvas bags over my shoulders. My daughter had awakened. I put my hand out and she caught my fingers. Her tender hand is still slightly indented at the knuckles instead of knobbed like a grown-up person's. We walked through the utilitarian doors, past the television perpetually and soundlessly tuned to a religious station, and checked ourselves in. We were given the room at the end of the hallway where we could sleep, undisturbed, long into the morning.

Dozing off with my daughter's small hand in mine was so relaxing in every way that I felt, myself, like a true queen of peace. Behind my eyelids pictures moved and I saw us walking down the hill, toward the graveyard lighted softly by solar lanterns. By day, our reservation graveyard is a gaudy place with lots of toys left for the deceased, plates of food, cigarettes placed on top of gravestones or sticking in the ground. Cigarettes because it takes a lot of tobacco to walk your road to the other side, where no lung disease is ever going to bother you again. There are photographs attached to the stones in waterproof cases or even expensively carved by waterjet into polished granite. Those faces are always smiling, unaware of what is coming. What they got. Yet the effect of it all is to make the dead seem happy and contented, while the living are left to deal with the hard sorrows. So I like the night graveyard better, the one we visit now in our margin of consciousness before we travel the dim tangle of neural pathways by which we will arrive at morning, where there will be pallid eggs and raisin toast to eat downstairs in the friendly kitchen, and the Sisters to talk to about all that has happened since we visited last.

—Louise Erdrich

The inn could have been the set of an L.A. noir film which dealt in broken dreams, and violence. A two-storied quadrangular building of red brick with regularly spaced off-white balconies and off-white air conditioners looked onto a generously sized garden. In the center of the garden, a large empty swimming pool with an interior of fading blue paint and cracked cement. Rusted stepladders at either end extended halfway down into the pool. A magnificent peacock roamed the gardens, like a movie star who finds herself dropped into obscurity but is determined to maintain standards. A peahen, guinea fowls, and a black and white cat made up its entourage.

Eleven of us had stopped for the night at the inn in Larkana, a band of travelers from Karachi who had come to visit the nearby ancient site of Mohenjodaro. At sunset, the inn manager laid out a long table in the garden, so we could eat beside the swimming pool and listen to each other's ghost stories. Eventually, in varying states of terror from the stories, nine of our party wandered back to their rooms until it was just my old friend Zain and me in a darkness broken only by the low-wattage bulbs of the inn. That's when something more unwanted than ghosts appeared: two men whose questions about the foreigners traveling with us identified them as being from Military Intelligence (the other mark of who they were was their lack of need to explain who they were before they launched into questions).

By now the second adult male in our group—Bilal—had walked out into the garden as well, and stood nearby listening as one of the men, with a neat mustache and a red polo shirt, pulled out a pad of legal paper and started to question me (he had started with Zain, because of the gender pecking order, but Zain had only just met the foreigners for the first time that morning and couldn't be of much help). The British citizen with Pakistani antecedents didn't interest the man from MI particularly. But then he turned his attention to The Blonde (every L.A. noir movie needs one).

What is her husband's name? he said. She has no husband, I answered. And her source of income? She's a writer. So her father supports her, he asserted. Is he a businessman? No, I said, she supports herself. The man looked pained by my evasions. No one earns a living from being a writer, he said. What is her real source of income?

Somehow we got through the income question, but landed straight into the peculiarity of a single woman who doesn't live with her parents. How is this possible? said the man from MI, at which point Zain launched into a long speech about the lack of family values in the West. This was, as he intended, convincing enough to move the conversation along. To which countries had my friend traveled? Did she have siblings and what did they do for a living? Had she been to Pakistan before, and why? Had she been to India? What were her books about? On our way to Larkana our van had stopped at the mausoleum of the Bhutto family—what had she said about it? She said it made her feel sad, I replied, though in fact we hadn't talked about it at all. This could be interpreted in many ways, said the man. What kind of sad? I decide to look appalled. There were many bodies buried there, I said. The second man, who had been silent until now, turned to his partner. It's a graveyard! he said. Exactly, I said. A graveyard! Where is the individual of any humanity who wouldn't feel sad in a graveyard? (Urdu allows for an extravagance of expression that came in handy at this point.)

What does she think about the Bhutto family? the man persisted. On some instinct I said, Why don't I call her out so you can ask her yourself? For the first time, the balance of power between us shifted. No, no, he said. She's a guest here; I can't disturb her.

I pressed home my advantage. I have answered your questions with an open heart, I said, and now it's getting late and I have an early flight. How long do you intend to keep me here? The man looked distressed. I have also spoken to you with an open heart, he said. At this point the inn manager, who had been smoking a few feet away, tapped the man on the shoulder and said, Let her go now. Very soon after, he did.

They kept Zain a few minutes longer, but he too took the route of outrage rather than compliance and the interrogation concluded. Once we were all back indoors Bilal, who had been listening to the whole exchange, said, What they wanted from you was money.

Zain and I replayed every detail of the encounter to each other. The truth of what Bilal said became evident. The inn manager and these two men—who were not from Military Intelligence at all—were in on the scam together.

Just wait, Bilal said. Tomorrow morning the inn manager will give us an inflated bill that will include the sum of money he'd hoped to extract from us. And so it proved. Zain demanded a breakdown of costs, and the bill reduced by half. By the time we were on the flight to Karachi I had tamed the encounter into a story of much hilarity. (The Blonde—a biographer of Eleanor Marx who cut her teeth on antiapartheid activism—particularly enjoyed my description of her as someone who studied literature, goes to see ancient ruins, and writes biographies of people who died more than a hundred years ago, and therefore can't possibly be expected to have any political opinions about the present.)

But beneath all the hilarity, there existed this truth: The inn manager and his accomplices could run such a scam because in all of us who have grown up in Pakistan there exists a terror of the men who proffer no ID, never explicitly state whom they work for, but maintain the right to ask any questions and carry out any actions in the name of security.

The plane dipped its wings; I looked down on Larkana, home of the Bhutto family, who dominate the imagination of Pakistan as no other family does. It wasn't just the inn, but the city—no, the nation itself—which was the set of broken dreams and violence.

—Kamila Shamsie

"Hey, are any of you guys easy sleepers?"

It was a bright July night in 1978. The question was asked by one of the hippy types whom Social Services had given the task of looking after the welfare of the teenage horde that descended on the center of Reykjavík every weekend from late May to early September from the early '50s to the end of the '80s. I was doing the rounds with some school buddies, circling the block that took us from the parliament square, past Hótel Borg and the three discotheques we would start trying to get into as soon as we could pass for childish-looking twenty-years-olds, past the old pharmacy and the co-op shop, to the parking lot by the city's main taxi station.

We were the third generation of kids practicing this circular wandering that was so much a thing in itself that when Jean-Paul Sartre and Simone de Beauvoir visited Iceland in 1951 and Sartre was asked what had made the biggest impression on him during his stay, he answered that after the poem "Sonatorrek" by the Viking poet Egill Skallagrímsson—in it the poet revenges his son by writing against the ocean that took him—what most fascinated him was the sight from his hotel room of the town's teenagers practicing pure existence by putting action before thought in the streets below.

On this sunny summer night in 1978 there was no world-famous philosopher watching us from above, but my positive answer to the question if some of us guys were easy sleepers was the first step I ever took into the mysteries of the man who in those days was considered the author of Iceland's only original donation to the art of philosophy, Dr. Helgi Pjetursson.

In his early days Dr. Pjetursson was a world-known natural scientist specializing in geology, and many of his discoveries are still recognized as groundbreaking contributions to, amongst other things, the history of the Ice Age. But by his own account his geological studies paled in comparison with his most important work, namely, his research into the nature of sleep and dreams, formulated in series of books called *Nýall*, or *Annals of the New*. In the epilogue of the first volume Dr. Pjetursson writes:

"*Nýall* is above all a scientific work. It is based upon all that has been best achieved in science and philosophy in the past, and it amends it and adds to it, in such a way that it heralds the dawn of an age of science here on earth."

On a somewhat humbler note he explained his endeavor as "some Icelandic attempts at cosmology and biology" and "some Icelandic attempts to understand life in the universe."

And what was it Dr. Pjetursson's Icelandic attempts had revealed to him?

In short, that in our dreams we are connected with people on other planets. That we see with their eyes, feel what they feel, do whatever they are doing, but because their experience is processed in our brains we do not realize that it is not our own. That these beings, scattered all over the universe, are people or creatures who have died and whose astral bodies, or Kirilian aura, have been

11

transported from their birth planet—we are only once begotten and born of a mother organism—by means of a beam called The Beam of Life and used as blueprints to reassemble them in corporeal form on their new home planets. That a force called the "Law Of Coordination" decides if our next planet will be friendly or hostile. And finally, that through mediums we can have conversations with our "dream-givers." It is a communication that happens without any delay in the transmission because thought travels faster than light.

Welcome to *Cosmobiology*!

The hippy who asked the question turned out to be a student of psychology at the University of Iceland and a follower of Dr. Helgi Pjetursson's theories. As a part of his final thesis he needed guinea pigs for his dream trials. I raised my hand:

"I am an easy sleeper!"

The tests were conducted in a research laboratory normally reserved for the students of the biology department, a rudimentary setup on the top floor of a warehouse with a garage on the street level and the offices of some questionable importers on the two floors between. I guess psychology students with unorthodox ideas about the nature of dreams have to make do with whatever comes their way, but the place looked impressive enough to a fifteen-year-old kid from the suburbs who until then had seen only laboratories from sci-fi films on television.

Next to the hospital trolley that would be my bed that night there were long and wide plastic tubes hooked up to an impressive stack of machinery. Dark shadows floated back and forth under their translucent shell. They belonged to my fellow test creatures, three brown trout from Lake Thingvallavatn who were having their sense of smell measured.

I put on my pajamas, brushed my teeth, and lay down on the trolley. The hippy-turned-psychology student connected a great number of wires to my scalp. He plugged the bundle into the impressive machinery. I pulled up the blanket and fell asleep.

Each time the brain scan showed that my REM sleep was on the wane I was woken up to recount what I had just dreamt.

As science has it, I was not informed about the nature of the test beforehand, but as I was about to leave the laboratory on the morning it was finished, the psychology student told me that he was looking for evidence of two consciousnesses being at play in our minds when we dream. Unfortunately, I had failed in dreaming a dream that supported his thesis. Still, as a thank-you for my participation in the tests, he wanted to give me some books.

He handed me a plastic bag with the six volumes of *Nýall* by Dr. Helgi Pjetursson, nicely bound and printed in blue on the orders of the scientist, who believed that a blue text makes for deeper understanding between author and reader.

The following winter I dove into the blue sentences of Dr. Pjetursson.

Through a bus driver I discovered that a splinter group from the *Nýall Society* met every Thursday night in the old town of Reykjavík. With the help of Gudrún the Medium, a middle-aged woman who worked in a fish factory during the day but served as a gateway between worlds in her spare time, the *Nýallists* practiced their science by talking to people who by dying had gained direct experience of the cosmobiological universe and could bear witness to the fact that all of Dr. Pjetursson's ideas were right. During coffee breaks members of the group shared their ideas about various subjects that occupied them. One was trying to prove that the Keops pyramid was built as a monument to the greatness of the Icelandic language; another had found evidence in the Bible that on the day of the crucifixion Jesus Christ had been four years old; a third was occupied with questions about what the static noise of radios really was.

My teenage mind swimming in Dr. Pjetursson's theories on death and dreams, at these meetings all my cravings for the weird were catered to—until the summer of 1979, when I found my next source of inspiration, Surrealism. There I was provided with a key element in the life of any young man, and one that was wholly missing from the Nýall: The Erotic.

I will always be thankful for my year with the *Nýallists*. And till the end of my days I will cherish my copy of the superbly named *Íslendingar á öðrum hnöttum* (*Icelanders on Other Planets*). A booklet written under the influence of Cosmobiology, it is an attempt by an Icelandic farmer to connect with his dead wife through automatic writing which results in a literary genre that can only be called "Peasant Science Fiction." If Dr. Helgi Pjetursson was as right about this subject as he was about the Ice Age, it is the best handbook for the afterlife I've ever read.

So, I am prepared.

The day I suddenly wake up in the glowing moss of a yellow mountainside, naked but warm from the reddish light of two suns, where five-legged birds flit through the air meowing like cats, and I see a small group of people walking toward me dressed as Icelandic peasants at the turn of the twentieth century, I will know I have died.

I will remember that at the moment of death I was beamed across the depths of space, to a distant galaxy, a foreign solar system, to a new planet where my body was reassembled according to my aural blueprint.

It will be the first day of the second stage of my everlasting life.

"Oh, there he is!"

One of the men from my welcoming group will raise me to my

feet—he looks like my father in his confirmation photograph, and I will soon discover that he actually is my deceased father—and two women (the younger one has pale blue skin and furry hands, as she has come here from a different world from ours) will wrap me in a blanket woven from the three-layered, green wool of the bus-sized sheep grazing in the valley below.

I have arrived. Now it is my turn to provide strange dream experiences to the easy sleepers back home on Earth.

—Sjón

F or a short while after the death of Seamus Heaney in 2013, the rumor floated around Dublin that the airport might be named after him. With flights from JFK. Or Reagan International. Or Charles de Gaulle. Or Benazir Bhutto. Maybe a fatal touchdown from George Bush International. Or even some flights that might have connected originally in Jorge Chávez or Il Carravagio or Frederico García Lorca International.

When it comes to departures and arrivals, the dead, and even the living, meet in many forms.

At Dublin Airport I can never remember whether the Departures gates are upstairs or downstairs. Somehow it matters very much. I get confused at times, especially in the brand-new Terminal Two. I stray to the Arrivals area when really I want to leave. Or upon arriving, I'll wander past the Departures gates and ponder if I made a mistake in touching down in the first place. There goes that old dead self leaving twenty-nine years ago, wearing skinny jeans, dragging a torn backpack. The new self walks the other direction, wider, slower, formal, with a new rhythm to his accent. All those ideas that once made him soar along a foot from the ground are somehow forgotten. At the rank downstairs he can't remember if it's a "taxi" or a "cab" that he should hail. No matter. The low-tide smell of the city returns.

A few years ago I used to make a habit, upon arriving in Dublin, of going to see my favorite Irish writer, Ben Kiely. I'd go by bus, or foot, or bicycle, or taxi, to his house on the Morehampton Road. He and his partner Frances would open the door and take me in, even unannounced. Ben had been important to me since at a young age I first read his short stories, which I still believe are amongst the finest of the twentieth century.

This time around, though, I was working far too hard at being busy. I had only about an hour and a half before I went to the airport again. Small matter. I drove my rental car into Donnybrook and pulled up outside 119 Morehampton Road and looked for a parking space, but there was none. A Garda car came up behind me. Its lights flashed. I gave them a wave and moved on.

I did an illegal turn down near the shops in Donnybrook. A woman in a brand-new Merc gave me the middle finger. I blew her a kiss. She didn't laugh. I reversed again and corrected, slowly crawled up the street.

Still no parking. A bus behind me blared. I was in, it seems, the wrong lane. I would have blared my horn if I was behind me too—in life we seem to want to split our feathers and leave both halves in flight. To hell with it, I pulled the car up onto the pavement and hit the hazard lights. If nothing else, I'd just drop the book through the letter box. But again the cops pulled up behind me. This time a Ban Garda got out and told me with a distinct lack of ceremony that I'd better move or else I'd be fined. That meant I would miss my departure, which meant, in essence, that I would miss my arrival home. But wasn't I home anyway?

I began to feel what I can only call an emigrant's panic. To be a man of two countries, his hands in the dark pockets of each. These were streets I used to know. Nothing was the same. I grew more and more desperate, charging down streets, looking for a parking space, looking for the correct turn back to Kiely's house. The miles clicked up on the car until eventually I was up beyond Milltown and caught in a traffic jam for the M50 motorway.

My confession: I sat in the traffic jam and had a fair idea that Ben would die sometime soon. He had survived a long time and he had given his readers and friends an inordinate amount of pleasure, but here I was, stuck in a Dublin traffic jam, and only this story to tell, a book of mine in the front seat, a novel, signed to him, ungiven. Someone behind me beeped again. I was home and I didn't recognize where I sat. I saw the sign for the airport. I took it. Ben died a few months later.

Cooking our lives down under boiling heat, the one thing we can't evaporate away is our original country. It would do no moral good to depart from Heaney International. It's a brain-peeling process to walk through an airport with the knowledge that you might not be coming back for a long time. Sure, there is an arrival on the far side. But all arrivals are departures too. Like two mirrors put face-to-face, the leaving and the coming swallow each other at a thousand points, lost eventually in the black border of each other.

It's just as well that the supporters of Heaney decided to not to go ahead with the plan. All ports—but especially Irish ports—reek of sadness, even in the Arrivals area where the cheap balloons temporarily bob.

What is the scene of arrival and where is the point of departure? Good question for a poet. Heaney knew the answers.

A few years ago the busiest place in Dublin Airport was the short-term parking lot. There were several reasons for this. Ireland was diseased with money. The economy was on fire. Porsches pulled in. Range Rovers. Lamborghinis. The drivers parked their cars as close as possible to the terminal. Often their machines were too wide for one spot and they purposefully straddled two. They ran inside. A weekend trip in Lanzaroti. A Spurs game in London. A horse race in Paris. They didn't care how much the parking would eventually cost.

But every now and then an older, dented car stayed beyond a weekend. Then a few more days. The Dublin Airport employees glanced inside. Nothing too unusual. Some papers on the front seat. A set of keys in the well of the dashboard. Maybe a child's stuffed animal in the backseat, forgotten. A few more days passed until eventually the airport employees began to recognize these cars as part of a pattern. The papers in the front seat were mortgage demands. The keys in the dashboard were the keys of a house abandoned. The stuffed animal in the backseat was part of a life that a child would never know. These young Irish families were going away forever. There could be no return. Short-term parking. Long-term loss. Sydney, Chicago, Buenos Aires, Paris would be their next arrival.

To abandon everything is a familiar story, perhaps especially to a poet. What we look for, then, is some internal rhyme, most likely just out of reach.

—Colum McCann

In 1996, I was living alone on the ground floor of a musty old house at the edge of a Japanese town called Kabe in Hiroshima Prefecture. Kabe is built where the Ōtagawa River emerges from the mountains and enters the delta plain over which Hiroshima and its suburbs nowadays sprawl. In 1945 an American Boeing B-29 dropped an atomic bomb (famously named "Little Boy") onto the city. Uncounted hundreds or thousands of people not incinerated in the blast made their way north along the Ōtagawa in the vain hope of finding help. Many died of their burns before they reached Kabe, and many died of radiation poisoning in the days and weeks that followed. The precise number of total casualties as a result of the bomb is impossible to reckon, but estimates range from 90,000 to 166,000, with about half the deaths—45,000 to 83,000—occurring on the first day. By any measure, this is a hellish quantity of sudden death. In the Japanese context, this also means a vast number of restless ghosts denied the Buddhist funerary rites required for a smooth passage to the next world.

The house I lived in stood at the edge of a small rice field on the banks of a shallow, stony, water-noisy tributary of the Ōtagawa. This peaceful spot was one of the nicest locations I've ever lived in, and thanks to the river it was cool even in the hammeringly hot Japanese August. Being young, I felt that I owned an unlimited bank account of hours and days, so I'd often zone out and gaze at the river, its herons, and the steep flank of wooded mountain rising from its far bank. No great leap of the imagination was required to picture the irradiated human beings of all ages arriving fifty years earlier—right there, at the very same spot where I aired my futon, hung my laundry, and ate my granola. (I found that when I lived in or near Hiroshima, I couldn't not think about the A-bomb, daily.) Maybe these imaginings were a factor in what follows, or maybe "my" section of the river was what Irish mystics

19

call "Thin Places," where the screen between this world and an eternal one is thin, less a wall and more a membrane. I didn't know then and I don't know now.

I slept in the back room, divided from my living/eating/writing room by sliding *fusuma* screens, this being a common arrangement in Japanese houses. My house was set back some distance from the main Hiroshima-Mihara road, so no light from street lamps or neon signage fell on my bedroom window. The nocturnal darkness, then, was close to total. One night in early October I woke up feeling four linked certainties: first, that a ghost was standing at the end of my bed; second, that it really was a ghost and not a burglar, because my front door was locked and made a juddery racket when it was slid open; third, that the ghost was male and much older than my twenty-seven years; and fourth, that he didn't want me to look at him.

I didn't feel that I would be turned to salt if I *did* look, but I did feel that it was strongly advisable not to. I was scared by my visitor in a way I hadn't been scared before, and haven't been scared since. It wasn't the calculating "What do I do to get out of this?" fear of a near-mugging experience I once had at the Tottenham Court Road Tube station; not the fight-or-flight "*F**%+*ing Hell!*" shock-fear I get if a mad-eyed dog's suddenly barking in my face; and not the helpless terror I'd felt for a few seconds one time flying out of Florence when the airplane seemed to lose power. My fear that night in Kabe was more like an ongoing, low-level electrical shock, and if it resided in any organ it was my skin. I was able to analyze my situation, and my first thought was that the presence in my room was a trick of my mind or a leftover from a dream. I tested the theory by waiting a minute, until I knew I had to be properly awake. My sense of being watched didn't subside. I didn't sense any anger or malice in the presence: It was more a robust curiosity about what this pale lanky foreigner was doing in *his* house.

The logical thing to do in the circumstances was to explain myself. So I told my visitor my name, my birthplace, my age, my job, how long I'd be there, all with my eyes shut, and all in my clunky Japanese—why would a ghost in Hiroshima speak English? I wound up my self-introduction with the same "*Yoroshiku onegaishimasu*" you'd use when begging a favor or acceptance from a human agency. Maybe a minute passed, and I felt a new certainty that my visitor had gone, reasonably satisfied with the new tenant's account of himself. So, I switched on my lamp, checked that the front door was still locked—it was—and slid back into my futon. The adrenaline in my blood faded away, and I slept until my alarm clock told me it was time to get up and go and teach three classes of thirty to forty Japanese nonectoplasmic junior high school boys.

And that's the end. It's hardly "Oh, Whistle, and I'll Come to You, My Lad" or "The Monkey's Paw," I know: There were no unexplained footprints in the dust there the next day, nor did my upstairs neighbors ever mention that a man had once hanged himself in my back room. Nonetheless, that night is the closest I have to a real-life ghost story, and turned a ghost-disbeliever into a ghost-agnostic, at least. I half-hoped that I'd get another nocturnal visit before I left the musty old house in Kabe and moved into a newish apartment in the city, but it seems that for him, one encounter with the transient was ample.

—David Mitchell

In September 2012, after taking part in a literary festival in Vincennes, France, I took a four-hour train journey to Toulon to see a Leonard Cohen concert. I spent the afternoon wandering through the backstreets of the old city, and felt intimidated by my total lack of knowledge about the region. I bought comic book histories and Marseille soap. I took dozens of useless photographs of the flagpoles of the boats in the harbor, silhouetted against the sunlit Mediterranean. After the concert, stimulated by the music and by the impressive energy which Cohen, almost an octogenarian, had displayed on stage, I walked the same unrecognizable backstreets until dawn, until I became depressed by the movements of the drunken tourists around the few pubs still open, where the air was heavy with intimidation. The following morning I woke around lunchtime, ate a kebab, and headed to the train station.

Twenty minutes into the return journey to Paris, the passengers heard the sound of pebbles on the high-speed train tracks. I raised my eyes from the book I was reading and noted that the man sat opposite me had stopped looking at the screen of his laptop. The train slowed down and came to a halt. It was a cloudy day, almost 4 o'clock in the afternoon. Through the windows a somber-looking field tinged with shades of lead, clay, and moss-green could be seen. A voice from the cabin's loudspeaker informed us that there had been an "accident involving a person" and that we would be at a standstill until further notice. Almost all the passengers looked out the window at the same time, seeing only uncultivated fields and a few homes scattered in the distance. Not long after, and with a truly unexpected agility, police officers appeared, inspecting the train's exterior, making notes, and taking photos with tiny digital cameras.

Two train company employees came through the corridor of the carriage asking which passengers needed to make connections, as it would be two hours before the train got going again. A girl seated on a chair near me, on the opposite side of the carriage, asked the employees in a loud voice if she would be reimbursed for the delay. Everyone turned toward this girl, whose beauty, I thought, seemed to give safe conduct to her amoral tendencies. Her indelicacy created a sense of bewilderment in the other passengers, who began to whisper, but she was not put off by this and adopted an even more provocative tone, raising her voice to demand her rights. The man opposite me closed his laptop and began to laugh nervously. The woman in her forties sitting on the chair opposite the girl demanding compensation began to cry. My French is poor, but I was able to understand that the woman was muttering, through tears, something about the sadness of death, making explicit, for the first time, the concreteness of the suicide committed on the tracks.

The first reaction of the outraged girl was to puff, in the French manner, to express her disdain at the women's sentimentality. However, after this she fell silent, and stayed silent. From where I was, I could see her sink a little into the chair, her arms crossed, staring into the void; in her wide eyes fury was metamorphosing into something more ambiguous. The woman opposite her continued to cry for a few minutes and then stopped. A lasting silence took control of the carriage, a silence that seemed to extend from one tip of the high-speed train, stationary in the middle of the open countryside, to the other.

Lost as I was in my own thoughts, I didn't see how it began, but at some point silence gave way to a chain reaction that took control of all the passengers, who were now laughing and chatting with their neighbors. During the hiatus of my distraction, the teary woman and the indignant girl had become friends. The contents of their conversation escaped me, but they laughed and gesticulated, as if complicit in a sarcastic joke. In the period that followed until the train departed, the passengers on the Toulon-Paris line told each other where they came from and what they were doing with their lives, shared drinks and chocolates, exchanged favors. At times the blinking blue and red lights of a police vehicle were seen inside the carriage. The wait was long. The temperature rose and the atmosphere became infested by the smell of sweat.

The man opposite me wanted to know what I was reading. It was the recently released biography of David Foster Wallace, the American writer who hanged himself in 2008. I thought about the contrast between the two suicides: the anonymous individual who walked through the field and assumed a discreet position so that he could throw himself in front of a high-speed train at the decisive moment, and the cult author who put his papers in order and strung himself up by the neck when his wife left the house to go shopping. I concluded that any apparent contrast between the deaths was purely aesthetic, a question of style. I remembered an era in which I fantasized frequently about a spectacular suicide in the busy center of Porto Alegre, a man, not me, never me, jumping from the highest building of the city to meet the asphalt in the middle of the crowd and go out in the most scandalous way possible, perhaps taking some unlucky people with him. I considered that I had often imagined the world without me, the world after my death, the consequences of this death for those who cared about me, but I had never considered the act of my suicide in a serious or practical way. At that instant, the absolute conviction that I would never under any hypothesis kill myself died within me.

Later on, after disembarking in Paris, several passengers, myself included, walked to the front of the train instead of heading immediately for one of the platform exits and placed themselves, circumspect and feigning lack of interest, in front of the metallic bodywork and ironware; but they were perfectly clean and in an impeccable state, undamaged.

The passengers went their separate ways, and the camaraderie of the carriage now seemed a distant and somewhat estranged memory, something that had perhaps never happened. I then understood more clearly a feeling that had surprised me during the long wait for the unfolding of the accident involving a person, a feeling that I am unable to name even now, but which had to do with the relationship between that prodigious, gigantic machine, gliding over the tracks at more than two hundred kilometers per hour, and the fragile living bodies it carried along with such efficiency. Looking toward the driver's compartment, I couldn't help but think of the train as a clumsy, ignorant beast of burden that could not be blamed for its actions.

—Daniel Galera, translated from the Portuguese by Rahul Bery

Haruki Murakami

was born in Kyoto in 1949 and lives near Tokyo. His work has been translated into more than fifty languages, and the most recent of his many international honors is the Jerusalem Prize, whose previous recipients include J. M. Coetzee, Milan Kundera, and V. S. Naipaul. His debut short novels *Wind* and *Pinball*—nearly thirty years out of print, newly translated, and in one English language volume for the first time—were published by Knopf in August 2015.

Drive My Car

HARUKI MURAKAMI
TRANSLATED FROM THE JAPANESE BY TED GOOSSEN

Based on the many times he had ridden in cars driven by women, Kafuku had reached the conclusion that most female drivers fell into one of two groups. Either they were a little too aggressive or a little too timid. Luckily—and we should all be grateful for this—the latter were far more common. Generally speaking, women were more cautious than men behind the wheel. Of course, that caution was nothing to complain about. Yet their style of driving tended to irritate others on the road.

Most of the aggressive women, on the other hand, seemed convinced they were great drivers. In most cases, they showed nothing but scorn for their too timid sisters, proud that they at least weren't like that. They were oblivious to the gasps and slammed brakes that accompanied their sudden and daring lane changes and to the less than complimentary words directed their way by their fellow drivers.

Not all women belonged to one of those two groups, of course. There were those *normal* drivers who were neither too aggressive nor too cautious. Some could even be called expert. Nevertheless, somehow or other, even with them Kafuku usually sensed a certain tension. There was nothing concrete that he could point to, but he felt a kind of friction in the air from where he sat in the passenger seat, and it made him tense. His throat would turn dry, or he would start saying foolish, totally unnecessary things just to bury the silence.

Certainly there were good and bad male drivers too. Yet in most cases their driving didn't create the same charged atmosphere. It wasn't that they were especially laid back. In reality, they were probably tense too. Nevertheless, they seemed to be able to separate their tension and who they were in a natural—likely unconscious—way. They could converse and act normally even with their attention fixed on the road. As in, that belongs there and this belongs here. Kafuku had no idea where this difference between men and women drivers came from.

Kafuku seldom drew distinctions between men and women in his daily life. Nor was he apt to perceive any difference in ability between the sexes. There were as many women as men in his line of work, and he actually felt more at ease working with women. For the most part, women paid closer attention to details, and they listened well. The only problem occurred when he got in a car and found a woman sitting beside him with her hands on the steering wheel. That he found impossible to ignore. Yet he had never voiced his opinion on the matter to anyone. Somehow the topic seemed inappropriate.

Thus it was when Oba, who ran the garage where he serviced his car and who he had asked to help him find a personal driver, recommended a young woman, Kafuku looked less than thrilled. Oba smiled at his reaction. Yeah, I know how you feel, the mechanic's face said.

"But she's one heck of a driver. I can guarantee that, no problem. Why don't you meet her and see for yourself?"

"Sure, since you recommend her," Kafuku said. He needed to hire a driver as quickly as possible, and Oba was someone he trusted. He had known him for fifteen years, an impish man with hair that bristled like wire. When it came to automobiles, Oba's word was as good as gold.

"To be on the safe side, I'm going to take a look at your wheel alignment, but assuming that's OK you can pick up your car the day after tomorrow at two p.m. Why don't I ask the girl to come then too, so you can check her out, maybe have her drive you around the neighborhood? You can level with me if you don't like her. No skin off my nose if you don't."

"How old is she?"

"Never got around to asking. But I would guess in her mid-twenties," Oba said. Then he gave a slight frown. "Like I said, she's a great driver, but . . . "

"But?"

"Well, how should I put this . . . she's not exactly the congenial type."

"In what way?"

"She's brusque, shoots from the hip when she talks, which isn't often. And she smokes like a chimney," Oba said. "You'll see for yourself when you meet her, but she's not what you'd call cute either. She almost never smiles, and she's a bit *homely*, to be honest."

"That's not a problem. I'd feel uncomfortable if she were too pretty, and there could be nasty rumors."

"Sounds like it might be a good match then."

"Apart from all that, she's a good driver, right?"

"Yeah, she's solid. Not just 'for a woman,' but as a driver, pure and simple."

"What kind of work is she doing now?"

"I'm not too sure. I think she scrapes by as a convenience store clerk, courier service driver, stuff like that. Short-term jobs she can drop right away when something better pops up. She came here on a friend's recommendation looking for work, but things are a bit tight, and I can't take on anyone full-time right now. I give her a shout when I need extra help. But she's really reliable. And she never takes a drink."

Kafuku's face darkened with the mention of liquor, and his fingers unconsciously rose to his lips.

"The day after tomorrow at two it is, then," Kafuku said. Brusque, closemouthed, not at all cute—he was intrigued.

Two days later, at two in the afternoon, the yellow Saab 900 convertible was fixed and ready to drive away. The dented right front fender was returned to its original shape, the painted patch blending almost perfectly with the rest of the car. The engine was tuned, the transmission readjusted, and new brake pads and wiper blades installed. The car was freshly washed, its tires polished, its body waxed. As always, Oba's work was flawless.

Kafuku had owned the car for twelve years and put nearly a hundred thousand miles on it. The canvas roof was showing its age. When it poured he had to worry about leaks. But for the time being, Kafuku had no intention of buying a newer vehicle. Not only had the Saab never given him any major trouble, he was personally attached to it. He loved driving with the top down, regardless of the season. In winter, he wore a thick coat and wrapped a scarf around his neck, while in summer he donned dark sunglasses and a cap. He would drive around the city, shifting gears with great pleasure and raising his eyes to take in passing clouds and birds perched on electric wires whenever he stopped at a traffic light. Those moments had been a key part of his life for many years. Kafuku walked slowly around his car, inspecting it closely like a horse before a race.

His wife had still been alive when he had purchased it new. She had chosen the yellow color. During the first few years, they had often gone out for drives together. Since his wife didn't have a license, Kafuku had always been the one behind the wheel. They had taken a number of road trips as well, to places like Izu, Hakone, and Nasu. Yet, for what was now nearly ten years, he had always driven alone. He had seen several women since his wife's death, but none had ever sat beside him in the passenger's seat. For some reason, the opportunity had never arisen. Nor had he ever taken the car outside the city, apart from those times when work made it necessary.

"There's some inevitable wear and tear, but she's in good shape," Oba said, running his palm over the dashboard as if petting the neck of a large dog. "Totally reliable. Swedish cars of this age are built to last. You have to keep your eye on the electrical system, but they're fundamentally sound. And I've been looking after this baby really well."

While Kafuku was signing the necessary papers and going over the itemized bill, the young woman showed up. She was about five foot five, not at all fat but broad-shouldered and powerfully built. There was an oval-shaped, purple birthmark on the nape of her neck to the right that she seemed to have no qualms about exposing. Her thick jet-black hair was fastened at the back, to keep it out of her way. No matter how you looked at her she could hardly be called a beauty, and there was something off-putting about her face, as Oba had suggested. The remnants of teenage acne dotted her cheeks. She had big, strikingly clear eyes that looked out suspiciously on the world, their dark brown irises all the more striking for their size. Her large, protruding ears looked

31

like a pair of satellite dishes erected in some remote landscape. She was wearing a man's herringbone jacket that was a bit too heavy for May, brown cotton pants, and a pair of black Converse sneakers. Beneath the white long-sleeved T-shirt under her jacket was a pair of larger-than-average breasts.

Oba introduced her to Kafuku. Her name was Watari. Misaki Watari.

"There are no kanji for 'Misaki'—it's written in hiragana," she said. "If you need a resumé I can get one." Kafuku detected a note of defiance in her voice.

"No need for a resumé at this stage," he said, shaking his head. "You can handle a manual shift, correct?"

"I prefer manual," she said in an icy tone. She sounded like a dyed-in-the-wool vegetarian who had just been asked if she ate lettuce.

"It's an old car, so there's no GPS."

"I don't need it. I worked as a courier for a while. I've got a map of the city in my head."

"Why don't we take a little test drive? The weather's good so we can put the top down."

"Where would you like to go?"

Kafuku thought for a moment. They were not far from Shinohashi.

"Take a right at the Tengenji intersection and then drive to the underground parking lot at the Meijiya supermarket so I can do a bit of shopping. After that we'll head up the slope to Arisugawa Park, and then down past the French Embassy and onto Meiji Avenue. Then we'll swing back here."

"Got it," she said. She asked for no further details about the route. Taking the key from Oba, she quickly adjusted the driver's seat and the mirrors. It appeared she already knew where all the buttons and levers were located. She stepped on the clutch and tested the gears. Then she pulled a pair of green Ray-Ban sunglasses from the pocket of her jacket and put them on. She turned and nodded to Kafuku to signal she was ready to go.

"A cassette player," she said as if to herself, glancing at the audio system.

"I like cassettes," Kafuku said. "They're easier than CDs. I use them to rehearse my lines."

"Haven't seen one of those for a while."

"When I started driving they were all eight-track players," Kafuku said.

Misaki didn't reply, but her expression suggested eight-track players were something new to her.

As Oba had guaranteed, she was an excellent driver. She operated the car smoothly, with no sudden jerks. The road was crowded, and had frequent stoplights, but she was focused on holding the engine's RPMs steady; the movement of her eyes told him that. When he closed his own eyes, though, he found it next to impossible to tell when she shifted. Only the sound of the engine let him know which gear the car was in. The touch of her foot on the brake and accelerator pedals was light and careful. Best of all, she was entirely relaxed. In fact, she seemed more at ease when driving. Her blunt, impersonal expression became softer, and her eyes more gentle. Yet her lack of words remained the same. She would answer his questions and nothing more.

The absence of conversation, though, didn't bother Kafuku. He wasn't good at small talk. While he didn't dislike talking to people he knew well about things that mattered, he otherwise preferred to remain silent. He sat back in the passenger seat and idly watched the city streets go by. After years behind the wheel, the view from where he now sat seemed fresh and new.

He had her parallel park several times on busy Meiji Avenue, a test she passed easily with a minimum of wasted effort. She had a good feel for the car, and her timing was perfect. She smoked only when they were stopped at traffic lights; Marlboros seemed her brand of choice. The moment the light changed she snuffed out the cigarette. Her butts had no lipstick on them. Nor were her fingernails polished or manicured. She seemed to wear virtually no makeup.

"Mind if I ask you a few questions?" Kafuku said when they were approaching Arisugawa Park.

"Go right ahead."

"Where did you learn to drive?"

"I grew up in Hokkaido, in the mountains. I started driving in my early teens. You have to have a car in a place like that. The roads are icy almost half the year. You can't avoid becoming a good driver."

"But you don't learn how to parallel park in the mountains, do you?"

She didn't answer that. Doubtless she found the question not worth bothering with.

"Did Oba explain to you why I need a driver all of a sudden?"

Misaki answered in a flat, emotionless voice, her eyes trained on the traffic ahead. "You're an actor, and you're on stage six days a week at the moment. You have always driven to the theater. You don't like taxis or taking the subway. That's because you rehearse your lines on the way. Not long ago you had a minor accident and your license was suspended. Because you'd been drinking a little, and there was a problem with your eyesight."

Kafuku nodded. It felt as if someone were describing her dream to him.

"The eye exam the police required turned up a trace of glaucoma. It appears I have a blind spot. On the right side, in the corner. I had no idea."

The amount of alcohol involved was negligible, so they had been able to hush it up; no one had leaked it to the media. But theater management couldn't ignore the problem with his eyesight. As things stood, a car might approach him from behind on his right side, and he would miss seeing it. Management thus insisted that he stop driving, at least until tests showed the problem had been fixed.

"Mr. Kafuku?" Misaki asked. "Is it all right if I call you that? It's not a stage name?"

"It's an unusual name, but it's really mine," Kafuku said. "The kanji mean 'House of Good Fortune.' Sounds auspicious, but there hasn't been any payoff as far as I can see. None of my relatives is what you could call wealthy."

After a period of silence, Kafuku told her how much she would be paid per month for being his chauffeur. Not a lot of money, but it was all his theater could afford. Although his name was well known, his status ranked below that of TV and movie stars, for there was a limit to how much money could be made on the stage. For an actor in his class, hiring a personal driver, even if only for a few months, was an exceptional luxury.

"Your work schedule will be subject to change, but these days my life is centered around the theater, which means your mornings are basically free. You can sleep till noon if you wish. I'll make sure you can quit by eleven—if I have to work later than that I'll take a taxi home. You will have one day off every week."

"I accept," Misaki said simply.

"The work shouldn't be that taxing. The hard part will be waiting around for hours with nothing to do."

Misaki did not respond. Her lips were set in a straight line. The look on her face said that she had tackled a ton of far more difficult jobs.

"I don't mind if you smoke while the top is down," Kafuku said. "But please don't when it's up."

"Agreed."

"Do you have any conditions?"

"Nothing in particular." She narrowed her eyes as she carefully downshifted. "I like the car," she added.

They drove the rest of the way without talking. When they arrived back at the garage, Kafuku called Oba out to give him the news. "I've decided to hire her," he announced.

Misaki started working as Kafuku's personal driver the next day. She would show up at his Ebisu apartment building at half past three in the afternoon, take the yellow Saab out of the underground garage, and drive him to a theater in Ginza. They drove with the top down unless it was raining. Kafuku practiced his lines on the way, reciting with the cassette recording. The play was a Meiji-era adaptation of Chekhov's *Uncle Vanya*. He played the role of Uncle Vanya. He knew the lines by heart, but ran through them anyway to calm his nerves before a performance. This was his long-standing habit.

As a rule, they listened to Beethoven string quartets on the way home. Kafuku never tired of them—he found them perfectly suited to thinking, or, if he preferred, thinking about nothing at all. If he wanted something lighter, he chose classic American rock. Groups like the Beach Boys, the Rascals, CCR, the Temptations, and so on. The popular music of his youth. Misaki never commented on his selection. He couldn't tell if his music pleased or pained her, or if she was listening at all for that matter. She was a young woman who didn't show her emotions.

Under normal circumstances, Kafuku found reciting his lines in the presence of others stressful, but those inhibitions vanished with Misaki. In that regard, he appreciated her lack of expressiveness and her cool, distant personality. However he might roar beside her when rehearsing, she acted as though she heard nothing. Indeed it was quite possible that her attention was solely focused on the road. Perhaps driving put her in a Zen-like frame of mind.

Kafuku was in the dark as to what Misaki thought of him as a person. Was she kindly disposed, or unimpressed and disinterested, or did she loathe him and put up with him just to keep her job? He had no idea. In fact, though, it didn't matter to him all that much how she felt. He liked the smooth and sure way she handled the car, her lack of chatter, and the way she kept her feelings to herself.

When the night's performance ended, Kafuku washed off his stage makeup, changed his clothes, and left the theater as quickly as possible. He didn't like dawdling around. He knew almost none of his fellow actors. He would call Misaki on his cell phone and have her drive to the stage door to pick him up. When he stepped outside the yellow Saab would be waiting for him. By the time he got back to his Ebisu apartment it would be a little after ten-thirty. This pattern repeated itself on a nightly basis.

He had other work as well. He spent one day a week shooting a drama series at a TV studio in the middle of the city. It was your garden-variety detective show, but the audience was large and it paid well. He played a fortune-teller who assisted the female lead detective. To prepare for the role, he had dressed in fortune-teller's garb and set up a desk on the street, where he told the fortunes of a number of passersby. Word had it that many of his prognostications had hit the mark. When his day of shooting ended he went straight from the studio to the theater in Ginza. That was the risky part. On weekends, after the matinee, he would teach a night class at an acting school. He loved working with young actors. Misaki ferried him around for all these activities. She drove him from place to place without the slightest fuss, always on time, so that Kafuku grew used to sitting beside her in the Saab's passenger seat. On occasion, he even fell fast asleep.

When the weather grew warmer, Misaki replaced her herringbone jacket with a lighter summer jacket. She always wore a jacket while working. Probably it was her equivalent of a chauffeur's uniform. With the rainy season, the roof was left up more frequently.

Sitting there in the passenger seat, Kafuku often thought of his dead wife. For some reason, he recalled her more frequently now that Misaki was doing the driving. His wife had been an actor too, a stunning woman two years his junior. Kafuku was what was generally known as a character actor, usually asked to play supporting roles that were quirky in some way or other. He had a long and narrow face, and had begun balding when still quite young. Not the leading-man type. His beautiful wife, on the other hand, was a real leading lady, and her roles and income reflected that status. As they got older, however, he became known as a skilled actor with a distinctive persona, while her star waned. Since each respected what the other was doing, the shifts in their popularity and income never caused problems.

Kafuku adored his wife. He had fallen deeply in love with her when they met (he was twenty-nine), and this feeling had remained unchanged until the day she died (he had been forty-nine). He hadn't slept with another woman in all their years of marriage. The urge had never arisen, although he had received his fair share of opportunities.

His wife, however, slept with other men on occasion. As far as he knew, there had been four such affairs. In other words, there were four men who had shared her bed for periods of time. She had never breathed a word to him, of course, but it hadn't taken long to figure out that she was sleeping with some other man in some other place. Kafuku had a sixth sense about such things, and his love for her made it impossible for him to ignore the signs, however much he would have liked to. It was easy to tell who her lovers were, too, from the way she talked about them. Invariably, they were fellow actors working on the same film. Most were younger. The relationship would continue for the few months they were shooting the movie and die a natural death when the filming stopped. The same thing had happened four times, always following the same pattern.

Kafuku hadn't understood why she felt the need to sleep with other men. And he still didn't. Their relationship as a married couple and as life partners had been excellent from the beginning. When time permitted, they talked with passion and honesty about a wide variety of subjects, and strove to trust one another. He had thought they were a most compatible pair, both spiritually and sexually. Others in their circle also regarded them as an ideal match.

He regretted that he had not summoned his resolve while she was still alive to ask her about her affairs. It was a regret that visited him frequently. He had been oh so close to putting the question to her. He would have asked: What were you looking for in those other men? What did you find lacking in me? But it had been mere months before the end, and she was suffering terribly as she struggled against her approaching death. He didn't have the heart to demand an answer. Then, without a word of explanation, she had vanished from Kafuku's world—the question never ventured, the answer never proffered. He was lost in such thoughts at the crematorium as he plucked her bones from the ashes. So lost that when someone spoke in his ear he did not hear him.

Needless to say, picturing his wife in the arms of another man was painful for Kafuku. It could be no other way. When he closed his eyes, the details of their lovemaking would rise unbidden and then fade away, only to rise again. He hadn't wanted to imagine such things, but he couldn't help it. The images carved away at him like a keen blade, steady and unrelenting. There were times he'd thought it would have been far better to never have known. Yet the principle that, in every situation, knowledge was better than ignorance lay at the core of his way of thinking—it was from that stance that he faced the world. However agonizing, it was necessary to confront *the facts*. Only through knowing could a person become strong.

Most excruciating of all, though, had been living a normal life with a partner whose secret he knew—the effort it required to keep *her* in the dark. Smiling calmly when his heart was torn and his insides were bleeding. Behaving as if everything was fine while the two of them took care of the daily chores, chatted, made love at night. Not something that a normal person could pull off. But Kafuku was a professional actor. Shedding his self, his flesh-and-blood being, to embrace a role was his calling. And he embraced this one with all his might. A role performed without an audience.

Yet if you put these things aside—excluded, in other words, the fact that she conducted occasional affairs with other men—their married life was calm and contented. Their careers proceeded smoothly, and they had no financial worries. Over the course of their nearly twenty years together, they made love countless times; for him, at least, the sex had been entirely satisfying. After she contracted uterine cancer and, in what seemed a mere instant later, passed away, he had been lucky enough to meet several women who, in the natural course of things, he had taken to bed. Yet he never experienced the same intimate joy with them that he had with his wife. All he felt was a mild sense of déjà vu, as if he were reenacting a scene from his past.

Kafuku's office needed specific information to process Misaki's paychecks, so he had to ask her to provide her address, the location of her family register, her birth date, and her driver's license number. She was living in an apartment in downtown Akabane, her family register was in Nakatonbetsu-cho on the island of Hokkaido, and she had just turned twenty-four. Kafuku had no idea where Nakatonbetsu-cho was in Hokkaido. But the fact that she was twenty-four grabbed his attention.

Kafuku's wife had given birth to a baby who had lived only three days. It was a girl. She died her third night in the hospital nursery. Her heart stopped without warning. When they found her the next morning she was already cold. The hospital said that she had been born with a defective heart. There had been no way to verify their story. Nor would finding the true cause of death have restored her to life. For better or for worse, they had not yet given her a name. Had she lived, she would have been twenty-four years old. Kafuku always marked the birthday of this nameless child by joining his hands in prayer. Then he would think about how old she would be had she lived.

As one would expect, the sudden death of their child wounded Kafuku and his wife, suspending them in a dark, heavy void.

It took them a very long time to get back on their feet. They secluded themselves in their apartment, where for much of the time they lived in virtual silence. Words, they felt, could only cheapen the emotions they were feeling. She began drinking immoderate amounts of wine. He, for a time, became a passionate, almost fanatical practitioner of calligraphy. It was as if he felt that the black symbols flowing from his brush onto the pure white paper could somehow lay bare the workings of his heart.

Nevertheless, by supporting each other, slowly but surely, the two of them recovered from their wounds enough to pass through that dangerous period. Now their focus on their work was even more intense. When they took on new roles they immersed themselves totally, voraciously. She told him that she had no more desire for children, and he agreed to help make sure she never got pregnant again. He was happy to do whatever she wanted.

Thinking back, he realized that it was then that her love affairs began. Perhaps the loss of their child had reawakened her sexual desire. But that was pure conjecture on his part. No more than another *perhaps.*

C an I ask you something?" Misaki said.
Kafuku had been looking out the window at the passing scenery, lost in thought. He turned to her in surprise. They had been driving around together for two months, and rarely had she initiated a conversation.

"Of course," Kafuku said.

"Why did you become an actor?"

"A college friend of mine, a girl, asked me to join her theater club. I'd never been interested in acting. I wanted to play baseball. I'd been the starting shortstop on my high school team, and was pretty confident of my defensive ability. But I wasn't quite good enough for our college team. So I figured, what the heck, I might as well take a stab at something new. I wanted to spend more time with that girl, too. After I'd been acting for a while, though, it dawned on me that I really liked it. Performing allowed me to be someone other than myself. And I could revert back when the performance ended. I really loved that."

"You loved being someone other than yourself?"

"Yes, as long as I knew I could go back."

"Did you ever not want to go back?"

Kafuku thought for a moment. No one had asked him that before. They were heading for the Takebashi exit on the Tokyo Metropolitan Expressway, and the road was jammed.

"There's no other place to go back to, is there?" Kafuku said.

Misaki didn't venture an opinion.

They were silent for a while. Kafuku removed his baseball cap, inspected its shape, and stuck it back on. Next to them was a tractor-trailer with too many wheels to count, a huge rig which made their yellow Saab convertible feel transitory, ephemeral, like a tiny sightseeing boat floating next to an oil tanker.

"This may be out of line," Misaki said, "but it's been on my mind. Is it OK if I ask?"

"Shoot," Kafuku said.

"Why don't you have any friends?"

Kafuku cast an inquisitive eye at Misaki's profile. "How do you know I don't have any?"

Misaki shrugged. "I've been driving you around for two months now, so I guess I can figure out that much."

Kafuku studied the tractor-trailer's enormous tires for a long moment. "There haven't been many people I could call true friends," he finally said. "I wonder why."

"Even when you were a child?"

"No, I had lots of pals back then. But once I grew up I no longer felt the need for them. Especially after I got married."

"You mean having a wife meant you didn't need friends anymore?"

"I guess so. She and I were great pals, too, after all."

"How old were you when you got married?"

"Thirty. We were in the same movie. She had a major supporting role, and I had a bit part."

The car inched its way forward through the jam. The roof was closed, as it always was when they drove on the expressway.

"You don't drink at all?" Kafuku changed the subject.

"My body can't handle alcohol," Misaki said. "And my mother was a problem drinker, which may have something to do with it."

"Does her drinking still cause problems?"

Misaki shook her head from side to side. "My mother's dead. She was driving drunk, lost control of the steering wheel, went into a spin, and flew off the road and into a tree. She died almost instantly. I was seventeen at the time."

"Poor woman," Kafuku said.

"What goes around comes around," Misaki said without emotion. "It was bound to happen sooner or later. The only question was when."

They were silent for a while.

"And your father?"

"I don't know where he is. He left home when I was eight and I haven't seen him since. Haven't heard from him either. Mother always blamed me for his leaving."

"Why?"

"I was their only child. If I'd been prettier, Father never would have left. That's what Mother always said. It's because I was born ugly that he abandoned us."

"You're not ugly," Kafuku said quietly. "Your mother just preferred to think of it that way."

Misaki gave a slight shrug. "Normally she wasn't like that, but when she was drinking she would go on and on. Repeat the same stuff over and over again. It hurt me. It's bad, I know, but I was relieved when she died."

This time the silence was even longer.

"Do you have friends?" Kafuku inquired.

Misaki shook her head. "Not a single one."

"Why?"

She didn't answer. Eyes narrowed, she was focused on the road.

Kafuku tried to take a nap, but sleep wouldn't come. The car edged forward and stopped, edged forward and stopped, as she deftly shifted gears. In the adjacent lane the tractor-trailer moved ahead and fell behind, like the shadow cast by some enormous fate.

Kafuku gave up trying to sleep. "The last time I became friends with someone was nearly ten years ago," he said, opening his eyes. "Perhaps 'someone like a friend' would be more accurate. He was six or seven years younger than me, a heck of a nice guy. He liked to drink, so we drank and talked about all kinds of things."

Misaki nodded and waited for him to continue. Kafuku hesitated for a moment before deciding to take the plunge.

"To tell you the truth, he was one of my wife's lovers. He didn't know that I knew, though."

It took Misaki a long moment to get her head around what she had just heard. "You mean he was having sex with your wife?" she said at last.

"That's right. I think he was having sex with my wife on a regular basis for three or four months."

"How did you know?"

"She hid it from me, of course, but I could tell. It would take too long to explain how. But there was no question. My imagination wasn't playing tricks."

When they stopped for a moment, Misaki reached up with both hands to adjust the rearview mirror. "Didn't that get in the way of your becoming friends?"

"Quite the opposite," Kafuku said. "I made him my friend precisely because he had slept with my wife."

Misaki didn't say anything. She waited for him to go on.

"How can I put this . . . I wanted to understand. Why she slept with him, why he was the one she wanted. At least that was my motive in the beginning."

Misaki took a long, deep breath. Her chest rose beneath her jacket, then sank back. "But wasn't that awfully painful? Drinking and talking with a man you knew had slept with your wife?"

"It wasn't easy," Kafuku said. "It made me think things I would prefer to have ignored. Remember things I would rather have forgotten. But I was acting. That is my profession, after all."

"Becoming somebody different," Misaki said.

"That's right."

"And then going back to who you are."

"That's right," Kafuku said. "Whether you want to or not. But the place you return to is always slightly different than the place you left. That's the rule. It can never be exactly the same."

A fine rain began to fall. Misaki worked the wipers for a while. "So then did you figure it out? Why your wife slept with him?"

"No," Kafuku shook his head. "I never understood. He possessed a few attributes that I lacked. All right, *a lot* of attributes, I guess. But I could never figure out which of those caught her fancy. Our actions aren't based on specifics like that—we can't pinpoint why we do what we do. Relationships between people, especially between men and women, operate on—what should I say—a more general level. More vague, more self-centered, more pathetic."

Misaki thought for a moment. "But still," she said, "you stayed friends with him even though you didn't understand, right?"

Kafuku took off his baseball cap again and placed it on his lap. "It's hard to explain," he said, rubbing the top of his head with his palm. "Once you really get into a role it's hard to find the right moment to stop. No matter how it taxes your emotions, you have to go with the flow until the performance has taken the shape it must, the point where its full meaning becomes clear. It's the same with music. A song doesn't reach a proper end until it arrives at a final, predetermined chord. Do you understand what I mean?"

Misaki drew a Marlboro from her pack and placed it between her lips. But she never smoked when the top was up, and it stayed unlit.

"So was the guy still sleeping with your wife when you were friends?"

"No, he wasn't," said Kafuku. "If he were it would have been, how should I say . . . too complicated. We became friends not long after my wife's death."

"So were you *real* friends? Or was it all just acting?"

Kafuku thought for a while. "It was both. It's gotten so I have a hard time drawing a clear line between the two. In the end, that's what serious acting is all about."

From the beginning, Kafuku had been able to feel something approaching affection for the man. His name was Takatsuki, and he was a tall, good-looking fellow, the classic romantic lead. He was in his early forties and not an especially skilled actor.

Nor did he have what one could call a distinctive presence. His range of roles was limited. As a general rule, he played nice guys, although sometimes a touch of melancholy would cloud his otherwise cheerful profile. He had a loyal following among middle-aged women. Kafuku bumped into him on occasion in the green room at the TV studio. Some six months after his wife's death, Takatsuki came up to introduce himself and express his condolences. "Your wife and I were in a film together once. I owed her a lot," Takatsuki said, humility written on his face. Kafuku thanked him. As far as he knew, chronologically speaking, this man was the last of his wife's string of lovers. It was soon after the end of their affair that his wife had gone to the hospital for tests and been diagnosed with advanced uterine cancer.

"Forgive me, but I'd like to ask a favor," Kafuku said when the formalities had concluded. This was his chance to broach what he had in mind.

"Is there something I can do?"

"If it's all right with you, I'd like you to grant me some of your time. To talk about my wife. Maybe have a few drinks and remember her together. She often spoke of you."

Takatsuki looked surprised at this sudden turn in the conversation. Perhaps "shocked" would be more accurate. His immaculate eyebrows inched together as he cautiously studied Kafuku's face. He seemed to be trying to discern what, if anything, might lie behind the invitation. But he could read no intent in the older man's expression. All he saw was the kind of stillness you might expect from someone who not long before had lost his wife of many years. Like the surface of a pond after the ripples had spread and gone.

"I was only hoping to talk about my wife with someone who knew her," Kafuku added. "To tell the truth, it can get kind of rough when I'm sitting at home all by myself. I know it's an imposition on you, though."

Takatsuki looked relieved. His relationship with the man's wife did not seem to be under suspicion.

"It's no imposition at all. I'd be happy to make time for something like that. I just hope I won't bore you." A faint smile rose to his lips as he said these words, and the corners of his eyes crinkled with compassion. An altogether charming expression. If I were a middle-aged woman, thought Kafuku, my cheeks would be turning pink right now.

Takatsuki mentally flipped through the schedule he kept in his head. "I think I have plenty of time tomorrow night. Do you have other plans?"

Kafuku replied that he was also free then. He was struck by how easy it was to read Takatsuki's emotions. The man was transparent—if he looked into his eyes long enough, Kafuku thought, he could probably see the wall behind him. There was nothing warped, nothing nasty. Hardly the type to dig a deep hole at night and wait for someone to fall in. But neither, in all likelihood, a man destined to achieve greatness as an actor.

"Where shall we meet?" asked Takatsuki.

"I leave it to you," Kafuku said. "Tell me a place, and I'll be there."

Takatsuki named a well-known bar in Ginza. He would reserve a booth, he said, so that they could talk frankly without having to worry about being overheard. Kafuku knew the spot. They shook hands goodbye. Takatsuki's hand was soft, with long slender fingers. His palm was warm and slightly damp, as if he had been sweating. Perhaps he was nervous.

After he left, Kafuku sat down on a chair in the green room, opened his right hand, and stared hard at his palm. The sensation left by the handshake was still fresh. *That hand*, those fingers, had caressed his wife's naked body. Slowly and deliberately, exploring every nook and cranny. He closed his eyes and breathed deeply. What in heaven's name was he trying to do? Whatever it was, he felt, he had no choice but to go ahead and do it.

Sipping single malt whiskey in the booth at the bar, Kafuku came to one conclusion. Even now, Takatsuki was deeply attached to his wife. He still had not grasped the immutable fact of her death, that the flesh he had known was now a pile of charred bone and ash. Kafuku could understand the way he felt. When Takatsuki's eyes grew misty recalling her, he wanted to reach out to console him. The man was quite incapable of hiding his emotions. Kafuku sensed he could trip him up with a trick question if he so chose, induce him to confess everything.

Judging from Takatsuki's way of talking, Kafuku's wife had been the one to call a halt to their affair. "It's best we not meet anymore," was probably how she had put it. And she had followed up on her words. A relationship of several months brought to a sudden close. Nothing long and drawn out. As far as Kafuku knew, that was the pattern of all her amours (if they could be called that). But it seemed Takatsuki couldn't handle such a quick and casual break. He must have been hoping for a more permanent bond.

Takatsuki had tried to visit her during the final phase of her cancer, but had been flatly refused. She had seen almost no one since being admitted to the city hospital. Other than hospital staff, only three people were permitted in her room: her mother, sister, and Kafuku. Takatsuki seemed filled with regret that he had not been able to see her during that time. He had not even known she had cancer until a few weeks before her death. The news had hit him like a thunderbolt, and still hadn't entirely sunk in. Kafuku could relate to that. Yet their feelings were far from identical. Kafuku had watched his wife waste away day by day as the end drew near, and had plucked her pure white bones from the ashes at the crematorium. He had passed through all the stages. That made a huge difference.

As they reminisced about his wife, it hit Kafuku that he was the one doing most of the consoling. How would his wife feel if she observed them sitting together like this? The idea aroused a strange emotion in Kafuku. But he doubted the dead could think or feel anything. In his opinion, that was one of the great things about dying.

One other thing was becoming clear. Takatsuki drank way too much. There were many heavy drinkers in Kafuku's line of work—why were actors so susceptible to alcohol?—so he could tell Takatsuki's drinking was not the healthy, wholesome kind. In Kafuku's considered opinion, there were two types of drinkers: those who drank to add something to who they were, and those who sought to subtract something. Takatsuki clearly belonged to the latter group.

Kafuku could not tell what it was he was trying to get rid of. Maybe weakness in his character, or trauma from his past. Or perhaps something in the present was causing his problem. Whatever it was, he was trying like mad either to forget it or to numb the pain it caused, which made it necessary to drink. For every drink Kafuku took, Takatsuki downed two and a half. Quite a pace.

Then again, he might just be tense. He was, after all, sitting face-to-face with the husband of the woman with whom he had been secretly having an affair. That was bound to put him on edge. But Kafuku guessed there was more to it. A man like Takatsuki could probably only drink this way.

Kafuku drank at a careful, steady rate while keeping a close eye on his companion. When the number of glasses mounted and the younger man began to relax, Kafuku asked him if he was married. I've been married ten years and have a seven-year-old son, Takatsuki answered. Due to certain circumstances, however, he and his wife had been living apart since the previous year. A divorce was likely, and the question of who would get custody of the child loomed large. What he wanted to avoid at any cost was being unable to visit his son freely. He needed the boy in his life. He showed Kafuku his child's photograph. A handsome, sweet-looking kid.

Like most habitual drinkers, the more alcohol Takatsuki drank the more loose-lipped he became. He volunteered information he shouldn't have without being asked. Kafuku took on the role of listener, interjecting an encouraging word here and there to keep his companion talking and offering carefully selected phrases of comfort when consolation seemed appropriate. All the while he was piling up as much information as he could. Kafuku acted as though he had only the warmest feelings for Takatsuki. This was not a hard thing to do. He was a born listener, and he did *truly* like the younger man. In addition, the two of them had one big thing in common: both were still in love with the same beautiful, dead woman. Despite the difference in their positions, neither had been able to get over that loss. They had a lot to talk about.

"Why don't we meet again?" Kafuku suggested when the evening was winding down. "It was a pleasure talking with you. I haven't felt this good for a long time." Kafuku had taken care of the bar tab in advance. It seemed not to have dawned on Takatsuki that someone would have to pay. Alcohol led him to forget a lot of things. Some were doubtless very important.

"Certainly," Takatsuki said, looking up from his glass. "I'd love to get together again. Talking to you has taken a weight off my chest."

"I feel that our meeting was somehow preordained," Kafuku said. "Perhaps my dead wife brought us together."

There was some truth to that.

They exchanged cell phone numbers. Then they shook hands and parted.

Thus the two men became friends. Drinking buddies, to be more accurate. They would contact each other, meet at a bar, and talk about a variety of subjects. Not once did they share a meal. Bars were their only venues. Kafuku had never seen Takatsuki eat anything more substantial than a light snack to accompany his liquor. For all he knew, the guy might never eat solid food. Except for the occasional beer, the only drink he ever ordered was whiskey. Single malt was his preference.

Their topics varied, but at some point the conversation would always turn to Kafuku's dead wife. Kafuku would relate episodes from her younger days while Takatsuki listened intently. He looked like a researcher plumbing a key informant's memory to assemble a comprehensive database about someone. Kafuku found himself enjoying those moments.

One night, the two were drinking in Aoyama at a small, nondescript bar tucked away on a narrow lane behind the Nezu Museum. The bartender was a quiet man of about forty, and a skinny gray cat was curled up on a display shelf in a corner of the room. It appeared to be an alley cat that had moved in for the time being. An old jazz record was spinning on the turntable. Both men liked the feel of the place, and had gone there several times before. For some reason, it often rained on the nights they met, and this night was no exception—a thin drizzle was falling outside.

"She was a wonderful woman," Takatsuki said, studying his hands on the table. They were attractive hands for a man already

53

in middle age. There were no wrinkles around his eyes, either, and his fingernails were tended with care. "You were fortunate to find her, Mr. Kafuku, and to have shared a life together."

"You're right," Kafuku said. "I guess I was happy then. But that much happiness can lead to an equal amount of pain."

"In what way?"

Kafuku picked up his glass and swirled the chunk of ice in it. "I worried that I might lose her. Just imagining that made my heart ache."

"I know that feeling," Takatsuki said.

"How so?"

"I mean . . . " Takatsuki said, groping for the right words. "Losing someone that wonderful."

"On general principle."

"Yes," Takatsuki said. He nodded several times as if trying to convince himself. "I can only imagine what it must be like."

Kafuku fell silent. He let the silence linger as long as possible. At last he spoke.

"In the end, though, I lost her. Gradually in the beginning, then completely in the end. Like something being eroded away bit by bit. The process began slowly until finally a tidal wave swept it all off, roots and all . . . Understand what I mean?"

"I think I do."

Like hell you do, Kafuku said in his heart.

"Here's what hurts the most," Kafuku said. "I didn't *truly* understand her—or at least some crucial part of her. And it may well end that way now that she's dead and gone. Like a small, locked safe lying at the bottom of the ocean. It hurts a lot."

Takatsuki thought for a moment before speaking.

"But, Mr. Kafuku, can any of us ever perfectly understand another person? However much we may love them?"

"We lived together for nearly twenty years," Kafuku said. "As man and wife, but also as trusted friends. We were able to talk frankly about anything and everything, or so I thought. But maybe it wasn't really like that. Perhaps—how should I put this?—I had what amounted to a fatal blind spot."

"Blind spot," Takatsuki echoed.

"There was something inside her, something important, that I must have missed. If I saw it, perhaps I failed to recognize it for what it was *in fact*."

Takatsuki chewed his lip for a minute. He drained his glass and called to the bartender to bring him another drink.

"I know what you mean," he said.

Kafuku stared hard at him. Takatsuki met his gaze for a few seconds and looked away.

"In what sense do you know?" Kafuku said in a low voice.

The bartender brought a fresh glass of whiskey on ice and replaced Takatsuki's wet coaster with a new one. They remained silent until he had left.

"In what sense do you know?" Kafuku repeated.

Takatsuki pondered this question for a moment. Kafuku glimpsed movement in his eyes. He's wavering, he concluded. Battling the urge to reveal something. In the end, though, Takatsuki managed to quell whatever had shaken him.

"I don't think we can ever understand all that a woman is thinking," he said. "That's what I wanted to say. No matter who that woman may be. So I doubt the blind spot you speak of is yours alone. If that's what you wish to call it, then we men are all living with the same sort of blind spot. So I don't think you should blame yourself."

"All the same, you're speaking in generalities," Kafuku said after some thought.

"That's true," said Takatsuki.

"But I'm talking about my dead wife and me. I don't want to jump to general principles so easily."

"From what I can gather," Takatsuki said after a long silence, "your wife was a wonderful woman. I am convinced of that even as I realize my knowledge of her is no more than a hundredth of yours. If nothing else, you should feel grateful for having been able to spend twenty years of your life with such a person. But the proposition that we can look into another person's heart with perfect clarity strikes me as a fool's game. I don't care how well we think we should understand them, or how much we love them. All it can do is cause us pain. Examining your own heart, however, is another matter. I think it's possible to see what's in there if you work hard enough at it. So in the end maybe that's the challenge, to look inside your own heart as perceptively and seriously as you can and make peace with what you find there. If we hope to *truly* see another, we have to start by looking within ourselves."

Takatsuki's speech seemed to have emerged from deep inside. A hidden door had swung open, if only for a short time. His words were clear and charged with conviction. He wasn't acting, that was for sure. His acting chops weren't that good. Kafuku said nothing, just looked straight into his eyes. This time Takatsuki met his gaze and held it for a long time. They could see a certain sparkle of recognition in each other's eyes.

They shook hands once again on parting. A fine rain was falling outside. After Takatsuki had walked off into the drizzle in his beige raincoat, Kafuku, as was his habit, looked down at his right palm. It was *that hand* that caressed my wife's naked body, he thought.

Yet strange to say, on this day the thought did not suffocate him. Instead, his reaction was, yes, such things do happen. They do happen. After all, it's just a matter of flesh and blood. No more than a pile of bone and ash in the end, right? There has to be something more important than that.

If that's what you wish to call it, then we men are all living with the same sort of blind spot. The words rang in his ear for a very long time.

"So did the friendship last?" Misaki asked, her eyes fixed on the line of cars in front of them.

"It continued for about six months, give or take. We'd get together at a bar every two weeks or so and drink together," Kafuku said. "Then it ended. I ignored his phone calls. Made no attempt to contact him. After a while he stopped calling."

"I bet he found that strange."

"Probably."

"You may have hurt his feelings."

"I guess so."

"Why did you break it off so suddenly?"

"Because there was no need to keep acting."

"You mean there was no need to stay friends once you didn't have to act?"

"Yes, there was that," Kafuku said. "But there was another reason too."

"What was it?"

Kafuku fell silent. Misaki glanced at him occasionally, the unlit cigarette clamped between her lips.

"Go ahead and smoke if you want," Kafuku said.

"Huh?"

"You can light that thing."

"But the roof is closed."

"I don't care."

Misaki lowered her window, lit the Marlboro with the car lighter, and took a deep drag. Her eyes narrowed in pleasure. She exhaled slowly, directing the smoke out the window.

"Tobacco's a killer," Kafuku said.

"Being alive is a killer if you look at it that way," Misaki said.

Kafuku laughed. "That's one school of thought."

"That's the first time I've seen you laugh," Misaki said.

She had a point, Kafuku thought. It had been a long time indeed since he had laughed, not as an act, but for real.

"I've been meaning to tell you this for some time," he said. "But there's something very attractive about you. You're not homely at all."

"Thank you very much. My features are plain, that's all. Like Sonya's."

Kafuku looked at Misaki in surprise. "I see you've read *Uncle Vanya*."

"I hear little bits of it every day, so I wanted to know what it was about. I get curious too, you know," Misaki said. "'Oh, how miserable I am! I can't stand it. Why was I born so poorly favored? The agony!' A sad play, isn't it."

"A sad play indeed," Kafuku said. "'Oh, how unbearable! Is there no help for me? I am forty-seven now. If I live till sixty I still have thirteen years to endure. Too long. How shall I pass those thirteen years? What will help me get through the days?' People only lived to about sixty back then. Uncle Vanya was fortunate he wasn't born into today's world."

"You were born the same year as my father. I checked."

Kafuku didn't respond. He took a handful of cassettes and scanned the songs on the labels. But he didn't play one. Misaki was holding the lit cigarette in her left hand with her arm out the window. Only when the line of cars crept forward and she had to use both hands to steer and shift gears did she place it between her lips for a moment.

"To be honest, I wanted to punish that guy," Kafuku said as if confessing to something. "The guy who slept with my wife." He put the cassettes back in their container.

"Punish him?"

"Make him pay for what he did. My plan was to put him off his guard by pretending to be his friend, find his fatal flaw, and use it to torture him."

"What kind of fatal flaw?" Misaki asked, knitting her brow in thought.

"I didn't think that far ahead. He was a guy who let his defenses down when he drank, so I was sure something would turn up sooner or later. I could use whatever it was to cause a scandal—create a situation that would destroy his reputation. I figured it would be a piece of cake. When he went through divorce arbitration he'd probably lose the right to see his son, which would be a terrible blow. I doubted he could recover from that."

"That's pretty dark."

"Yeah, it's dark for sure."

"And it was all to take revenge on him for sleeping with your wife?"

"It was slightly different than revenge," Kafuku said. "I wasn't able to forget what had taken place between them. I worked really hard at it. But I failed. The image of her in another man's arms was stuck in my mind, as real as life. As if there was a demon with nowhere else to go clinging to a corner of the ceiling, eyes fastened on me. After my wife's death, I expected the demon would disappear if I just waited long enough. But he didn't. Instead his presence grew even stronger. I had to get rid of him. To do that I had to let go of the rage I was holding in."

Kafuku wondered why he was telling all this to a young woman from Nakatonbetsu-cho in Hokkaido, a girl young enough to be his daughter. Yet once he started he found he couldn't stop.

"So you thought you'd try to punish him," the girl said.

"Yes, that's true."

"But you didn't, did you?"

"No, I didn't," Kafuku said.

Misaki looked relieved to hear that. She gave a small sigh and flicked her lit cigarette onto the road. He guessed that was what people did in Nakatonbetsu-cho.

"I can't explain it very well, but at a certain point a lot of things didn't seem like that big a deal anymore. Like the demon had left me all of a sudden," Kafuku said. "The rage vanished. Or maybe it was never rage in the first place."

"Whatever it was, I'm glad for your sake that it left. That you never seriously hurt anyone."

"I think so too."

"But you never did figure out why your wife slept with that fellow, why *it had to be him*, did you?"

"No, I never grasped that. It's still a big question mark for me. He was a nice, uncomplicated guy. And I think he truly loved my wife. It wasn't just a romp in the hay for him. Her death hit him hard. Being turned away from her sickbed at the end hurt him a lot too. I couldn't help liking the guy, even thought we could become friends."

Kafuku broke off. He was trying to trace the course of his feelings to find the words that best matched reality.

"In fact, though, he was a man of little consequence. He had a good personality. He was handsome, with a winning smile. He got along with everybody. But he wasn't someone who commanded much respect. He was a weak man, and a second-rate actor. My wife, though, had a strong will and great depth of character. She was the type of person who could think things through on her own. So how could she fall for a *nonentity* like that and go to bed with him? It's still a thorn in my heart."

"It sounds like you take it as an insult. Is that how it is?"

Kafuku thought for a moment. She had a point. "You may be right," he said.

"Isn't it possible that your wife didn't fall for him at all?" Misaki said simply. "And that's why she slept with him?"

Kafuku regarded Misaki's profile as if gazing at a distant landscape. She worked the wipers a few times to remove the drops from the windshield. The newly installed blades squeaked like a pair of squabbling twins.

"Women can be like that," Misaki added.

Kafuku couldn't think of what to say. So he kept silent.

"To me, it's a kind of sickness. Thinking about it doesn't do much good. My father's walking out on my mother and me, my mother's constant abuse—I blame the sickness for those things. There's no logic involved. All I can do is accept what they did and try to get on with my life."

"So then we're all actors," Kafuku said.

"Yes, I think that's true. To a point, anyway."

Kafuku settled back in his leather seat, closed his eyes, and tried to focus his mind on the sound of the engine when she shifted gears. But he couldn't catch the precise moment. It was all too smooth, too mysterious. He could only make out a slight gradation in the engine's hum. It was like the wings of a flying insect, now drawing closer, now fading away.

Time to take a nap, Kafuku thought. Sleep deeply and wake up. Ten or fifteen minutes would be enough. Then back to the stage, and the acting. The bright lights, the rehearsed lines. The applause, the falling curtain. Leaving oneself for a brief time, then returning. But the self one returned to was never exactly the same as the self one left.

"I'm going to sleep a little," Kafuku said.

Misaki didn't answer. She quietly studied the road. Kafuku was grateful for her silence.

Aleksandar Hemon

was born in 1964, in Sarajevo, Bosnia and
Herzegovina. He began writing fiction in English
in 1995 and was awarded a "genius grant" from
the MacArthur Foundation in 2004. He is the
author of *The Question of Bruno, Nowhere Man,
The Lazarus Project,* and *Love and Obstacles.*
His collection of autobiographical essays, *The
Book of My Lives,* was published by Farrar, Straus
and Giroux in March 2013. His latest novel is
The Making of Zombie Wars, and this fall he
will publish *Behind the Glass Wall,* a nonfiction
chronicle of the United Nations. He lives in Chicago
with his wife and two daughters.

In Search of Space Lost

ALEKSANDAR HEMON

Whenever I write about my parents I am compelled to open with the following statement: My parents arrived in Canada at the height of the war in Bosnia. They had left Sarajevo in the spring of 1992, just as the siege got under way, wandered as refugees around Bosnia and Serbia, and finally, in December of 1993, landed in Hamilton, Ontario, a dismal steel-mill town thirty miles from Toronto. They brought nothing with them, except for Mak, the family Irish setter. This displacement is the central event of their life, what split it into the before and the after. Everything after the rupture took place in a damaged, incomplete time—some of it was forever lost, and forever it shall so remain.

Upon their arrival in Hamilton, they at first lived in a two-bedroom rental apartment on the fifteenth floor of a nondescript building, paid for by the Ontario government and modestly equipped with donated secondhand furniture. They took English classes with other refugees and immigrants, acquiring words for things they lost or didn't have. The very scarcity of possessions reminded them that they were foreigners living in someone else's space, relatively comfortable as it might have been, and that their home space—Sarajevo, Bosnia—was now in the before, beyond their reach.

Back in Bosnia, my family possessed property, which is to say, we had spaces we called our own. Not only did we live in an apartment that was pretty big by the standards of socialist housing, but we also had a couple of cabins (one each to be inherited by my sister and me) on Jahorina, a mountain outside Sarajevo. My parents loved the mountain; nearly every weekend, they would drive to Jahorina, with or without their children.

They insisted it was the nature (always good for you) that drew them, but they loved the cabins because they could keep busy. My parents are the kind of people who always have to be doing something, ever in the middle of a number of short- and long-term projects; the kind of people who believe they'll die the day they have nothing to do. Thus Mother cleaned and organized the cabins, pickled vegetables, roasted peppers on an outdoor grill my father built, etc. Meanwhile, Father had a workshop in the cabin basement; he'd build a nail-less table; restore an old chair, extending its life span indefinitely; construct shelves for our Sarajevo apartment; design and develop the who-knows-whats of handymen, which his unhandy son could never truly appreciate. Upon the return from Jahorina at the end of the weekend, Mother would often complain that Father hadn't left the basement the whole weekend, except to eat and sleep.

Now I understand that in the mountains, as well as in Sarajevo, they were perpetually invested in constructing their life, in continuously defining and refining the space in which it unfolded. In a country marked by many generations of abysmal poverty, where socialism was the ideology of the day, there was little money to get the goodies; and there were few goodies to get. The quality of life had to be built from scratch—construction instead of consumption. The vague, distant goal of my parents' lifetime project was to enjoy a modest retirement living in Jahorina, a theme park of their hard work, where everything around them spoke of their time in the world.

With their displacement to Canada, they lost all that, and much more. At the beginning of their life in Hamilton they had to find work and learn the basic ways of being in North America, with no family, no friends, no neighborhood, but only the illogical vagaries of the English language, plus cars, malls, and long, dreary winters devoid of mountains.

After a while, though, things started to look up a bit. First, more family arrived: two of my father's brothers with their broods, some cousins, and even some friends. Now they could get together to reminisce about their previous life and pool their knowledge of and kvetch about the ways "Canadians" did things. Moreover, my parents got hired as superintendents in a forty-apartment building, which included a modest salary plus rent-free lodging. Mother cleaned, collected rent, chitchatted with tenants as she used to with her Sarajevo neighbors, and kept things in order, while Father did repairs in the building and took care of the garbage, all the while working in a factory, at a job well below his engineer qualifications but just above his knowledge of English.

Most important, the vast basement of the building was big enough for my father to carve out some space and set up a workshop. He had just started beekeeping again (one of his lifelong projects). The germ (two weak hives) of his future apiary on a farm outside Hamilton was donated by a fruit producer, who depended on bees' pollinating to increase the yield from his orchards. In his basement workshop, Father not only constructed hives and frames, but also restored the pieces of furniture wasteful Canadians commonly dumped in the garbage. He even experimented with drying meat in the basement: He hung some pork, lightly smoked elsewhere, near a window with a ventilator. It was edible, but far from being impressive, or even enjoyable, although my father insisted it was as good as any dried meat.

The meat-drying debacle, however, pointed to one of the crucial issues related to my family's displacement. They, as many immigrants do, identified themselves by way of the food they ate—food was one of the few conduits of continuity between the before and the after. Among my family in Canada and their friends, much time was spent debating dietary and other differences between *them* (Canadians) and *us* (people from Bosnia and the former Yugoslavia): *Their* bacon was soggy; *they* didn't know how to make sausage; *their* sour cream was not thick enough; *they* didn't eat things we ate; *they* were fat and incapable of truly enjoying life because *they* worried about getting fat all the time.

My father would occasionally return from a simple mission of fetching milk with a couple of lamb heads he discovered in the remote corners of the supermarket. He'd demand that my mother boil them, which she refused to do. Much of the lamb heads' beyond-dog-food-factory afterlife was spent in the fridge, their eyes bulging in morbid surprise whenever it was opened. Father would finally deal with Mother's boycott by boiling the heads himself and then sit defiantly at the table to pick lamb brains with a tip of a knife, As my mother scoffed, he relished not only the alleged taste, but also the fact that lamb heads, given the satisfaction they provided, were ridiculously cheap in Canada.

Because my parents grew up in poverty and worked hard for everything that they would eventually lose, they were tormented by Canadian wastefulness. To them, and Father in particular, there were always so many uses for things nobody seemed to want. Once, the real estate company that employed them decided to replace a large number of old refrigerators in the building, their warranty life span ending. My father was thus instructed to remove the fridges from the apartments and leave them by the garbage shed, where they would be picked up and taken away to a dump. He could not get over all those good, perfectly function-ing fridges ending up as scrap metal—to his poverty-conditioned mind the waste was unimaginable. He talked to everyone he knew in Hamilton, beginning with family, to ask them if they needed another fridge; he called me in Chicago, only to be disappointed that I had little need for extra refrigeration. Mother, who could be described as a pathologically honest person, was beside herself over his trying to give away someone else's property. She begged me to interfere, but I could not help, as I was not, I hasten to admit, up to the task of dealing with the difficult ethical conun-drum the situation presented: Does waste still rightfully belong to someone who wasted it?

The fridge overabundance, however, offered a possible solu-tion to the smoked meat problem. At a family get-together, my father and his brothers spontaneously brainstormed: Suppose they take two of those old fridges, rip out the plastic lining, put them on top of each other, drill a hole in between and another one on top, attach an improvised tin chimney, then stick the chimney out of the basement window—they could smoke meat in the basement! My mother was desperate, and complained to me that their obsession with smoking meat blinded them to the laws and civilized customs of Canada. There was nothing I could do, of course. Fortunately, the project was canceled when they discovered a farm outside Hamilton, owned by a Slovenian, where you could select and personally meet your pig before it was slaughtered and smoked to your heart's (and stomach's) content.

The irreducible problem with living in an apartment building was that my parents were always in someone else's space, so when they had a chance to buy a house in a cul-de-sac they grabbed it with their calloused hands. The house was modest, with a small backyard and a structure that the real estate agent referred to as The Barn. It was, in fact, a workshop, which one of the previous owners—an Austrian-born engineer—built for himself. In no time the family joke became that my father bought The Barn and the house came with it. My mother claims that my father lives in The Barn and comes to the house only to eat and sleep.

For some immigrants, property is what they own, what gives them legitimacy—their piece of the foreign land, which becomes home by virtue of belonging to them. But for my parents the house, The Barn, and the piece of land they acquired were but half-empty shells to be filled out with their projects, a space for their agency. A deed was not enough to make that space their own—like the early settlers, they needed to reshape it to fit who they were.

In the fifteen years they've lived there they've undertaken a number of projects that transformed the space into a domain for their self-(re)actualization. My father added a chimney to the house, which required his carrying bricks up the ladder to the roof, my mother fretting (when I called to inquire how it was going) that he might fall and crack his spine. The chimney allowed them to place a wood-burning stove in the basement, so that when I call in the winter to check in, their report often features a quaint fire crackling in the stove as Canadian snow is falling outside. They also unloaded, with my uncle's help, a truckload of soil in the corner of their backyard so as to establish a vegetable garden, where every summer they grow tomatoes, peppers, onions, cucumbers.

The list of additions and improvements to the original property is long and impressive, while The Barn has become the veritable headquarters of all the (re)building projects. This is where Father built an outdoor table and benches so that in the summer they can lounge in a deep shade and proudly consume their meals entirely (the requisite meat notwithstanding) from what they've harvested in their own garden. Most important, The Barn is where Father's many beekeeping operations take place: where he makes his hives and frames, extracts honey, keeps a shelf (that he built himself) entirely dedicated to the propolis reserves.

All this requires: a wall of screwdrivers; boxes of nails and screws of all sizes; electric tools he buys behind my mother's back, or with the Home Depot gift certificates I give him for Christmas; plastic buckets and jars for honey; old sweaters and overalls he wears to work, which he refuses to let Mother wash lest they disintegrate; a refrigerator containing pots, which had been there for so long that they contain mysterious ecosystems; various objects collected for no obvious purpose other than avoiding wastefulness—say, a tray full of dull knives etc. There is also a wood-burning stove; a cord phone he picks up when I call; an ancient stereo that allows him to hum along with the CDs of choral music or listen to the immigrant programs in the many languages he can understand (Bosnian, Serbian, Croatian, Ukrainian, Polish, Russian) and the many he cannot. Clusters of plastic bags hang off the nails in the crossbeams, weighted with stuff (hinges, nozzles, bolts, abrasive paper) that might become useful for some undetermined future project.

And then there is one wall that in its random, perplexing combination of fragments looks like an art installation: a magazine cover with a picture of Jane Fonda and the headline "Me Jane"; an incredibly tangled extension cord hanging on a nail; a 2007 calendar from the Louvre featuring *Mona Lisa* inside a picture frame too big for it, with another empty frame on top; a road map of Europe, a begrimed mirror obscuring Scandinavia; a couple of stopped clocks, showing different times, one of them partially covering Fonda's face; a single bulb, thumbtacked in its packaging right above the mirror; an unused timer above that. It was late December last time I visited The Barn, and there were two mature pumpkins on the floor.

Other than the honey in plastic buckets and jars, nothing that enters The Barn ever leaves it—it is a waste-free space. Some native-born stranger versed in reality-TV diagnoses would see it as a place of hoarding, but everything in it makes perfect sense not only to my father, but to me as well: The inside of The Barn is the inside of my father's head, the clutter an emanation of his mind, the overpopulated territory of his personal sovereignty.

And there is more: Behind that "Me Jane" wall there is an additional room he built to house a circular saw, above which smoked meat hangs to dry, as the smokehouse, immediately beyond The Barn, tends to be overcrowded. With the smokehouse, which he built brick by brick, the meat-smoking issue was resolved: Chunks of bacon, hocks, loins, and sometimes salmon hang inside. Next to the smokehouse is a brick oven—which he, yes, also built, in order to roast meat using the *sač* method (a conical cast-iron lid topped with ashes and ambers covers a pan).

And then there is a wood storage area under a roof which Father, of course, improvised himself. If you walk under that roof, between tall stacks of firewood needed for the stoves, smokehouse, and brick oven, you come upon another shack which contains more stuff. I'm not sure what's in it, but whatever it is, it must be very valuable, as in that Zen parable in which a master responds to the question "What is the most valuable thing in the world?" by saying "A dead cat's head—because you can put no value on it."

If The Barn is the mind, the apiary is the soul. There are between twenty and forty hives in a small clearing facing east just beyond the clutter complex. In the summer, it is abuzz with the bees getting out to do their work, a sight and sound so pleasing that Father has placed a chair (recovered from the garbage) just above the hives so that he can sit in his throne and enjoy his domain. At the foot of the chair there is a little tombstone reading "Mak 2006." The ashes of Mak, our first and only family dog, are scattered there. If my father ever experiences transcendence, this is where it takes place, an instant before the hum of working bees causes him to doze off.

The sovereignty of the domain is, however, precarious, ever in need of protection. Although every year my parents return to Sarajevo for a couple of months at the end of the (usually long) winter, they are reluctant to leave their territory in the summer: They worry about the heat scorching the garden, about bee swarms escaping the hives without supervision, about burglars, about any number of unforeseeable things. Once upon a time they left their home and never went back. Protecting and maintaining the space they have in Canada has become their primary, overarching project.

And they're willing to fight for it. The greatest of the battles, so far, was the one against raccoons. One summer, not so long ago, a family of raccoons living in the back woods discovered the pleasures of my father's apiary. They came upon some empty hives and figured out a way to lift the tops, pull out the frames, and then scrape and lick off honey residues. My father would find his hives toppled over, frames and tops strewn around, many of them damaged—recalling the demise of his apiary in back home, where drunken Serb soldiers had spitefully destroyed his hives, thereby ending the history of the Hemons' beekeeping in Bosnia and Herzegovina. Attracted into the domain by the smell and taste of honey, the raccoons also stole vegetables from the garden,

ALEKSANDAR HEMON

chased away feral cats my mother liked to feed, and were most certainly eyeing the smokehouse.

Following one particularly egregious raid, Father put the hives back where they belonged and replaced the frames and tops; then he nailed one corner of the top to each hive, so that you (being human) would have to lift the top slightly, then swing it to the side to get to the frames. In no time, the inhuman raccoons figured out how to overcome that obstacle, and the battle intensified. Father would call me to rant about raccoons, those devious, evil animals, and declare his determination to end their incursions by ending their lives. At family get-togethers spontaneous brainstorms were now devoted to means of raccoon entrapment and subsequent liquidation.

One day, I called and the first thing my mother said was: "Your father is going crazy about those raccoons. I don't know what to do. You've got to talk to him." She had just watched a local news story about a man who killed a raccoon with a shotgun, which was illegal in the city of Hamilton, where only Animal Control was to handle wildlife. "Your father does nothing but plot how to kill those raccoons." Apart from being the kind of animal lover who chats with squirrels and worries about feral cats when they miss a meal she has put out for them, she worried that my father could be arrested: The TV showed the raccoon killer entering a police car handcuffed. Sometimes, I'd have them both on the phone—Father in The Barn, Mother in the kitchen—and they'd argue, essentially, over jurisdiction: He claimed his right to kill the raccoons, as they were trespassing on his domain; she insisted on the fact that they were in Canada, where laws were to be obeyed.

Finally, my father devised a trap which allowed him to capture four baby raccoons. He imprisoned them in a deep barrel, on top of which he placed a heavy piece of flat wood. He was confident

74

there was no way they could get out. He expected the mother raccoon to come look for her babies and fall into the same trap. He patrolled his domain diligently, hoping to catch the mother before she figured out a way to escape, then exterminate the whole pest family.

But. on one of his patrols, he discovered that the piece of wood had been pushed off the barrel and that now three of the baby raccoons in the barrel managed to escape, only one remaining. Apparently, they'd climbed on one another's shoulders, making a raccoon ladder of sorts, lifted the lid, and gotten away. They left behind the volunteer, probably the youngest one, to deal with my father's fury. He'd made a tactical mistake of not killing them right away and lost the battle. To his credit, Father acknowledged his defeat and released the last raccoon.

But he turned his anger on my mother and her softhearted animal loving—it was because of her nagging that he hadn't exe-cuted the baby raccoons. They'd argue on the phone with me with such intensity that they wouldn't hear me hang up. When they calmed down and we talked again, I urged Father to call Animal Control, telling him they would take care of it, and eventually he did and they did. It was always the most obvious and diplomatic solution, but Father's obsession, now I understand, was related to his jurisdiction principle: His domain was his responsibility.

Unlike the raccoons, I'm in awe of my parents. The lazy, terri-ble clichés available in the North American mainstream culture present immigrants, at best, as innocent new arrivals. In the con-descending native imagination, immigrants are swallowed and digested by the host culture and its practices, which are presum-ably so recondite as to make new immigrants akin to children. What such platitudes fail to see is the resourceful transformative power of immigrants, even of those who, like my parents, arrive in their mid-fifties with a scant knowledge of English. My parents did what the early North American settlers had done once upon a time: They transformed the space they found themselves in. Even if my parents didn't have to decimate the natives, they did have to deal with bureaucracy and papers, with finding jobs and getting fired, with the language deficiency so encouraging to condescension, all the while constructing a space that could be indelibly their own.

The domain that my parents have built for themselves is perfectly sovereign. In it they do and create things that allow them to be themselves; this is where they have agency, a bubble outside of which they are reduced to passivity inflicted by history. Their house, The Barn, and the backyard is one place where they're not refugees. Time they could not regain, but space they could, and they did.

Ghassan Zaqtan

a Palestinian living in Ramallah, is one of the
most prominent poets writing in Arabic. His
poetry and prose have been translated into
several languages. A translation of his poetry
into English, *Like a Straw Bird It Follows Me*,
won the Griffin Poetry Prize in 2013.

When This Happens

GHASSAN ZAQTAN
TRANSLATED FROM THE ARABIC BY FADY JOUDAH

When things become light and imprisoned shadows
in their firm forms disassemble,
and the genies climb bougainvilleas and garden fences,
and the planks of cactus filter out of intimate order,

and when he sees the genies, actually sees them,
resting on the doorsteps of houses, on minaret crescents
and in damp benedictions at dawn,

when a genie on the wooden shelf calls to him, by his name,
in his mother's room which he remembers less well lately,
and how that used to hurt him, send a fear his way
to stir up his murk.

And the lepers hanging on oaks climb down
while their scared eyes shine in the grove on the slope,
the oaks he found in the Christian novel that he doesn't recall
exactly how it made it into his book collection.

When they liberate themselves
from the book and the miracle's riddle
and take a stroll like opened suitcases on the roads
in nearby villages, their bare faces, their smiles
difficult to believe.

Their feet touch the ground, they bend down
to pick up stones just because
stones remember their distant childhood
and their cracked fingers that a curse had plowed.

When he hears his dog's monotone bark
as if coming from ancient abandoned wells
in the hidden valley of his mind, by the river bank
where soldiers shot his limping dog dead
there thirty years ago.

And the new homes on the mountains disappear, dissipate
opaque in construction spray, cranes, and fabricated rooms
built any which way for guards and laborers,
and only a single light remains, whose source is unknown,
a secret spring that removes its mask to breathe.

When he sees dead trees and the ones that caterpillars
uprooted, and lumberjacks, their saws and scarred axes.

When he sees her rise in ditches, gathering her twigs,
she has the confidence of the dead and the trepidation of a ghost,
she rises in affected figures:

Couches in living rooms, benches in gardens, shelves,
employee offices, ascetic café chairs, wardrobe closets
where she leaves fabric behind hanging in a gorge hopelessly
like bodies raised high.

When she walks to the mountain like a happy family
coming home after a costume party
and when he notices the kids
that the dead patrols and deceived queues forgot about

and notices the screams caught in night traps
and people who cross the cold dark mountain
and sodden fields toward the homes they miss.

His heart knows, but he doesn't know how it knows this,
that he has reached his country.

Etgar Keret

was born in Ramat Gan and lives in Tel Aviv. A recipient of France's Chevalier de l'Ordre des Arts et des Lettres, he is a lecturer at Ben-Gurion University of the Negev and author of five short story collections and, most recently, *The Seven Good Years: A Memoir*. His work has been translated into thirty-seven languages and has appeared in *The New Yorker*, *The Paris Review*, and *The New York Times*, among many other publications, and on the NPR radio program *This American Life*, where he is a regular contributor.

Mellow

ETGAR KERET
TRANSLATED FROM THE HEBREW BY SONDRA SILVERSTON

Ten minutes before the scheduled time, I was already waiting downstairs with my small bag. It held a fresh copy of my recently published first book, two pens for autograph signing, and a pack of Kleenex for whatever emergencies might arise. I was excited. This wouldn't be my first time giving a reading in front of an audience, but it was the first time I'd be getting paid for it, and outside of Tel Aviv to boot, in Rosh Pina, with a van to pick me up and take me back, like I was a real professional. The van that pulled up was shiny and new, and the smiley, curly-haired driver said his name was Aviram. After five minutes on the road, he asked me, "So how's my driving?" I said it was great. And it really was. A few traffic lights later, he asked me about his driving again, saying I should be honest with him. "Fantastic," I replied, "really. I wish I knew how to drive so well."

"And how about the way I merge into traffic," he asked. "Calm? Cool? Or do I project a little bit of stress?"

"Calm, very calm," I said, "but also very alert."

That answer made Aviram happy. "I'm asking," he said, "because this is my first day on the job and I don't want to screw up."

"It's my first day on the job too," I admitted, "the first time I'm being paid for a reading, and I don't want to screw up either."

"Wow," Aviram said, honking at a van that cut us off, "I hope it works out for both of us," and after a brief pause, took a round tin box out of his shirt pocket and added, "I have an idea. How about I roll us a joint to calm us down? I mean, it's our first time and everything." I told him I'd rather not. I didn't want to be stoned when I got to the event.

"Don't worry," Aviram persisted, "I'll make us a mild one so we don't get wasted. Something that'll relax us enough to maximize our performance." I explained that grass had a really strong effect on me, and that what was mild for him might completely waste me. "But *you* can smoke," I added, "that's totally okay with me."

Aviram sighed. "It doesn't work like that," he said. "If I smoke alone, I'll start having these thoughts about you ratting me out. You know, paranoia and stuff. But if you smoke with me, I'll be okay because if you rat me out, then you're in trouble too." I shrugged, and we kept driving in silence. When he got onto the highway, he asked me about his driving again, and I complimented him again. "Listen," Aviram said, "maybe you could just take a drag or two? Not really smoke, you know. Just inhale enough so I don't get stressed." I nodded. It would take at least another two hours to get to Rosh Pina, and Aviram did not look relaxed at all.

He rolled the joint with one hand as he drove. "I'll make us a skinny one," he told me twice while he was rolling, "so we don't zone out. We need to be sharp." It was already dark when he lit the joint and handed it to me. I took a puff; it was delicious. I took another two or three puffs. Maybe more. Then I handed the joint back to him. He took a few puffs too. "The truth is," he said, "that it's a lot safer to drive when you're stoned. It mellows you out." I told him he drove really well even before the joint.

"Thanks," he said and took another long drag, "but now I'm driving even better."

And he really did do a nice job of passing two tourist buses and one van full of goats. "This is good grass," he said. "I grow it myself." It really was good grass, the kind that bubbles in your brain but also drips into your muscles. After a few minutes, I couldn't move. I tried to turn my head toward him, but couldn't. I tried to tell him that, but talking was hard too. "Great," Aviram said, and tossed the roach out the van window. "Now we're all set."

By the time we reached Rosh Pina, the paralysis had weakened slightly. I could move my body and speak, but still felt very stoned. "I'll wait for you here," Aviram said, pointing to the parking lot outside the hall where I was supposed to read. "How long will the whole thing take? An hour and a half? Two hours?"

"Two at the most," I mumbled, and as I dragged myself out of the van, I also managed to say, "Probably less." I began to walk toward the hall. It wasn't easy. There was a huge flight of stairs at the entrance. The audience had already begun to arrive, and the people walking up the stairs seemed to be doing it without effort or fear, but to me, it seemed a little scary. The last thing I wanted to do at my first reading was fall down the stairs and make a fool of myself, so I decided not to take the chance and climbed up on all fours. It went fairly well and felt safe enough.

Halfway up, I met a tall, thin woman named Rina who introduced herself as the event organizer. I nodded hello because in my current position, there was no way I could extend a hand without falling. Rina asked how the drive was and if everything was okay. I told her that the drive was great and that I felt terrific. She accompanied me to the top of the stairs, where I felt safe enough to straighten up, and showed me the hall. She said that in her opinion, there were more than a hundred people in the audience, and that was a wonderful turnout for a town as small as Rosh Pina. She asked me whether I needed anything before I started the reading, and when I said no, she glanced at her watch and at the audience in the hall and said, "Good, so let's get started."

After Rina gave me a brief introduction, I walked onto the stage and sat on the bar stool next to the microphone. I opened the book to the first page and stared at it for a few seconds. It looked like a collection of oil globs floating on water, constantly changing shape in a fairly mesmerizing way. I stared at them a little longer. It was beautiful. I couldn't read anything, but it was really beautiful. Someone in the audience coughed, reminding me that I shouldn't keep staring at that hypnotic display. I was supposed to read; that was the unwritten agreement between me and that Galilee audience. But I couldn't. I recalled that my brother once told me that if you're too stoned, the best thing is to eat something sweet because sugar neutralizes the effects of the drug, and thinking about eating something sweet turned me on. I really felt like eating something sweet because it might help me finally start reading. But not only. Regardless of anything else, something sweet sounded like a great idea now. I moved the microphone closer to my mouth and looked at the audience. I said good evening, told them how glad I was to be there and that I felt a little weak, probably because my blood sugar levels had dropped. Then I asked whether anyone in the audience who happened to live close to the hall might have an extra piece of cake at home, because if I ate some cake, I'd feel better. An elderly woman with flowing white hair who was sitting in one of the last rows stood up and said that she lived really close by and that she'd finished baking a cheesecake right before coming here. She said she'd be happy to go home and bring it for me if it would help me feel better. I thanked her and asked the rest of the audience if they were willing to wait until she came back. The murmuring in the hall sounded to me like "yes," and the lady with the white hair set out on her way. I waited for her on the stage. The audience was quiet, and so was I. Time moved slowly, but that woman really did live close by because after what felt like an eternity but was actually, according to the hands on the clock, only twelve minutes, she returned to the hall with a tray of cheese-and-crumb cake. She handed me the tray, along with a knife and a few paper napkins, and after thanking her, I spoke into the microphone, asking if anyone wanted a taste. This time, the audience murmur sounded like a "no." I sliced a piece of cake. The thought of walking off the illuminated stage and eating somewhere else never entered my mind, so I sat there and ate it. It was fantastic. Just soft and sweet enough, and the crumbs were the perfect crunchy contrast to the smooth, fluffy cake. I complimented the lady on her baking skills and again asked if anyone had changed their mind and wanted a taste of that miracle cake. When no requests came from the audience, I just cut myself another slice.

Seven minutes on the clock—that's how long it took me to eat that whole cake. When I finished, I felt much better. I opened to the first page of the book again. The letters continued to swirl like oil globs on water, but now I had the taste of that fantastic cake in my mouth. "True," the soothing sweetness on my tongue said, "you can't read, but who said you have to read at a reading? You can just give a talk." Cheered by that refreshing thought, I tossed the book over my shoulder, stood up from the bar stool, and began speaking. I don't really remember about what, I only remember that my words blended well with the taste of the cake and the quiet, patient audience. When I'd spoken enough, I thanked the audience and walked off the stage. A few people came up to me and asked for autographs. They looked very pleased. Aviram, who was waiting for me in the van, less so. "Thank God," he said, "I was beginning to think you weren't coming back." Apparently the event had gone on for more than three hours.

I slept all the way back, and when we arrived, Aviram woke me up and said, "See? I told you it'd work out for both of us today." When I got out of the van, still a little shaky, he said, "*Ya'allah*, see you at the next event." I shook his hand goodbye and he insisted on a hug.

I woke up at 11 the next morning with a stomachache. The first thing I did, even before drinking my coffee, was to call the car company and tell them that the driver I'd had the day before was excellent, very careful and courteous. When it's someone's first day on the job, it's really important to put in a good word. The hoarse voice on the other end of the line thanked me and said that Aviram had quit that morning and was going back to agricultural work.

"Why?" I asked.

"I don't exactly know," the hoarse guy admitted. "All I know is that he picked up a children's writer at nine o'clock and they argued on the way. Fifteen minutes ago, he came to the office and returned the car keys to me. He said he dropped the writer off at some interchange. I didn't really understand why, he just said something about the guy not being as nice as the writer from last night."

Six years after the cheesecake reading, I went back to Rosh Pina. I was afraid they'd never invite me again, and when the invitation arrived, I decided that this time, I'd come prepared with a well-organized lecture, informative but light, profound yet loaded with jokes. I was a little stressed before the event, but when I got onto the stage, the fear vanished and the lecture and the reading went really well. Afterward, some people came over and asked me to sign their books, and the elderly woman with the long white hair, now even a little longer, was among them. "It was interesting," she said as she handed me her book to sign, "not as special as the last time, but still, interesting."

Anne Carson

was born in Canada and teaches ancient
Greek for a living.

SAPPHO DRIVES UPSTATE (Fr. 2)

ANNE CARSON

I saw two old white horses in a field,
in the corner of a field,
in the shade,
who had sought the shade,
thoughtfully.
glancing not quite at each other but past,
holding their heads close, their heads aligned,
standing
as they had stood many times,
a thousand times,
standing so,
weak moments, strong moments,
shivering slightly,
a cool breeze sliding down the apple branches or
All this—
you tore a hole, pushed your arm through, hit the switch.

Tahmima Anam

is the author of two novels: *A Golden Age*, which was awarded the Commonwealth Writers' Prize for Best First Book, and *The Good Muslim*. In 2013 she was selected as one of Granta's Best of Young British Novelists. She lives in London with her family.

Garments

TAHMIMA ANAM

One day Mala lowers her mask and says to Jesmin, my boyfriend wants to marry you. Jesmin is six shirts behind so she doesn't look up. After the bell, Mala explains. For months now she's been telling the girls, ya, any day now me and Dulal are going to the Kazi. They don't believe her, they know her boyfriend works in an air-conditioned shop. No way he was going to marry a garments girl. Now she has a scheme and when Jesmin hears it, she thinks, it's not so bad.

Two days later Mala's sweating like it's July. He wants one more. Three wives. We have to find a girl. After the bell they look down the row of sewing machines and try to choose. Mala knows all the unmarried girls, which one needs a room, which one has hungry relatives, which one borrowed money against her wage and can't work enough overtime to pay it off. They squint down the line and consider Fatima, Keya, Komola, but for some reason or other they reject them all. There's a new girl at the end of the row but when Mala takes a break and limps over to the toilet she comes back and says the girl has a milky eye.

There's a new order for panties. Jesmin picks up the sample. She's never seen a panty like it before. It's thick, with double seams on the front, back, and around the buttocks. The leg is just cut off without a stitch. Mala, she says, what's this? Mala says, the foreign ladies use them to hold in their fat and they call them Thanks. Thanks? Yep. Because they look so good, in the mirror they say to the panties, Thanks. Jesmin and Mala pull down their masks and trade a laugh when the morning supervisor, Jamal, isn't looking.

Jesmin decides it won't be so bad to share a husband. She doesn't have dreams of a love marriage, and if they have to divide the sex that's fine with her, and if he wants something, like he wants his rice the way his mother makes it, maybe one of them will know how to do it. Walking home as she did every evening with all the other factory workers, a line two girls thick and a mile long, snaking out of Tongi and all the way to Uttara, she spots a new girl. Sometimes Jesmin looks in front and behind her at that line, all the ribbons flapping and the song of sandals on the pavement, and she feels a swell in her chest. She catches up to the girl. Her name's Ruby. She's dark, but pretty. Small white teeth and filmy eyes. She's new and eager to make friends. I'm coming two, three hours from my village every morning, she complains. I know, Jesmin says. Finding a place to live is why I'm doing this.

The year Jesmin came to Dhaka she said to her father, ask Nasir chacha to give you his daughter's mobile contact. Nasir chacha's daughter Kulsum had a job in garments. Her father nodded, said, she will help you. Her mother, drying mustard in front of their hut, put her face in the crook of her arm. Go, go, she said. I don't want to see you again. Jesmin left without looking back, knowing that, once, her mother had another dream for her, that she would marry and be treated like a queen, that all the village would tell her what a good forehead she had. But that was before Amin, before the punishing hut.

Kulsum did help her. Put in a good word when she heard they were looking. She has a place, a room in Korail she shares with her kid and her in-laws. Her husband works in foreign so she lets Jesmin sleep on the floor. She takes half of Jesmin's pay every month. You're lucky, she tells her, I didn't ask for the money up front. But now her husband's coming back and Jesmin has to find somewhere else. She has another relative, a cousin's cousin, but he lives all the way out in Mogbajar and Jesmin doesn't like the way he looks at her. There's a shanty not far from the factory and she heard there were rooms going, but when she went to look, the landlord said, I can't have so many girls in my building. What building? Just a row of tin, paper between the walls, sharing an outside tap. But still he told her he wasn't sure, had to think about it. If you had a husband, he said, that would be a different story.

When Jesmin joined the line, she started as Mala's helper. She tied her knots and clipped the threads from her shirt buttons. The Rana strike was over and Mala's leg was broken and the bosses had their eye on her, always waiting to see if she'd make more trouble. Even now, Jamal gives her a look every time she walks by, waiting to see if she takes too long in the toilet. They would have got rid of her a long time ago if her hands weren't so good, always first in the line, seams straight as blades of grass, five, seven pieces ahead of everyone.

To make the Thanks you have to stretch the fabric tight against your left arm while running the stitch. Then you fold it, stretch again, run the stitch back up, till the whole thing is hard and tight. Jesmin trims the leg and takes a piece home. She pulls it up over her leg. Her thigh bulges in front and behind it. She doesn't understand. Maybe the legs of foreign ladies are different.

Jesmin and Mala know a foreign lady, Miss Bridgey. She came to the factory and asked them a few questions and wrote down

95

what they said. How many minutes for lunch? Where is the toilet? If there's a fire, what will you do? In the morning before she came Jamal lined everyone up. There's an inspector coming, he said. You want to make a good impression. Jamal liked to ask a question and supply the answer. Are we proud of the factory? Yes we are! What do we think of Sunny Textiles? We love SunnyTex! That day they opened all the windows and did the fire drill ten times. Then Miss Bridgey showed up and Jesmin could see the laugh behind Jamal's face. He thought it would be a man in a suit, and there was this little yellow-haired girl. Nothing to worry. Aren't we lucky? Yes we are.

When Miss Bridgey comes back Jesmin is going to ask her about the Thanks. But right now they have to explain the whole thing to Ruby. Mala's doing all the talking. We marry him, and that way we can tell people we are married. We give him a place to stay, we give him food, we give him all the things a wife gives. If he wants sex we give him sex. When she mentions the sex Jesmin feels her legs filling up with water. Why don't we get our own husbands? Ruby asks. She's green, she doesn't know. Ruby looks like she's going to cry. Then she bites her full lip with a line of those perfect little teeth and she says, okay, I'll do it.

When Jesmin was born, her mother took a piece of coal and drew a big black mark behind her ear. Jesmin went to school and learned the letters and the sums before any of the other children. The teacher, Amin, always asked her to sing the national anthem on Victory Day and stand first in the parade. Amin said she should go to secondary. He said, meet me after school. He taught her sums and a, b, c. He put his hand over her hand on the chalk.

Miss Bridgey comes a few days later and she takes Jesmin aside. I'm worried about the factory, she says. Has it always been this bad? Jesmin looks around. She takes in the fans in the ceiling, bars on the windows, rows and rows of girls bent over their machines. It's the same, she says. Always like this. This place good. This place okay. We love SunnyTex! But why, she asks Miss Bridgey, do the ladies in your country wear this? She holds up the Thanks. Miss Bridgey takes it from her hand, turns it around, then she laughs and laughs. Jesmin, you know how expensive these are?

On the wedding day Dulal comes to the factory. He's wearing a red shirt under the gray sleeveless sweater they made last year when the SunnyTex bosses decided to expand into knitwear. Jesmin and Mala and Ruby stand in front of him, and he looks at them with his head tilted to the side. Take a look at my prince! Mala says. He's got a narrow face and small black eyes and hair that sticks to his forehead. Now it's time to get married so they set off on two rickshaws, him and Mala in the front, Jesmin and Ruby following behind. They are all wearing red saris like brides do, except nobody's family has showed up to feed them sweets or paint their feet.

Jesmin watches the back of Mala and Dulal. She knows that Mala's brother died in Rana. That Mala had held up his photo for seven weeks, hoping he would come out from under the cement. That she was at the strike, shouting her brother's name. That her mother kept writing from the village asking for money, so Mala had to turn around and go back to the line. Mala's face was cracked, like a broken eggshell, until she found Dulal. Now she comes to the factory, works like magic, tells her jokes, does her overtime as if it never happened, but Jesmin knows that once you die like that, on the street or in the factory, your life isn't your life anymore.

This morning Jesmin went to the shanty to talk to the landlord. I'm getting married. Can I stay? He looked at her with one side of

his face. Married? Show me the groom. I'll bring him next week,
she said. He took one more drag and threw his cigarette into the
drain and Jesmin thought for sure he was going to say no, but
then he turned to her and said, what, I don't get any sweets?
Then he slapped her on the back, and she shrank, but it was a
friendly slap, as if she was a man, or his daughter. Next she went
to Kulsum. I found a husband. Good, she said, you're getting old.
Now I don't have to worry about you.

Jesmin sees marriage as a remedy. If you are a girl you have
many problems, but all of them can be fixed if you have a husband. In the factory, if Jamal puts you in ironing, which is the
easiest job, or if he says, take a few extra minutes for lunch, you
can finish after hours and get overtime, you can say, but my husband is waiting, and then you won't have to feel his breath like
a spider on your shoulder later that night when the current goes
out and you're still in the factory finishing up a sleeve. Everything is better if you're married. Jesmin is giving Ruby all this
good advice as their rickshaw passes the Mohakhali flyover but
the girl's eyes are somewhere else. Bet she had some other idea
about her life. Jesmin puts her arm around Ruby's shoulder and
notices she smells very nice, like the biscuit factory she passes
on the way to SunnyTex.

Jesmin is the only one who can sign her name on the wedding
register. The others dip their thumbs into ink and press them
into the big book. The kazi takes their money and gives them a
piece of paper that has all their names on it. Jesmin reads it out
loud to the others.

After, Dulal wants to stop at a chotpoti stall. Three men, friends
of his, are waiting there. They look at the brides, up and down,
and then they stick their elbows into Dulal's side and Dulal smiles
like he's just opened a drawerful of cash. Who's first? they ask

him. The old one, he replies, not bothering to whisper it. Then that one, he says, pointing to Jesmin. Next week Kulsum said she would let Jesmin string a blanket across and take half the bed. Her in-laws will be on the other half and she'll take the kid and sleep on the floor. Best for last, eh? his friend says. Dulal looks at Ruby like he's seeing her for the first time and he says, yeah, she's the cream.

The friends take off and then it's just the brides and groom. They sit on four stools along the pavement. Jesmin feels the winter air on her neck. Where's your village? Dulal asks, but before she can tell him, she hears Ruby's voice saying, Kurigram. Something in the sound of her voice makes Jesmin think maybe Ruby wants to be the favorite wife. She notices now that Ruby has tied a ribbon in her hair. They finish their plates and Mala holds hands with Dulal and they take off in the direction of her place. Jesmin and Ruby are taking the bus to Kulsum's. Ruby's giving Kulsum some of her pay so she can stay there too, just until they find her somewhere else.

Jesmin wants to say something to mark the fact that they are all married now. She can't think of anything so she asks Ruby if it gets cold in her village. Yes, she says, in winter sometimes people die. I'm from the south, Jesmin tells her, it's not so bad but still in winter, it bites. They hug their arms now as the sun sets. I wonder what they're doing, Ruby says. Do you think he's nice? He looks nice.

They're doing what people do, she tells Ruby, at night when no one is looking. They arrive at Kulsum's. She can share your blanket, Kulsum says, throwing a look at Ruby until Ruby takes the money out of her bag. They warm some leftover rice on the stove Kulsum shares with two other families at the back of the building. The gas is low and it takes half an hour to heat the rice, then they crush a few chilies into it. I have three younger sisters, Ruby says, even though Jesmin hasn't asked about her family. Where are they? Home and hungry, she says, and Jesmin gets a picture in her mind of three dark-skinned girls with perfect teeth, shivering together in the northern cold. What about you? Ruby asks. A snake took my brother, Jesmin says, remembering his face, gray and swollen, before they threw it in the ground. Hai Allah! Ruby rubs her hand up and down Jesmin's back. His forehead was unlucky, Jesmin says, pretending it wasn't so bad, like this wasn't the reason everything started to go sour, her parents with nothing to look forward to, just a daughter whose head was a curse and the hope that next year's rice would come up without a fight.

It's freezing on the floor. Jesmin is glad for Ruby's back spreading the warm into their blanket. You are kind, Ruby mumbles as she falls asleep, and Jesmin can see her breathing, her shoulders moving up and down. She lies awake for a long time imagining Mala with their husband. The watery feeling returns to her legs. Ruby shifts, moves closer, and her biscuit smell clouds up around them. Jesmin takes a strand of Ruby's hair and puts it into her mouth.

When she gets to SunnyTex the next morning Mala is already at her machine with her head down. Jesmin tries to catch her eye but she won't look up, and when they break for lunch she disappears and Jesmin doesn't see her until it's too late. Finally it's the end of the day and Maya is hurrying along in the going-home line. What d'you want? She squints as if she's looking from far away and when Jesmin asks her what the wedding night was like, she says, it wasn't so bad. That's all? You'll find out for yourself, don't let me go and spoil it, and then her face bends into a smile. She won't say anything else.

After their shift is over Jesmin tells Ruby, let's go to a shop. I don't have any money, Ruby says. Don't worry, we'll just look.

They walk to the sandal shop at the end of the street. They stare at the wall of sandals. Ruby takes Jesmin's hand and squeezes her fingers. It's so nice she can almost feel the sandals on her feet.

The week is over and finally it's Jesmin's turn. She scrubs her face till Kulsum scolds her for taking too long at the tap. She wears a red shalwar kameez. Ruby wants to do her hair. She makes a braid that begins at the top of Jesmin's head and runs all the way down her back. Her fingers move quickly and Jesmin feels a shiver that starts at her neck and disappears into her kameez. Ruby reaches back and takes the clip out of her own hair and puts it into Jesmin's. She feels it tense her hair together.

All day while they're sewing buttons onto check shirts Jesmin can feel the clip pulling at her scalp. Mala, she says, I'm feeling scared. At first Mala looks like she's going to tell her something, but her eyes go back to her sewing machine and she says, all brides are scared. Don't worry, I tested him out for you. Equipment is working tip-top.

After work Dulal is standing outside the SunnyTex gate. He puts his finger under her chin and stares into her face like he's examining a leg of goat. His breathing is ragged and his cheeks are shining. She notices how dirty his shirt is under the sweater and she starts to wonder what sort of a man would want three wives all at once. She shakes her head to knock the thoughts out of it. She has a husband, that's what matters. The road unfolds in front of them as they walk home, his hand molded onto her waist.

Kulsum is wearing lipstick and she tells her kid, look, your khalu has come to visit, give him foot-salaam, and her kid kneels in front of Dulal and touches his sandal. In the kitchen they pass around the food. Jesmin puts rice on Dulal's plate, and the bigger piece of meat. Kulsum gets a piece too and the rest of them do with gravy. She's given him the mora from under the bed so he sits taller than everyone else. The gravy is watery but Jesmin watches Kulsum's kid run his tongue all across his plate. She thinks about Ruby. It's Thursday and she's gone home on the bus to spend the weekend with her brothers. Jesmin fingers the clip, still standing stiff on the side of her head.

Now it's time and they lie down together. The blanket is strung across but Jesmin can see the outline of Kulsum's mother-in-law, her elbow jutting into their side of the bed. Dulal turns his face to the wall and says, scratch my back. He squirms out of his shirt and she runs her fingers up and down his back and soon her nails are clogged with dirt. He takes her hand and pulls it over to the front of his body, and then he takes out his thing. His hand is over her hand, and she thinks of Amin and the chalk and the village, fog in the winter and the new season's molasses and everything smelling clean, the dung drying against the walls of her father's hut. Her arm is getting sore and Dulal's breath is slow and steady, his thing soft as a mouse. She thinks maybe he's fallen asleep but then he turns around and she feels the weight of him pressing down on her. He drags down her kameez and tries to push the mouse in. After a few minutes he gives up and turns back around. Scratch my back, he says, irritated, and finally he falls asleep with her hand trapped under his elbow.

The next day is Friday and Dulal says he's going to spend it with his sister, who lives in Uttara. Jesmin was hoping they could go to the market and look at the shops, but he leaves before she can ask. She takes the bus to Mohakhali. Mala's neighbor looks Jesmin up and down and says to her, so your friend is married now. Look at her, like a queen she is. Mala's wearing bright orange lipstick and acting like something good has happened to her. She's talking on her mobile and Jesmin waits for her to finish. Then she asks, is it supposed to be like that?

Mala looks up from the bed. You couldn't do it?

What, what was I supposed to do?

She grabs an arm. Did he put it in?

No.

She curses under her breath. But I told him you would be the one.

The one to what?

The one to cure his, you know, not being able to.

Jesmin struggles to understand. You told me his equipment was tip-top.

Mala shrinks from her. It occurs to Jesmin that she never asked the right question, the one that has been on everyone's mind. Why does a guy working in a shop, who doesn't get his hands dirty all day, want a garments girl, especially a broken one like Mala? Jesmin stares at her until Mala can't hold her eye anymore. Mala looks down at her hands. I paid him, she says.

You paid him?

Then he started asking for more, more money, and I didn't have it, so I told him you and Ruby would fix him. That's the only way he would stay.

She's got her head in her hands and she's crying. She rubs her broken leg, and Jesmin thinks of Rana, and Mala's brother, and her own brother, and she decides there's nothing to be done now but try and fix Dulal's problem, because now that they were married to him, his bad was their bad.

What next?

Try again, try everything. Mala hands her the tube of lipstick. Here, take this.

That night Jesmin asks Kulsum for a few sprays from the bottle of scent she keeps in a box under the bed and Kulsum takes it out reluctantly, eyeing her while she pats some of it onto her neck. Jesmin draws thick lines across her eyelids and smears the lipstick on hard. Dulal cleans his plate and goes outside to gargle into the drain. She stands with him at the edge of the drain and after he rinses and spits he looks up at the night. There's all kinds of noise coming from the compound, kids screaming, dogs, a radio, but up there it looks quiet. Maybe Dulal's looking for a bit of quiet, too. Fog's coming, she says. She asks about his sister. Alhamdulillah, he tells her, but doesn't say, I will take you to meet her. I hate winter, he says instead, makes my bones tired.

Winter makes her think of the sesame her mother had planted, years ago when she was a baby. The harvest was for selling, but after the first season the price at the market wasn't worth the water and the effort, so she gave it up. But still the branches came up, twisted and pointy every year, tearing the feet off anyone who dared walk across the field. Only Amin knew how to tread between the bushes, his feet unscarred, the soles of his feet always so soft. Jesmin ran them across her cheeks and it was like his palm was touching her, or the tip of his penis, rather than the underside of his big toe, that's how delicate his feet were. I'm only here to talk, he said, telling her the story of Laila and Majnu. From Amin she learned what it was to be swallowed by a man, like a snake swallowing a rat, whole and without effort. He pressed his feet against her face, showing her the difference between a schoolteacher and a farmer's daughter, and she licked the salt between his toes, and when she asked when they would get married, he laughed as if she had told him the funniest joke in the world. And then his wife went to the Salish, and the Salish decided she had tempted Amin, and they said, leave the village. But not before you are punished. And into the punishing hut she went, and when she came out, she looked exactly like she was meant to look, ugly and broken. Like a rat swallowed by a snake.

Just like Mala looked after they told her the search was over and she would never see her brother again. Now Jesmin is wondering if something happened to Dulal that made him feel like the rest of them, like a small animal in a big, spiteful world.

Maybe that's why, she offers, speaking softly into the dark. He turns to her. What did you say?

Maybe that's why, you know, it's not—it's not your fault.

He comes close. His breath is eggy. That's when, out of nowhere, one side of her face explodes. When she opens her eyes she's on the ground and everyone is standing over her, Kulsum, her kid, her in-laws, and Dulal. The kid tugs at her kameez and she stands up, brushes herself off. No one says anything. Jesmin can taste lipstick and blood where she's bitten herself.

In the morning Jamal takes one look at her and runs her to the back of the line. You look like a bat, he says, you should've stayed home. What if that inspector comes nosing around? Her eye is swollen so she has to change the thread on the machine with her head tilted to one side. Ruby's back from her village and when she sees Jesmin she starts to cry. Don't worry, Jesmin says, it's nothing. She takes a toilet break, borrows a compact from Mala and looks at herself. One side of her face is swallowing the other. When she comes out Ruby's holding a chocbar. She presses it against Jesmin's cheek and they wait for it to melt, then they tear open a corner and take turns pouring the ice cream into their mouths.

They go home. Dulal isn't there. Now look what you did, Kulsum says. They wait until the mosquitoes come in and finally everyone eats. When the kerosene lamp comes on and she's about to bed on the floor with Ruby, Dulal bursts in and demands food. She makes him a plate and watches him belch. The food's cold, he says. After, it's the same, lying there facing his back, holding his small, lifeless thing, except this time Ruby's on the floor next to Kulsum and her kid. Scratch my head, Dulal mutters. He falls asleep, and later, in the night, she hears him cry out, a sharp, bleating sound. She thinks she must have dreamt it because in the moonlight his face is as mean as ever.

On the day of Ruby's turn, she looks so small. When she's cut too much thread off her machine, Jamal scolds her and she spends the rest of the day with her head down. But after lunch she goes into the toilet and when she comes out she's got a new sari on and the ribbon is twisted into her hair like a thread of happy running all around the back of her head. Dulal comes to the gate and when he sees Ruby his face is as bright as money. Ruby says something to Dulal and he laughs. Jesmin watches them leave together, holding hands, her heart breaking against her ribs.

Jesmin covers her ears against the sound of laughter.

In the punishing hut, the Salish gathered. The oldest one said, take off your dress. When her clothes were on the ground he said, walk. They sat in a circle and threw words like rotten fruit. She's nothing but a piece of trash. Amin said: her pussy stinks like a dead eel. She is the child of pigs. She's a slut. She's the shit of pigs. Walk, walk. Move your hands. You want to cover it now? Where was your shame when you seduced a married man? Get out now. Get out and don't come back. Afterward, they laughed.

Jesmin covers her ears against the sound of laughter.

It's Friday. She packs her things and says goodbye to Kulsum. The kid wraps his legs around her waist and bites into her shoulder. She hands money to the landlord and he waves her to the room. There's a kerosene lamp in one corner, and a cot pushed up against another. Last year's calendar is tacked to the wall. The roof is leaking and there's a large puddle on the floor. She sees her face in the pool of water. She sees her eyes and the shape of her head and Ruby's clip in her hair. She opens her trunk and finds the pair of Thanks she stole from the factory. She holds it up. It makes the silhouette of a piece of woman. She pulls the door shut and the room darkens. She takes off her sandals, her shalwar. She lies on the floor, the damp and the dirt under her back, and drags the Thanks over her legs. When she stands up she straddles the pool of water and casts her eyes over her reflection. There is a body encased, legs and hips and buttocks. The body is hers but it is far away, unreachable. She looks at herself and hears the sound of laughter, but this time it is not the laughter of the Salish, but the laughter of the piece of herself that is closed. She knows now that Ruby will fix Dulal, that she will parade with him in the factory, spreading her small-toothed smile among the spools of thread that hang above their heads, and that Dulal will take Ruby to his air-conditioned shop, and her sisters will no longer be hungry, and Jesmin will be here, joined by the laughter of her own legs, no longer the girl of the punishing hut, but a garments girl with a room and a closed-up body that belongs only to herself.

The door opens. Jesmin turns to the smell of biscuits.

Helen Simpson

is the author of five short story collections,
including *Getting a Life* and *In-Flight
Entertainment*. She was the first *Sunday
Times* Young Writer of the Year and has also
received the Hawthornden Prize and the
American Academy of Arts and Letters' E. M.
Forster Award. Her next short story collection,
Cockfosters, will be published later this year.
She lives in London.

Arizona

HELEN SIMPSON

18:07 NEEDLES

"Can you feel that?"

"Ouch. Yes."

"Good."

"A sort of pulling sensation. Is that right?"

"'The therapeutic ache.' Yes."

She felt like a violin being tuned, she thought as she stared up at the ceiling. The twisting of the hair-fine needles along with the checking of various pulse points made it feel like some sort of fine-tuning was going on.

"And that?" asked Mae again, turning another needle.

"Yes, but not as strongly," Liz replied.

It seemed to work by administering little shocks to get things moving again. Stalled fluids. All the chronic stuff doctors hated, that's what it was supposed to be good for; autoimmune conditions, IBS, asthma, backache. From what she'd understood.

"Was the migraine less severe this time, would you say?" asked Mae. "In terms of intensity?"

"No," said Liz. "Unfortunately not. Worse, if anything. Flashing lights, nausea; flat on my back in a darkened room. But it may all simply disappear when I hit the menopause! You said so last time."

"That does happen sometimes," said Mae, raising her eyebrows slightly and smiling. "I'm not offering empty hope."

They lapsed back into silence while Mae stood and held Liz's wrist, testing her pulse. Quite a lot of any acupuncture session seemed to be filled with this careful pulse-taking. As far as she had understood, there were twelve different pulse points, six along each wrist, all useful for reading the selfsame central pulse in subtly different diagnostic ways. And the changes in pulse quality which happened when Mae slid a new needle into one of the body's eight hundred or so acupuncture points provided her with clues as to what should be done next. Or something like that. At any rate it was a quiet painstaking business as well as a leap of faith, and Liz was finding it surprisingly restful.

The room was bare and clean and bright though without the strip-lit glare of the hospital space where she had last week seen the specialist. "Be happy," he had said, patronizingly, at the end of an inconclusive appointment. Her GP had snorted when she told her this: "Another consultant telling a middle-aged woman she's hysterical." Certainly his advice had not been noticeably more scientific than anything Mae had said so far.

"So, what are you working on now?" asked Mae, returning her arm carefully to the table.

"I'm finishing a paper on the Risorgimento for a conference at Senate House next week. Mazzini's identification of liberty with blood sacrifice, all that."

"The Risorgimento?"

"It was the big freedom movement of the nineteenth century."

"Yes, yes," murmured Mae mock-seriously, then: "I don't know what you're talking about but it all sounds very impressive."

Mae had been recommended to Liz by an insomniac colleague in the history faculty. He had earnestly assured her that he felt better than he had done for months and that a needle between the brows was a sovereign remedy against sleeplessness; Liz had decided to go along with an open mind.

"He <u>was</u> quite impressive, Mazzini. In exile all those years. He never gave up. Though Marx did call him 'that everlasting old ass.'"

"History passed me by," shrugged Mae. "I couldn't take the rules at school, the lack of freedom. I did no work. I was a rebel."

"I was a swot," said Liz. "I've never really stopped being one."

"Um," said Mae. "I was quite wild."

"It doesn't seem to have done you any harm!"

"I don't know about that."

They lapsed back into silence. How strange and welcome, thought Liz, the distant intimacy which had sprung up between them. They could afford to say anything that came into their heads since they had zero contact with each other outside this bare quiet room. Lying on Mae's padded table seemed to liberate all sorts of illuminated ramblings, which, combined with the sporadic nature of the treatment, made for an unusually dreamy, intermittent sort of conversation.

18:15 GOTHIC

While she had been taking Liz's health history in the preliminary session, Mae had laughed and commented that the two of them happened to be almost exactly the same age. Born in the same month fifty years ago, they were coalescing a step deeper into middle age. What would it be like, now wondered Liz, this shift away from the heightened sensitivity which regularly, tidally, made itself felt in advance of blood? And, parrying her own embarrassed, automatic accusation of self-indulgence: Why <u>shouldn't</u> the private life of the body be acknowledged as it crossed this new threshold?

"Aren't we supposed to feel fear and loathing about it?" she said now.

"I don't," said Mae. "Do you?"

"No," said Liz, with slight surprise. "But other people seem to. Younger women. Men. I haven't mentioned it to anyone else except you, because of that."

"It does creep men out," admitted Mae. "The very mention of it. But then, so does any mention of periods."

"Even the language is Gothic, isn't it—the 'Curse,' and the 'Change.'"

"'The Change!'" said Mae. "Very doomy, yes. But menopause isn't much better. It even *sounds* miserable and moany."

"Moanapause."

They both started to laugh, quietly.

Sometimes when she woke from a flabbergasting dream Liz would lie very still to see if she could net it before it fled; perfectly still, eyes closed, not moving her head, as if the slightest shift would tip the story-bearing liquid, break its fragile meniscus and spill the night's elusive catch. Here she had to be still too, even rocking gently with laughter as she was now, in order not to displace the various long fine silvery needles which bristled from her face and arms and fingers and toes, and which quivered slightly as she moved.

"Also, had you noticed?" she said, once their laughter had died away. "Calling a woman 'menopausal' is the ultimate insult."

"I thought that was the c-word," said Mae, eyes downcast, professionally circumspect. "The ultimate insult."

"Except that's a noun, and 'menopausal' is an adjective. 'Menopausal' is used to write you off, isn't it."

"Yes."

"Whereas the c-word carries more hatred."

"It's what men call other men," commented Mae.

"Is it? Yes, you're right—I suppose it is."

"In Russia they call it your moneymaker," said Mae. "The c-word."

"How nasty! No, we're not having that."

Les Grandes Horizontales, she thought, gazing up at the ceiling; wasn't that what they used to call the courtesans of nineteenth-century Paris? At least we're now allowed paid employment in other areas—equal pay, sometimes. But yes, upwardly mobile; vertical job opportunities. In much of the world, anyway.

"In Chinese traditional medicine they call it the Gate of Mystery," added Mae, after a long pause. "Also, the coital muscle."

"Hmm. Interesting. But neither of those will do either really."

"No."

"There's always vagina, of course, but I've never liked that because I did Latin at school, Caesar's Gallic Wars, and it's Latin for 'scabbard.' Still, I suppose it's the best of a bad bunch."

There was a pause.

"I'm certainly not calling it a 'coochie' or a 'foofoo' or whatever the latest suggestion is," she added.

"No," said Mae. "I find I don't want to personalize it in that way."

"You're right. Neither do I. And that's how it should be. That's OK. If there was a good name they'd only take it and trash it."

18:19 AUGUST

It can be useful for chronic conditions that flare up, Mae had told her, mildly, at the start of these sessions. If it brings

113

inflammation down and holds it down, acupuncture can give more years not dominated by the condition; inflammation that flares up and feeds on itself is not great. As for the menopause, Mae had observed from her clients that it seemed to be pure luck of the draw as to how it affected you.

"Some women are unlucky and have a bad time," came her voice from behind Liz as she stood at the head of the table and checked the needles in her scalp. "Night sweats. Drenched sheets. They have to get up and change their sheets in the middle of the night."

"Not us!" said Liz, rolling her eyes back in her head at her like a racehorse.

"Of course not," said Mae drily.

They were quiet. Mae moved to the wooden chair in a corner of the room and sat checking her notes.

"It's interesting," she said at last. "Your migraines do tend to occur in the same week as your cycle."

That heavy dream-dogged sleep of the week before, thought Liz; the headache and slowness and central unwillingness to stir: would these disappear along with the heady waterlogged desire to be inward?

"I realize I think of the menopause as extra time," said Mae, after another pause. "If I'd been born elsewhere in the world I might easily have died long before now."

"Yes," said Liz. "Or, a hundred years ago, here, of course. Pure luck. It would help, though, if we knew whereabouts we were on the scale now, wouldn't it. Toward the end? In the middle?"

"I like to think we're somewhere around August," said Mae dreamily. "The very end of summer."

August, thought Liz: the sudden chill in the middle of bright-ness and warmth; confident wasteful growth starting to go to seed.

Something casual and wild about it. Confidence. Strength. The smell of dust, and sudden thunderstorms.

"I'll tell you my own idea of it," continued Mae. "Here and now. For us."

She paused and lifted Liz's arm again, silently counting for a few seconds.

"There's a sort of game I play when I'm trying to get to sleep where I parcel out the years," she continued. "So, up to the age of ten when you're still in waiting and time goes slowly, that's when you're in January and February. From ten to twenty it's March and April. Then it's May, which takes you all the way to thirty since you're fully in the world at last."

"OK," said Liz, smiling. "And at that rate, June is your thirties, July your forties, August your fifties."

"September until sixty-nine, that's autumn," continued Mae. "Early old age whatever anybody says. Then October is the seventies, which can still be early to middle old age if you're lucky; and November and December are middle to proper old age, because let's face it, we're probably not going to make it beyond a hundred."

"August sounds good," said Liz.

18:24 *SHIBUI*

"Now, if you'll close your eyes I'm going to try something new. I'm going to try some needles in the eye sockets."

"Really? Give me a moment," said Liz. "I could never have a face-lift, could I. OK. Go ahead."

She closed her eyes and freewheeled into her thoughts, breathing through the little shock as the needles were inserted one at a time.

"So how do you feel about looking older?" she asked, eyes still closed. "Do you care?"

The room was quiet for a while.

"It's harder in some professions than others," said Mae at last. "I have a client, she's an actress, she's quite famous. You know what they say about an older woman having to choose between her face and her bum? Well, she chose her bum and she tells me she wishes she hadn't."

"Serves her right."

"But still."

"Talking of which," said Liz, "had you noticed how you never can tell from a man's face how big his bum is going to be?"

Mae cast her gaze up at the ceiling and considered. There was silence.

"That's true," she conceded after a while. "That's very true."

There was a pause while they thought about this, Liz with her eyes shut and Mae gazing out the window, giggling gently, waves of submerged laughter rippling through them.

"She's also gone down the Botox route, this same client," continued Mae after a while. "She's had little bits of work done and she does look younger than her age. But *she* doesn't think she looks good, so what's the point? She groans when she looks in the mirror."

Yes, the challenge is to see whether you can carry on liking your own face, thought Liz. There is such a thing as the beauty of aging. The Japanese have a word for it, don't they—*shibui*. I leave anemones in their vase for as long as I can, tulips too, for those wild swoops they do on their way out, the way their stems curve and lunge and shed soot-dusted petals. In fact I like them best at that stage. I'm not a vase of flowers, though, am I.

"Is that all right?" asked Mae, adjusting a needle. "Can you feel that?"

"Ouch. Yes."

116

But let's not luxuriate in self-disgust, continued Liz, taking herself to task. We wouldn't riff on how hideous our grandmothers look—it's disrespectful of life, that sort of spite, for one thing. It's childish to criticize people for looking older. Including ourselves. And the spite comes from fear.

"I honestly don't think I've ever loved anyone less for growing older," she said now. "For looking older. Even friends where I've started off drawn to them by their looks. In fact, I usually love them more because they've become more vulnerable. I feel extra tenderness on top of everything else. I love them *more*. Don't you find that?"

"Mmm," said Mae. "Not sure."

Some of the people I've loved most in my life have been quite old, thought Liz. One or two have been *very* old—the ones who've continued to change and grow. And some of them—particularly the ones who've had worldly success—have probably been much nicer and more interesting older than in their unkind, powerful youth. They've acquired vulnerability.

"OK, then, say it hasn't made you love them less," said Mae. "Has it made you *fancy* them less, though?"

"Oh," said Liz. "Ah. Yes. Let me have a think."

"Because it's about that, isn't it," said Mae, starting to remove the needles from Liz's eye sockets with practiced deftness.

18:31 SEX

"Yes, it is interesting, all that," said Liz, opening her eyes. "I am interested in what happens about, um, sex. I mean, at what age that's supposed to stop."

Mae raised her eyebrows as she contemplated the fan of needles in her left hand, and looked thoughtful.

117

"They say," she said cautiously, "they say the menopause takes women one of two ways. Either they grow more libidinous. Or, the opposite."

"What, it can just turn off?" said Liz, also raising her eyebrows.

"Maybe it happens that one day you stop wanting to. And then you find you don't regret what you don't want."

"Maybe," said Liz doubtfully.

Liz was still married to the girls' father though there was little opportunity for sex anymore—most nights he was up and waiting for the return of one or the other of them, texting and swearing and generally on their case. Then there was always the possibility that a daughter would return early from a disappointing night and walk in on them. Their bedroom had become a general family meeting place over the years, incorrigibly domesticated— Christmas stockings; sick children being cosseted; a forum for passionate and extensive discussions about vital matters (like when bedtime was); a meeting place for postmortems of fascinating teen evenings and resumes of movies watched. He had suggested a bolt on the door; she had worried that would seem unfriendly; he had fixed one, nonetheless. "Oh yuk, gross, they're trying to have sex," came the voices from the other side. In the service of tact as when under parental rooves of their youth they persisted in grim silence, clenching their teeth.

"I do have clients who say they feel nothing but relief now that 'all that,' as they put it, is over," said Mae, opening a new packet of needles. "I'm going to try your right temple next."

Liz drew a long slow breath and closed her eyes again. Into her mind floated the lunchtime concert she'd attended at St Pancras Church last week, Schubert's *Death and the Maiden*. Most of the heads in the audience had been white or gray-haired. And she hadn't been able to help noticing the smell: nothing awful, just the subdued but unmistakable smell of under-washed jumpers and hair that had been left to go an extra day. They weren't expecting anything.

"I can't see how you wouldn't regret the loss of that," she said.

"Regret" was surely too dilute a word.

"I've heard it's sixty, sixty-five," she continued. "That sixty-five's about average. For women *and* men."

"It can go on to seventy," said Mae. "Eighty."

"*Eighty?*"

"It would be different, though," said Mae, thoughtfully. "Older. Different things."

"Yes?"

"Communication would be key."

"How do you mean?"

But Mae had lapsed into silence again.

18:37 SANDWICH

Her own girls, fifteen and sixteen, were at the start of it all. They still hadn't got used to their bodies gearing up, thought Liz with a pang; they oscillated between pride and outrage at the new conditions of life to which they now saw they would have to reconcile themselves (and in strict silence, too, publicly at least). Emerging into lunar beauty, they were virulently critical of her appearance and frighteningly sensitive about their own. They shudder at my arms, Liz thought, at my elbows; but they're savagely self-policing too. It's all part and parcel. I wish I could make them know how effortlessly beautiful they are.

"It's when you come out the other side," said Liz now. "Isn't it."

"The other side of what?"

"All *that*. The reproductive life. If you've had children. Even if you haven't. It's when you're returned to yourself. So they say."

"My middle daughter is in a bulimic phase just now," shrugged Mae. "Meanwhile my mother's lost it; she opens the door with nothing on."

"Wow."

"Yeah."

She twirled the needle in the crook of Liz's right elbow.

"Can you feel that?"

"Ouch. Yes. They call us the sandwich generation, you know," continued Liz. "They're trying to blame us again, of course. Caught between teenagers and aged parents and all because we left having children until our thirties. But it doesn't wash!"

She paused and scowled up at the ceiling.

"I know a woman of sixty-four who had her children in her early twenties," she continued, "and now she's having to deal with her ninety-three-year-old father as well as house one of her divorced daughters and provide hefty chunks of child care for various baby grandchildren."

"She doesn't have to," said Mae, coolly.

"True," admitted Liz, momentarily confounded.

There was a pause.

"Though sometimes it seems boundless, what you give," she added.

"It's not, though," said Mae. "Boundless. Is it."

"Isn't it?"

"Once in a while I leave them all to it, I always have done. Every now and then I need to cut loose. Travel."

"*How?*" said Liz.

"I call in a few favors," shrugged Mae, "set up some basic support. Youth hostels have no age limit. I have my life to think of too."

"How do you not feel guilty?" said Liz after a while.

"I do feel guilt but I react to it by just doing more of what I want to do. I take *more*."

The room was quiet again as they both considered this.

18:44 CAKE

"I still can't quite get over being able to walk out of the house without setting up an entire support system," said Liz. "Lists of food, emergency numbers, and so on."

"Yes."

"I've recently taken on a fantastic amount of work, and I'm really looking forward to it."

"Yes."

"I tell you, it's not vanity that's the issue, is it—it's employability. Keeping your place in the world. I want to carry on working. I'm doing the best work I've done in my life but—and I notice it every time I go for an interview—fifty is a black mark on the CV. They think you're their mum!"

"I'm going to get one of those fish-throats, I can see it coming," said Mae, pinching her neck pensively. "My mother had one so I don't see how I can avoid it."

"What do *you* say now, Mae, when people ask your age?"

"Sometimes I tell them to mind their own business," said Mae. "Sometimes I just stare at them. But I really don't care. I don't have to: It doesn't affect my work. What do *you* say?"

"I say, Guess! As in, guess the weight of the cake in the village tombola. In fact, I really do think if they ask your age they should insist on your weight as well—it's just as relevant to your health and fitness for the job."

"I don't think that would catch on," said Mae. "I don't think that would be very popular."

"Imagine if they stood there trying to guess your weight aloud as if you were a cake at a village fete!"

"Yes."

18:48 BLOOD

Mae stood holding Liz's forearm in a pulse-taking clasp, motionless as a statue.

"All this talk," said Liz, "and we're not even there yet. At least, I don't think I am. Are you?"

"No. Not really. Though I find there's a new unpredictability."

"Yes."

"Funny though," said Mae. "When blood appears after a long pause—seven weeks recently—I feel pride. Blood makes me feel strong and powerful. I'd hate to have another baby now, but it makes me proud to know I still could."

"Yes."

Yes, it would be strange to leave this behind, thought Liz; even at the times when internally she had been melting and trembling, crumbling, with hot joints, hot swollen breasts, it had been being in another state. But these new tides of thin heat flowing just under her skin, like shadows racing over hills when clouds cross the sun—these were interesting too. Inconvenient sometimes, but interesting.

"And now that the drama of our fertile years is drawing to a close . . . " continued Mae.

"Melodrama, more like."

"Will you mourn it? Will you mourn it as a little death?"

"*Petit mort*," said Liz. "Though it should be petite, as death is feminine in French. Petite mort. That's what they call orgasm in America, isn't it."

"Not in France?"

"I think they say *jouir* in France, as in, 'to enjoy.' It's weird to call it a little death, I think, when the actual experience is more like waking up."

"I thought it meant 'epilepsy,'" said Mae. "*Petite mort.*"

"That's *le petit mal.*"

She had even come to look forward to it over the years, each time it came round, the volatile week. Yes, it could be a nuisance in practical terms, but sometimes she felt cleverer, she felt as though she saw and understood more . . . . Nor was it false, the thin-skinned emotion that emerged at such times. Extravagant, more like, so that life appeared as lurid and backlit as an El Greco. Not untrue; not to be acted on, either.

"As for mourning it," she said now, considering Mae's query. "I suppose it's time passing, another step toward the grave if you see things in those terms; but I don't. No. Not unless it means I'll somehow feel less intensely; not unless it means emotion will become less powerful."

"I don't really see why that should happen," said Mae.

"What I wouldn't want is to get very cut-and-dried; you know, very blunt and dismissive and set in what I feel about everything."

"No."

"But then again sometimes I think I really wouldn't mind feeling less," said Liz perversely, with feeling.

They fell quiet, separately musing.

"I envisage the new state as being like Arizona," said Mae at last, opening a new packet of needles.

"Arizona?" said Liz, nonplussed.

"Yes," shrugged Mae.

"What, a desert?"

"No, not that. I see it as . . . It might be . . . "

"Phoenix. Tucson. Why *Arizona*?"

"I see it as arriving in another state," said Mae, slowly. "Brilliantly lit and level and filled with dependable sunshine."

"Oh!"

"In fact I can't quite believe in it," said Mae, "this promise of . . ."

She stopped again and fell silent.

"So that's it," said Liz. "We're about to emigrate."

It's true, isn't it, she thought. Already I'm not as quickly moved to tears as I was ten years ago; soon I'll have cried all my tears and only laughter will be left.

18:55 RISORGIMENTO

Mae walked round the table, peering closely at Liz's face and hair as she extracted the long needles one by one.

"Do they ever break off?" asked Liz, raising one hand gingerly to feel.

"Never," said Mae firmly.

"So I won't find the point of one in my scalp tonight when I come to wash my hair?"

"No! It doesn't happen. The needles are very fine but they're very strong as well. Now, careful as you sit up. Slowly."

"Yes," said Liz as she swung her legs off the edge of the table. "Oh! I feel really clearheaded. Alive."

"Good. Now, would you like to see how it goes or book a follow-up appointment?"

I want to go ahead unashamed, thought Liz as she reached for her bag. Is that possible? Unashamed. Brave! At the very least brave, because you've got to be. At every stage really, looking back, and this is no different. Except now there's no need to fit in because for the first time there's no particular template.

124

"I don't want just to accept it—I mean to enjoy it," she declared to Mae. "I like being here, now, this minute."

"Well, we're all living in time," said Mae, glancing at her watch. "That's fifty pounds, please."

"Cash, isn't it," said Liz. " I went to the machine on the way."

"Thanks. Women our age—it's different now, it's not the image that's put out, is it. Look at us! We're strong and active, we've raised children and earned money all our lives; we're fine. Look at you with your big lecture next week on . . . what was it?"

"The Risorgimento," said Liz.

"Yes. And while you're getting dressed, it's supposed to be a good thing as you get older if you can put on your socks or tights without sitting down or leaning against anything."

"What, like this?" laughed Liz, standing on one leg like a flamingo, unsteady, one arm flailing for purchase in the air, teetering, hopping from side to side, finding her balance.

"Yes," said Mae, laughing too. "Like that."

Ishion Hutchinson

was born in Port Antonio, Jamaica. His poetry collection, *Far District: Poems*, won the PEN/ Joyce Osterweil Award. Other honors include a Whiting Writers' Award and the Academy of American Poets' Larry Levis Prize. He teaches at Cornell University.

Windfall

ISHION HUTCHINSON

Away to the uncertain desert of Utah,

the land a rusting delirium of mortuaries,

I mark with gravel stones and bottle caps

those cousins to whom I cannot speak,

their mother just rigor mortis by the wharf

workmen gutted out for some yacht club

and a KFC, its stink a dreadful malebolge.

Cement dust specters the shore with rough

moonlight music; the surf no longer comes

to her louvers, where ibises, marsh morticians,

settled at sundown. Their faces shirr up

in my mud room, shouting *bingo! bingo! bingo!*

I seek in exile one incontrovertible windfall,

their laughter above the surf as we gather shells

to play, numbers skimming water like stones.

Garnette Cadogan

has written about culture and the arts for
various publications. He is currently at work
on a book on walking and is slowly at work on
a book on rock-reggae musician Bob Marley.
He lives in New York City.

Black and Blue

GARNETTE CADOGAN

"My only sin is my skin. What did I do, to be so black and blue?"
　　—Fats Waller, "(What Did I Do to Be So) Black and Blue?"

"Manhattan's streets I saunter'd, pondering."
　　—Walt Whitman, "Manhattan's Streets I Saunter'd, Pondering"

My love for walking started in childhood, out of necessity. No thanks to a stepfather with heavy hands, I found every reason to stay away from home and was usually out—at some friend's house or at a street party where no minor should be—until it was too late to get public transportation. So I walked.

The streets of Kingston, Jamaica, in the 1980s were often terrifying—you could, for instance, get killed if a political henchman thought you came from the wrong neighborhood, or even if you wore the wrong color. Wearing orange showed affiliation with one political party and green with the other, and if you were neutral or traveling far from home you chose your colors well. The wrong color in the wrong neighborhood could mean your last day. No wonder, then, that my friends and the rare nocturnal passerby declared me crazy for my long late-night treks that traversed warring political zones. (And sometimes I did pretend to be crazy, shouting non sequiturs when I passed through especially dangerous spots, such as the place where thieves hid on the banks of a storm drain. Predators would ignore or laugh at the kid in his school uniform speaking nonsense.)

I made friends with strangers and went from being a very shy and awkward kid to being an extroverted, awkward one. The beggar, the vendor, the poor laborer—those were experienced wanderers, and they became my nighttime instructors; they knew the streets and delivered lessons on how to navigate and enjoy them. I imagined myself as a Jamaican Tom Sawyer, one moment sauntering down the streets to pick low-hanging mangoes that I could reach from the sidewalk, another moment hanging outside a street party with battling sound systems, each armed with speakers piled to create skyscrapers of heavy bass. These streets weren't frightening. They were full of adventure when they weren't serene. There I'd join forces with a band of merry walkers, who'd miss the last bus by mere minutes, our feet still moving as we put out our thumbs to hitchhike to spots nearer home, making jokes as vehicle after vehicle raced past us. Or I'd get lost in Mittyesque moments, my young mind imagining alternate futures. The streets had their own safety: Unlike at home, there I could be myself without fear of bodily harm. Walking became so regular and familiar that the way home became home.

The streets had their rules, and I loved the challenge of trying to master them. I learned how to be alert to surrounding dangers and nearby delights, and prided myself on recognizing telling details that my peers missed. Kingston was a map of complex, and often bizarre, cultural and political and social activity, and I appointed myself its nighttime cartographer. I'd know how to navigate away from a predatory pace, and to speed up to chat when the cadence of a gait announced friendliness. It was almost always men I saw. A lone woman walking in the middle of the night was as common a sight as Sasquatch; moonlight pedestrianism was too dangerous for her. Sometimes at night as I made my way down from hills above Kingston, I'd have the impression that the city was set on "pause" or in extreme slow motion, as that as I descended I was cutting across Jamaica's deep social divisions. I'd make my way briskly past the mansions in the hills overlooking the city, now transformed into a carpet of dotted lights under a curtain of stars, saunter by middle-class subdivisions hidden behind high walls crowned with barbed wire, and zigzagged through neighborhoods of zinc and wooden shacks crammed together and leaning like a tight-knit group of limbo dancers. With my descent came an increase in the vibrancy of street life—except when it didn't; some poor neighborhoods had both the violent gunfights and the eerily deserted streets of the cinematic Wild West. I knew well enough to avoid those even at high noon.

I'd begun hoofing it after dark when I was ten years old. By thirteen I was rarely home before midnight, and some nights found me racing against dawn. My mother would often complain, "Mek yuh love street suh? Yuh born a hospital; yuh neva born a street." ("Why do you love the streets so much? You were born in a hospital, not in the streets.")

I left Jamaica in 1996 to attend college in New Orleans, a city I'd heard called "the northernmost Caribbean city." I wanted to discover—on foot, of course—what was Caribbean and what was

American about it. Stately mansions on oak-lined streets with streetcars clanging by, and brightly colored houses that made entire blocks look festive; people in resplendent costumes dancing to funky brass bands in the middle of the street; cuisine—and aromas—that mashed up culinary traditions from Africa, Europe, Asia, and the American South; and a juxtaposition of worlds old and new, odd and familiar: Who wouldn't want to explore this?

On my first day in the city, I went walking for a few hours to get a feel for the place and to buy supplies to transform my dormitory room from a prison bunker into a welcoming space. When some university staff members found out what I'd been up to, they warned me to restrict my walking to the places recommended as safe to tourists and the parents of freshmen. They trotted out statistics about New Orleans' crime rate. But Kingston's crime rate dwarfed those numbers, and I decided to ignore these well-meant cautions. A city was waiting to be discovered, and I wouldn't let inconvenient facts get in the way. These American criminals are nothing on Kingston's, I thought. They're no real threat to me.

What no one had told me was that I was the one who would be considered a threat.

Within days I noticed that many people on the street seemed apprehensive of me: Some gave me a circumspect glance as they approached, and then crossed the street; others, ahead, would glance behind, register my presence, and then speed up; older white women clutched their bags; young white men nervously greeted me, as if exchanging a salutation for their safety: "What's up, bro?" On one occasion, less than a month after my arrival, I tried to help a man whose wheelchair was stuck in the middle of a crosswalk; he threatened to shoot me in the face, then asked a white pedestrian for help.

I wasn't prepared for any of this. I had come from a majori-ty-black country in which no one was wary of me because of my skin color. Now I wasn't sure who was afraid of me. I was especially unprepared for the cops. They regularly stopped and bullied me, asking questions that took my guilt for granted. I'd never received what many of my African-American friends call "The Talk": No parents had told me how to behave when I was stopped by the police, how to be as polite and cooperative as possible, no matter what they said or did to me. So I had to cobble together my own rules of engagement. Thicken my Jamaican accent. Quickly mention my college. "Accidentally" pull out my college identification card when asked for my driver's license.

My survival tactics began well before I left my dorm. I got out of the shower with the police in my head, assembling a cop-proof wardrobe. Light-colored oxford shirt. V-neck sweater. Khaki pants. Chukkas. Sweatshirt or T-shirt with my university insignia. When I walked I regularly had my identity challenged, but I also found ways to assert it. (So I'd dress Ivy League style, but would, later on, add my Jamaican pedigree by wearing Clarks Desert Boots, the footwear of choice of Jamaican street culture.) Yet the all-American sartorial choice of white T-shirt and jeans, which many police officers see as the uniform of black troublemakers, was off-limits to me—at least, if I wanted to have the freedom of movement I desired.

In this city of exuberant streets, walking became a complex and often oppressive negotiation. I would see a white woman walking towards me at night and cross the street to reassure her that she was safe. I would forget something at home but not immediately turn around if someone was behind me, because I discovered that a sudden backtrack could cause alarm. (I had a cardinal rule: Keep a wide perimeter from people who might

133

consider me a danger. If not, danger might visit me.) New Orleans suddenly felt more dangerous than Jamaica. The sidewalk was a minefield, and every hesitation and self-censored compensation reduced my dignity. Despite my best efforts, the streets never felt comfortably safe. Even a simple salutation was suspect.

One night, returning to the house that, eight years after my arrival, I thought I'd earned the right to call my home, I waved to a cop driving by. Moments later, I was against his car in hand-cuffs. When I later asked him—sheepishly, of course; any other way would have asked for bruises—why he had detained me, he said my greeting had aroused his suspicion. "No one waves to the police," he explained. When I told friends of his response, it was my behavior, not his, that they saw as absurd. "Now why would you do a dumb thing like that?" said one. "You know better than to make nice with police."

A few days after I left on a visit to Kingston, Hurricane Katrina slashed and pummeled New Orleans. I'd gone not because of the storm but because my adoptive grandmother, Pearl, was dying of cancer. I hadn't wandered those streets in eight years, since my last visit, and I returned to them now mostly at night, the time I found best for thinking, praying, crying. I walked to feel less alienated—from myself, struggling with the pain of seeing my grandmother terminally ill; from my home in New Orleans, under-water and seemingly abandoned; from my home country, which now, precisely because of its childhood familiarity, felt foreign to me. I was surprised by how familiar those streets felt. Here was the corner where the fragrance of jerk chicken greeted me, along with the warm tenor and peace-and-love message of Half Pint's "Greetings," broadcast from a small but powerful speaker to at least a half-mile radius. It was as if I had walked into 1986, down to the soundtrack. And there was the wall of the neighborhood shop, adorned with the Rastafarian colors red, gold, and green along with images of local and international heroes Bob Marley, Marcus Garvey, and Haile Selassie. The crew of boys leaning against it and joshing each other were recognizable; different faces, similar stories. I was astonished at how safe the streets felt to me, once again one black body among many, no longer having to anticipate the many ways my presence might instill fear and how to offer some reassuring body language. Passing police cars were once again merely passing police cars. Jamaican police could be pretty brutal, but they didn't notice me the way American police did. I could be invisible in Jamaica in a way I can't be invisible in the United States.

Walking had returned to me a greater set of possibilities. And why walk, if not to create a new set of possibilities? Following serendipity, I added new routes to the mental maps I had made from constant walking in that city from childhood to young adulthood, traced variations on the old pathways. Serendipity, a mentor once told me, is a secular way of speaking of grace; it's unearned favor. Seen theologically, then, walking is an act of faith. Walking is, after all, interrupted falling. We see, we listen, we speak, and we trust that each step we take won't be our last, but will lead us into a richer understanding of the self and the world.

In Jamaica, I felt once again as if the only identity that mattered was my own, not the constricted one that others had constructed for me. I strolled into my better self. I said, along with Kierkegaard, "I have walked myself into my best thoughts."

When I tried to return to New Orleans from Jamaica a month later, there were no flights. I thought about flying to Texas so I could make my way back to my neighborhood as soon as it opened for reoccupancy, but my adoptive aunt, Maxine, who hated the idea of me returning to a hurricane zone before the end of hurricane season, persuaded me to come to stay in New York City instead. (To strengthen her case she sent me an article about Texans who were buying up guns because they were afraid of the influx of black people from New Orleans.)

This wasn't a hard sell: I wanted to be in a place where I could travel by foot and, more crucially, continue to reap the solace of walking at night. And I was eager to follow in the steps of the essayists, poets, and novelists who'd wandered that great city before me—Walt Whitman, Herman Melville, Alfred Kazin, Elizabeth Hardwick. I had visited the city before, but each trip had felt like a tour in a sports car. I welcomed the chance to stroll. I wanted to walk alongside Whitman's ghost and "descend to the pavements, merge with the crowd, and gaze with them." So I left Kingston, the popular Jamaican farewell echoing in my mind: "Walk good!" *Be safe on your journey,* in other words, *and all the best in your endeavors.*

I arrived in New York City, ready to lose myself in Whitman's "Manhattan crowds, with their turbulent musical chorus!" I marveled at what Jane Jacobs praised as "the ballet of the good city sidewalk" in her old neighborhood, the West Village. I walked up past midtown skyscrapers, releasing their energy as lively people onto the streets, and on into the Upper West Side, with its regal Beaux Arts apartment buildings, stylish residents, and buzzing streets. Onward into Washington Heights, the sidewalks spilled over with an ebullient mix of young and old Jewish and Dominican-American residents, past leafy Inwood, with parks whose grades rose to reveal beautiful views of the Hudson River, up to my home in Kingsbridge in the Bronx, with its rows of brick bungalows and apartment buildings nearby Broadway's bustling sidewalks and the peaceful expanse of Van Cortlandt Park. I went to Jackson Heights in Queens to take in people socializing around garden courtyards in Urdu, Korean, Spanish, Russian, and Hindi. And when I wanted a taste of home, I headed to Brooklyn, in Crown Heights, for Jamaican food and music and humor mixed in with the flavor of New York City. The city was my playground.

I explored the city with friends, and then with a woman I'd begun dating. She walked around endlessly with me, taking in New York City's many pleasures. Coffee shops open until predawn; verdant parks with nooks aplenty; food and music from across the globe; quirky neighborhoods with quirkier residents. My impressions of the city took shape during my walks with her.

As with the relationship, those first few months of urban exploration were all romance. The city was beguiling, exhilarating, vibrant. But it wasn't long before reality reminded me I wasn't invulnerable, especially when I walked alone.

One night in the East Village, I was running to dinner when a white man in front of me turned and punched me in the chest with such force that I thought my ribs had braided around my spine. I assumed he was drunk or had mistaken me for an old enemy, but found out soon enough that he'd merely assumed I was a criminal because of my race. When he discovered I wasn't what he imagined, he went on to tell me that his assault was my own fault for running up behind him. I blew off this incident as an aberration, but the mutual distrust between me and the police was impossible to ignore. It felt elemental. They'd enter a subway platform; I'd notice them. (And I'd notice all the other black men registering their presence as well, while just about everyone else remained oblivious to them). They'd glare. I'd get nervous and glance. They'd observe me steadily. I'd get uneasy. I'd observe them back, worrying that I looked suspicious. Their suspicions would increase. We'd continue the silent, uneasy dialogue until the subway arrived and separated us at last.

I returned to the old rules I'd set for myself in New Orleans, with elaboration. No running, especially at night; no sudden movements; no hoodies; no objects—especially shiny ones—in hand; no waiting for friends on street corners, lest I be mistaken for a drug dealer; no standing near a corner on the cell phone (same reason). As comfort set in, inevitably I began to break some of those rules, until a night encounter sent me zealously back to them, me having learned that anything less than vigilance was carelessness.

After a sumptuous Italian dinner and drinks with friends, I was jogging to the subway at Columbus Circle—I was running late to meet another set of friends at a concert downtown. I heard someone shouting and I looked up to see a police officer approaching with his gun trained on me. "Against the car!" In no time, half a dozen cops were upon me, chucking me against the car and tightly handcuffing me. "Why were you running?" "Where are you going?" "Where are you coming from?" "I said, why were you running?!" Since I couldn't answer everyone at once, I decided to respond first to the one who looked most likely to hit me. I was surrounded by a swarm and tried to focus on just one without inadvertently aggravating the others.

It didn't work. As I answered that one, the others got frustrated that I wasn't answering them fast enough and barked at me. One of them, digging through my already-emptied pockets, asked if I had any weapons, the question more an accusation. Another badgered me about where I was coming from, as if on the fifteenth round I'd decide to tell him the truth he imagined. Though I kept saying—calmly, of course, which meant trying to manage a tone that ignored my racing heart and their spittle-filled shouts in my face—that I had just left friends two blocks down the road, who were all still there and could vouch for me, to meet other friends whose text messages on my phone that could verify that, yes, sir, yes, officer, of course, officer, it made no difference.

For a black man, to assert your dignity before the police was to risk assault. In fact, the dignity of black people meant less to them, which was why I always felt safer being stopped in front of white witnesses than black witnesses. The cops had less regard for the witness and entreaties of black onlookers, whereas the concern of white witnesses usually registered on them. A black witness asking a question or politely raising an objection could quickly become a fellow detainee. Deference to the police, then, was sine qua non for a safe encounter.

The cops ignored my explanations and my suggestions and continued to snarl at me. All except one of them, a captain. He put his hand on my back, and said to no one in particular, "If he was running for a long time he would have been sweating." He then instructed that the cuffs be removed. He told me that a black man had stabbed someone earlier two or three blocks away and they were searching for him. I noted that I had no blood on me and had told his fellow officers where I'd been and how to check my alibi—unaware that it was even an alibi, as no one had told me why I was being held, and of course, I hadn't dared ask. From what I'd seen, anything beyond passivity would be interpreted as aggression.

The police captain said I could go. None of the cops who detained me thought an apology was necessary. Like the thug who punched me in the East Village, they seemed to think it was my own fault for running.

Humiliated, I tried not to make eye contact with the onlookers on the sidewalk, and I was reluctant to pass them to be on my way. The captain, maybe noticing my shame, offered to give me a ride to the subway station. When he dropped me off and I thanked him for his help, he said, "It's because you were polite that we let you go. If you were acting up it would have been different." I nodded and said nothing.

I realized that what I least liked about walking in New York City wasn't merely having to learn new rules of navigation and socialization—every city has its own. It was the arbitrariness of the circumstances that required them, an arbitrariness that made me feel like a child again, that infantilized me. When we first learn to walk, the world around us threatens to crash into us. Every step is risky. We train ourselves to walk without crashing by being attentive to our movements, and extra-attentive to the world around us. As adults we walk without thinking, really. But as a black adult I am often returned to that moment in childhood when I'm just learning to walk. I am once again on high alert, vigilant.

Some days, when I am fed up with being considered a troublemaker upon sight, I joke that the last time a cop was happy to see a black male walking was when that male was a baby taking his first steps. On many walks, I ask white friends to accompany me, just to avoid being treated like a threat. Walks in New York City, that is; in New Orleans, a white woman in my company sometimes attracted more hostility. (And it is not lost on me that my woman friends are those who best understand my plight; they have developed their own vigilance in an environment where they are constantly treated as targets of sexual attention.) Much of my walking is as my friend Rebecca once described it: A pantomime undertaken to avoid the choreography of criminality.

Walking while black restricts the experience of walking, renders inaccessible the classic Romantic experience of walking alone. It forces me to be in constant relationship with others, unable to join the New York flaneurs I had read about and hoped to join. Instead of meandering aimlessly in the footsteps of Whitman, Melville, Kazin, and Vivian Gornick, more often, I felt that I was tiptoeing in Baldwin's—the Baldwin who wrote, way back in 1960, "Rare, indeed, is the Harlem citizen, from the most circumspect church member to the most shiftless adolescent, who does not have a long tale to tell of police incompetence, injustice, or brutality. I myself have witnessed and endured it more than once."

Walking as a black man has made me feel simultaneously more removed from the city, in my awareness that I am perceived as suspect, and more closely connected to it, in the full attentiveness demanded by my vigilance. It has made me walk more purpose-fully in the city, becoming part of its flow, rather than observing, standing apart.

But it also means that I'm still trying to arrive in a city that isn't quite mine. One definition of home is that it's somewhere we can most be ourselves. And when are we more ourselves but when walking, that natural state in which we repeat one of the first actions we learned? Walking—the simple, monotonous act of placing one foot before the other to prevent falling—turns out not to be so simple if you're black. Walking alone has been anything but monotonous for me; monotony is a luxury.

A foot leaves, a foot lands, and our longing gives it momentum from rest to rest. We long to look, to think, to talk, to get away. But more than anything else, we long to be free. We want the freedom and pleasure of walking without fear—without others' fear—wherever we choose. I've lived in New York City for almost a decade and have not stopped walking its fascinating streets.

And I have not stopped longing to find the solace that I found as a kid on the streets of Kingston. Much as coming to know New York City's streets has made it closer to home to me, the city also withholds itself from me via those very streets. I walk them, alternately invisible and too prominent. So I walk caught between memory and forgetting, between memory and forgiveness.

Laura van den Berg

was raised in Florida. Her first collection of
stories, *What the World Will Look Like When
All the Water Leaves Us,* was a Barnes & Noble
Discover Great New Writers selection and a
finalist for the Frank O'Connor International
Short Story Award. Her second collection of
stories, *The Isle of Youth* (published by FSG
Originals in 2013), received the Rosenthal Family
Foundation Award for Fiction from the American
Academy of Arts and Letters. *Find Me* is her first
novel. She lives in the Boston area.

The Dog

LAURA VAN DEN BERG

The dog is dying. She is sure of it. His sleep is deep and dreamless. His black nose is hot and dry. One morning he doesn't eat his breakfast. One morning he is blind. She watches him run right into a wall. He stumbles back, shaking his head. She kneels in front of the dog and scratches his white chest. She imagines a cartoon halo of yellow stars turning above his head.

Our dog is dying. Don't you care that our dog is dying? This is what she wants to tell her husband, though there are limitations to how she can tell him anything these days—only by e-mail, and when she types out *Our dog is dying*, the words lack the necessary force. Besides, he would likely point out that the dog is more *hers* than *ours*. Five years ago, she found the dog late one night near their home in New Gloucester. He was skinny and spooked and collarless, trotting up and down a shadowed road. Coal black with a white chest and a white spot on top of his skull. The vet said he looked like a Bullador, a cross between a bulldog and a lab.

"There is nothing wrong with your dog," this same vet says when she takes him in.

"Check his eyes," the woman says. "He can't see a thing."

145

The vet shines a tiny flashlight in the dog's eyes.

"This dog can see as clearly as you or me." The vet clicks off the light and drops it into his coat pocket. He takes off his glasses, as though the removal of that barrier will help her to better understand. "It can be difficult to care for a dog on your own, if you're not used to it. It can be an adjustment."

Cars are adjusted. Backs are adjusted. Home entertainment systems are adjusted. Lives are not adjusted.

He's just a little man in a white coat, the woman thinks on her way out, the dog's red leash wrapped around her hand.

In the car, she looks out at all that her husband has chosen to leave behind: gas stations and twenty-four-hour diners and moose-crossing signs and liquor emporiums and bridges and pine trees. How did he get away with this? In the backseat, the dog whines in his crate.

At home, he collapses on the blue-tile floor of the kitchen and she stands over him, still holding his leash.

"Roll over." She draws a circle in the air with her finger. Usually he would turn over on his back and kick his heavy black paws and she would give him a biscuit, but instead he stays flat on the floor, still dying.

Our dog is dying, she writes in an e-mail. *He won't stop dying until you come home.* She imagines the message breaking into little bursts of data, shooting across time zones, across skies and oceans, until it locates her husband, who is sailing around the world in a boat called *The Alistair*. He left the Galápagos a month ago and might still be in the Marquesas Islands or on his way to Papua New Guinea. He has been gone for four months. Every other week she gets a terse, telegraph-style e-mail or a brief, staticky phone call.

(*continues on page 147*)

Introduction

[to Ben Huff's *The Last Road North*]

BARRY LOPEZ

Many years ago my life included some modest success as a landscape photographer. In 1981, following a benign encounter with a polar bear—in pack ice about a hundred miles off the coast of northwest Alaska—I put my cameras aside and continued down the road I'd been traveling as a writer. The short answer to why I never picked the cameras up again is that I knew, in the moments of that encounter with the bear, that I was not likely to become as articulate in both these languages as I would hope to be. And back then there was little question about which creative effort, if I were forced to choose, I would set aside.

Later, I wrote an essay called "Learning to See," about what happened on that fall day in 1981 in the Chukchi Sea. One thing I had to learn as a photographer, I implied, was the difference between art and mere technique or simple craft. Succinctly put, I did, and now know which sets of images arriving unannounced on my doorstep should be returned and which warrant clearing some space at my worktable, those pictures that call to be examined with deliberation, the way one might cautiously raise a pair of binoculars to study a herd of wild animals grazing unaware.

A few days after receiving a handful of such worthy prints, part of Mr. Huff's Dalton Highway project, I returned them to him with a brief note saying I was very taken with his images and wondering if he might send me more. I didn't say that, for me, he'd not only brought that industrial thoroughfare weirdly to life, he'd reified complex human attitudes toward it. I thought his pictures conveyed something many people might be vaguely aware of but that few of us would have any ready words for. His was not a pro forma report on a socially and politically complex feat of engineering, bolstered by easy ironies and clever setups. It was a confident inquiry, based on an artistic vision.

The Dalton, a highway I'm personally more prone to recall as the Haul Road, as if to set it apart from all other highways, rears its head in Huff's photos in a way I hadn't imagined it could. He evokes for me the menace, the seductive allure (that "call of the open road" magic), and the alien intensity that make this Silk Road from a future century such an apt symbol of our consumptive habits. Further, in his compassionate view of the bewildered and ambivalent human beings he meets on the road, Huff fastens on something of the particular grief that afflicts the modern era. Here are our nebulous fears at the dawn of the Anthropocene, a time of overheated economic exploitation, when even the farthest corners of the earth are being industrialized.

L ate in the boreal summer of the year I encountered the polar bear, I drove the Haul Road for the first time with two friends, both marine mammal biologists employed by the Alaska Department of Fish and Game. Our plan was to pick up a third biologist, waiting for us at the northern terminus of the road at Prudhoe Bay—on the verge of the Beaufort Sea—and from there to conduct a biological survey westward along the coast, using a sixteen-foot workboat which we were now towing up the Haul Road behind a truck. As we approached the southern slopes of the Brooks Range on a rising stretch of road, one of the four tires on the boat trailer collapsed. Second flat of the day.

As I exited the truck I caught sight of a female grizzly about two hundred feet away, rising up slowly on her hind legs. After a few moments of looking and probing the air, she dropped back onto all fours and continued grubbing in a marshy swale. Two cubs-of-the-year were with her. One of us loaded a high-powered rifle and stood by while the other two, with our backs to the bear, changed the tire.

In the time it took to repair and remount the tire, the bears drifted out of sight. The three of us drove off with a vague sense of trespass, with feelings of regret even, because we were all so wedded to the idea of being on time somewhere else. We'd made no time just to sit and watch the bears until they disappeared from our view into the folds of the tundra plain.

Back then, at a time when the Haul Road was not yet open to the public, a trucker had erected a hand-lettered sign near the Yukon River crossing, far to the south, a half sheet of plywood nailed to a post. On it he'd written something like "Whiteouts, Floods, Blizzards, Breakdowns, Tundra Fires, Landslides, Sheet Ice, Washouts—Hell of All Kinds Ahead," an assertion of his belief that the Dalton up ahead was no ordinary road. Here, instead, was the beginning of a manly adventure, one likely to impress the folks at home, a kind of Oregon Trail. Indeed, this was a comparable line, long and narrow, scribing a vast plain, a line with its own chain of Rocky Mountains to cross, a ribbon of crushed rock that underscored a uniquely American folklore of self-reliance, brute heroism, and Manifest Destiny. The impetuous advance of the track across the tundra represented a twentieth-century dream of ordained economic colonization. To suggest that the road vulgarized the countryside, as some think it does, would be unpatriotic.

I missed a lot on that two-day drive, years ago. Fortunately, however, when Mr. Huff's photographs arrived in the mail, I had a second chance. I saw how the road, which parallels the Alyeska Pipeline for much of its way, divides the landscape into two, sharply distinct spaces. On the wild side, the side opposite the pipeline, one looks off and off into unframed or raw space; on the other side, one gazes into culturally defined space, a domain of lines made by engineers. The road, then, represents a philosophical divide. To the wilderness side lies space free of the social and economic schemes of mankind. Here we find the undisturbed lineage, the uninterrupted natural history, of *Rangifer tarandus*, of *Ursus arctos* and the others; *Alopex lagopus*, the arctic fox; *Spermophilus undulatus*, the arctic ground squirrel: and *Plectrophenax nivalis*, the snow bunting. On the other side is space upon which meaning and purpose have been *im*posed. Again, on the unmanaged side, human imagination only *pro*poses purpose and meaning.

I cannot seem to help myself around this dichotomy that the Haul Road suggests between the disturbed and the undisturbed. I feel compelled to evaluate and finally to question the process that creates the division. Mr. Huff, alternatively, seems less inclined to address the merits of this process. His effort is more the posing of a question about human values than it is a moral statement. He portrays the people he photographs as innocent rather than naïve; and if we come to those images with the same reluctance to judge that he brought to making them, we can identify with these travelers. In the faces of some of them, Huff finds the confoundment and conflict that any one of our faces might carry, driving this industrial trace. Up ahead, in the oil fields, where the drill strings go deep into the bays of Heaven's last easy barrels, we can pull to the side of the road and turn the gasoline or diesel engine off, knowing in that silence how we're implicated. Everyone, of course, is to blame for the compromises here. Maybe Mr. Huff saw early on that insisting on identifying a particular enemy would have made his project tendentious.

As vistas open and close for a driver on the Haul Road, he or she might feel ingested by the land's deep corrugations and then suddenly exposed, the car riding the tundra like a ship's dory adrift in the pelagic ocean. As the road enters a blind turn or is exposed by feeble headlights in the benthic darkness of midwinter, we intuit, as Mr. Huff's passengers, the trickiness of successful navigation here in a region of the earth where both day and night can seem endless. Less obviously challenging for anyone curious enough—or brave enough—to embark on this road is Mr. Huff's suggestion that the contrast he has established between wild and domesticated space is more than a matter of divergent scenery. He realizes that most of us are, in fact, more comfortable with organized space, with architecture of some sort. Unorganized space, the scene yet-to-be-framed, however, appears to be the real point of departure for him in his quest for a revelatory conversation about human fate.

If one were to travel the Haul Road with Mr. Huff, my guess would be that topics like corporate rapaciousness, aggressive capitalism, peak oil, or vanishing cultures of either men or animals wouldn't much engage him. These are the stories we already know. Mr. Huff seems more focused on what we do not know, on what we need to find out. He presents, I think, the somewhat outré idea that nature is not disorganized, an emptiness waiting for some sort of architecture—a fence, a bit of roadside debris, a derelict vehicle—to give it meaning, but is distinguished by a high degree of design, design so intricate, so integrated, that it's hard to locate a point of entry, a starting point such as a fence might provide. By showing us an alternative to cultural space, his pictures offer an opportunity to discover tropes we simply cannot find by staring off into the cultural space from which so much of our trouble comes. When he shows us a landscape that one might posit is still owned by the animals, he is showing us what is *calling* to us from the future, a potential source of fundamentally different ideas about governance and economic and social organization. When he shows us the other side, the cultural side, he is showing us what is *forcing* us into the future.

Glance too quickly at these photographs and it's possible to think that Mr. Huff has limned a tragedy. What he is actually saying, though, is much more complex. If any road is finally to take us somewhere good, he appears to suggest, and not route us into the dead ends of despair and of comeuppance for our naïveté, we cannot ignore either margin in our search for clues. To declare for one side or the other would be the wrong way out of our predicament. Anyone, it seems to me, who wants to understand the impact of natural resource extraction on humanity and the earth, or who wants to consider the direction human cultures are taking in a time of dwindling natural resources, must opt for the road hardly anyone really wants to travel, however much we say we do. The Haul Road on a winter night. Hell of all kinds.

Mr. Huff's work avoids the temptation to cynically catalog human shortsightedness and foolishness in his effort to provoke a discussion we seem afraid to embark on, the quest for some as-yet-unknown form of human cooperation. The figurative Dalton Highway in his pictures might be the last road we can hope to set out on without having to deal with a firestorm, forced on us by our continuing reluctance to sit down together with the questions we seemingly can't bring ourselves to address as a nation.

The *Portland Press Herald* has run a story on her husband's voyage. In the kitchen, she reads it aloud to the dog. He talks about doldrums and brushes with pirates and the Bajau Sea Gypsies and death-defying storms. There is a photo of him hunting fish with a bamboo spear—is this really the man she married? The man who bathed the dog in the driveway in the summertime and made Mohawks out of his black fur? In the article, he talks about his plans for Borneo and Sri Lanka and Gibraltar. There is no mention of a wife and a dog.

"You only get one shot at life," her husband is quoted as saying.

"You only get one shot at being a major asshole," the woman says to the dog.

A neighbor comes by to see how she's doing. This neighbor, the reigning champion of New Gloucester's annual seafood chowder competition, is wearing a plaid headband and carrying a rolled-up copy of the *Press Herald*. She jabs at the air between them with the paper.

"This is the kind of thing men do when they realize they're going to die," she says.

Perhaps, but the woman's husband has always had an intense and peculiar relationship with the sea. Before the voyage, *The Alistair* was docked in Harpswell. He was always doing repairs to his boat—oil changes, hull reconstruction, gel-stripping—as though he knew its sturdiness would one day be tested. When they fought, he drove to Harpswell to spend the night on the water. On weekends, he gave sailing lessons to children and felt compelled to incorporate ocean survival skills: how to spear a fish, how to collect rain, how to fend off hypothermia with the Heat Escape Lessening Posture—HELP—where you pull your knees to your chest in the water. He would become upset when

147

parents canceled these lessons in the face of a thunderstorm or said their children had been frightened by the lectures on shark survival skills.

I have no shark survival skills, the woman thinks, looking at her neighbor. I don't even have a fucking plaid headband.

"I'll tell you who's dying," she says, and they go into the kitchen, where the dog is lying on his side. She can see his rib cage growing and shrinking under his skin. His eyelids are fluttering. His tongue is hanging out.

"Huh," the neighbor says. "Have you taken him to the vet?"

"Oh, the vet doesn't know!" She turns away from the dog and stares into the dry basin of the sink. Bits of lettuce are trapped in the drain. The sponge smells.

"What you need is a getaway," the neighbor says.

"What about the dog?"

"I'll ask around." With the edge of the newspaper she pushes back her headband. "I'll see what I can do."

For hours that night the woman stands in her backyard and watches the sky for planes. She remembers the last flight she took, a business trip to Minneapolis. She was seated next to a physicist who specialized in supermassive black holes. A supermassive black hole is made of billions of solar masses. A supermassive black hole resides in the center of every galaxy. Sitting there and waiting to eat us, the woman imagined on the plane, even after the physicist assured her that supermassive black holes were integral to the structural health of a solar system, that they meant us no harm. She has never looked at the sky in the same way since.

Are there black holes in the sea? she wonders now. What are the odds of her husband falling into one? On nights like this, the air cool on her arms, it seems impossible that she will ever see him again.

She turns around and the dog is at the sliding glass door. She opens the door and pets her thigh. She tries to get the dog to come out, to shit in the dirt, to roll in the grass, to dig and bark and run circles around the witch hazel tree.

"Come out, come out." She slaps her thigh so hard it stings. She can see her reflection in the door and it's like seeing her own ghost talking back to her, mimicking her every move.

The dog blinks. A gentle wag of the tail, a string of drool. This is all he has left.

Two days later the neighbor returns. This time she is holding an envelope with an address and a key inside.

"I've got a lake house for you," she says.

"This is Maine," the woman says. "There are lakes everywhere."

"Muscongous," the neighbor says. "Can't beat it."

The house turns out to be not on a lake but on a vast sound. From the GPS on her phone, she knows the sound leads out into the ocean. The house is a white New England saltbox with ridges of dust on the windowsills. She carries the dog into the house in his flannel and fleece bed and sets him in front of a fireplace. Her arms have gotten strong from lifting the dog.

By the cold fireplace the dog sleeps, snoring like he has a small motor inside him.

The woman wanders around outside. She finds a withered flower bed near the back of the house, crinkled purple buds that turn to dust when she touches them. One side of the house is covered in the buoys used to mark lobster traps in the water. These buoys are shaped like large bullets and painted weather-beaten greens and yellows and reds. She follows a gravel path down to the sound, where there is a dock and a white dinghy with an outboard motor. From the edge of the dock, she sees a scattering of small, wooded islands, fishing boats, a lone kayaker, a distant lighthouse.

149

When she returns, she finds the dog has pissed the bed. He is lying in a pool of warm, rank liquid, the motor inside him still running. She drags the bed outside. She rinses the dog with a garden hose. The water is cold and he shivers. She rubs him dry with a thin bath towel. She doesn't care what the vet says. She knows they are near the end.

That night, she uses her phone to write an e-mail to her husband. The e-mail says, *We are near the end.* She is talking about the dog, but likes the idea of its being open to interpretation. She likes the idea of him lying in his narrow bed, in the sway of the ocean, the signal just strong enough to receive her message, and wondering what on earth she might mean.

She has not yet realized that the signal on her own phone is too weak for the message to go through.

"Goddamn middle-of-nowhere Maine," she says to the dog after twenty-three tries.

At midnight, she clips the red leash to the dog's collar and walks him down the gravel path. At the dock, she lifts him into the white dinghy before lowering herself inside. His soft ears go flat against his head. He barks at her.

The dog has barked at her only once before, on the morning her husband left. For months, she had been arguing her points— folly, selfishness, credit card debt, the high probability of disaster or even death—but when the day came it was as though a door inside her locked. She would not be a good wife. She would not be pathetic or noble. She would not beg. She would not see him off. In the dawn hours, she lay on her side and pretended to sleep, even as she felt her husband rise, felt the bed grow lighter, felt the house empty, even after she felt the dog's hot breath in her face and heard him barking and barking, imploring her to *do something.* Even then she stayed still as a corpse.

Years ago, on Moosehead Lake, her husband taught her how to operate a motorboat. Now, in the dark, she tries to remember the steps. She finds the handle. She stands and pulls the rope. The engine growls, but there is no movement. The dog keeps barking. She pulls again and again. The dinghy jumps in the water. Finally the motor revs, drowning out the dog.

They putter out into the sound. It takes her some time to remember how to modulate the speed, how to push the handle one way to go faster, the other way to slow. In the moonlight, the dark lumps of island look like a maze. She slips by one island after another, finding her way through. She looks into the trees and wonders what might be living in there. When they pass the last island, the dog begins to lick her hand.

"That is no place for a dog," she shouts over the motor.

The dinghy presses into a cold wind. She feels the vibrations of the motor in her bones. She continues until she and the dog are surrounded only by water and sky. She watches thin clouds move over the stars like white tentacles. She thinks about supermassive black holes. She wants to keep going until they slip through the mouth of the sound and into the ocean.

Instead she cuts the engine. She sits in the dinghy and holds her knees to her chest, even though she is in no danger of hypothermia. She decides they need to make a plan. They cannot go any farther without a decent plan.

"Imagine this," she says to the dog.

They sail out into the Atlantic, past the border of Nova Scotia. They embrace the abyss. Day after day the sun beats down on them. They sweat and blister and peel. They grow new skins. She learns to snatch fish from the water with her bare hands. She feeds half of every catch to the dog. Birds shit on them. Sharks circle. They run out of gas and are at the mercy of the wind.

151

Storms rattle the dinghy and during these storms, she holds the dog tight and prepares to be inhaled into the supermassive black hole beneath, yet somehow they survive. They drink the rainwater that collects in the dinghy. She gets on her knees and laps. She learns from the dog, who has, in their time at sea, managed to stop dying. A seagull lands on the stern and she breaks its neck. She eats the eyes. She feeds the guts to the dog. She loses all sense of time: There is only dawn and dusk and searing day. She forgets she has a husband, forgets the details of his face, forgets all that the word "husband" is supposed to mean. She hallucinates that the dog is talking to her, that he is standing upright like a person and saying *We're almost to land* or *We are going to die tonight* or *Can't you see that I'm just a dog?*

Finally they come upon a hard brown line of land. The coast of the Western Sahara. They abandon the dinghy and trek out into the sand, never to be seen by anyone ever again, except for her husband, that now-long-forgotten husband, who one day finds himself approaching the coast of the Western Sahara, one of the last stops on his trip around the world. By now he is very tired and longing for home and curious to meet this wife who suddenly stopped e-mailing him, who made herself as unreachable as he. From the bow, he sees a woman riding a horse along the shore, a crown of salt crystals on her head, and a dog walking upright, speaking perfect English, and nothing about them looks at all familiar.

Fatin Abbas

was born in Khartoum, Sudan, and attended
university in the United Kingdom and the
United States. She is a graduate of the Hunter
College MFA Program in Creative Writing.

On a Morning

FATIN ABBAS

Dina picked up the camera bag, lifted the tripod under her arm, and, in the courtyard, stopped to look up. The light was mellow, caressing surfaces: the thatched roof of the gazebo that stood at the back of the compound, the clay walls of the storage room, the pale canvas of the tent set up by the office. Light like this was rare—it was only because of a haze of morning clouds, which might melt away at any moment—and so she hurried across the yard to the kitchen, where she found the boy Mustafa sweeping.

He glanced at her and smiled and then his eyes returned to the work. There were few formalities between them now. She didn't have to ask, as she used to, whether she could switch on the camera. He knew why she was there, that her work was watching him, and he'd accepted it, though not without some lingering bewilderment.

She unpacked her things—headphones, a piece of paper to check for white balance, batteries—then turned on the camera and framed the boy sweeping dirt. Sweat trickled into the crease of her one shut eye and through the other she watched his arms move, the cloudy sunlight hitting them just so, reflecting the smooth skin just so against the brown mud of the kitchen wall behind. At his feet the dust swirled up luminous from the uneven ground, rising, then unfurling out in a shadowy motion, the cloud thinning then dissipating in the morning air.

'Look,' he said, shading his eyes. Dina watched him through the lens. 'There'll be rain later.' His hand remained above his brow for an instant, and then he reached for the broom again.

In the background, echoing through her headphones as though from a faraway place, she could hear a salsa tune pulsating on the radio, and behind that the sound of water splashing in the street. The scent of baking bricks and dung came and went, carried by the river breeze, and still she looked, drifting between the face, the hands, the dust, the moving broom, so lost in looking that the pulse in her aching arm no longer felt like pain but only rhythm.

In the office Alex sat on a stool too low for the makeshift desk, a map spread out in front of him. The room was the only one built out of concrete in the compound. It was cramped, barely big enough for the table, chair, and two metal filing units set against the left-hand wall. A poster was pinned above them, showing the logo of the organization: a white globe floating above two green palms raised upward as though in prayer.

He'd spent the morning reading an agricultural report, but, bored, had pulled open one of the maps lying on the desk. He never got tired of looking at maps. He leaned forward on his elbows, eyes tracing the northern border, a line bolting straight across the Sahara. His gaze drifted down, following the river to its source as it meandered through the thick yellow belt of desert to the capital, where it split in two, a branch curving up toward the Ethiopian highlands in one direction and the other continuing south toward Lake Victoria. He stopped at a dot marking the town he was in now—Saraaya, at the boundary between north and south. Here the desert merged into grasslands, swaths of pale green that became darker and denser toward the tropical south of the country.

He'd come to this town to make a map, sent by his organization to chart farmlands, villages, grazing routes, water wells, district lines as part of an information-gathering mission. The maps that existed were outdated, drawn up by the British more than fifty years ago and still used by the local authorities; a good map was needed to give direction to the organization's aid efforts in the area.

He wanted to begin, but two weeks into his stay he was still waiting for official permission from the authorities. And his surveying equipment, which should have arrived a week ago from Khartoum, had been shipped to the wrong town, a hundred kilometers away, and was only now on its way over.

A shadow blocked the light coming through the window opposite him and when he looked up he saw William, the translator, looming in the frame.

Teeth flashed in a smile beneath glinting eyes. 'Good morning,' said William.

Even from a few feet away Alex could smell William's cologne. He had begun to wear it recently, and Alex thought it had something to do with the pretty new cook who had started working in the compound.

He raised his nose in the air and sniffed. 'What's this?' He paused, sniffed again. 'Has my translator turned into a lemon tree?'

William grinned, his long, handsome face bashful. 'It's a new cologne,' he said in a lilting accent, drawing out the vowels. 'Maybe you could do with some yourself.'

It occurred to Alex that he didn't make a very pretty picture. Framed in the window, he sat shirtless, his chin overgrown with stubble, his dark hair dangling in wet tendrils around his ears. Sunburnt skin was peeling off his nose. In contrast, William was a picture of elegance: His shirt glowed crisply white against the dull clay walls of the houses behind him. His hair was buzz-cut close to his scalp so that the line between it and the broad, dark forehead was almost impossible to discern.

'Any news?' asked Alex. 'About the authorization?'

'Not yet,' said William. 'But soon. Any day now.'

It was the same answer that William always gave him.

'It's been two weeks. How much longer am I supposed to wait?'

He was suddenly irritated by the neatness of William's white shirt.

'I'll talk to them again tomorrow,' said William. 'But I can't rush the authorities. They will slow things down even more if I push them.' He leaned back from the window. 'I'll be inside. Call me if you need me.'

He stepped away and disappeared around the corner, before Alex had a chance to say anything more.

William unlocked the gate to the compound and entered, walked past the plants and the old tires and the sacks of sand piled by the door. He saw Dina and Mustafa by the storage room, heard the rhythmic swoosh of Mustafa's broom like an accompaniment to the tempo of the Spanish music coming from the radio under the gazebo.

His heart clattered in his rib cage. He had tossed and turned all night in bed thinking of Layla—there, now, in the cool darkness of the kitchen. He had plotted and considered what he was about to do: walk into the kitchen and, under the pretense of seeking a glass of water, linger to make conversation about the weather, the crops, the seasonal arrival of the nomads. Then he might venture into more intimate questions: ask her where she lived, about her family.

He stopped by the office wall, smoothed his white shirt, ran his tongue over his teeth. Since meeting Layla his body was not his own, existing only as she perceived it in his imagination. Now, in anticipation of her presence, he was suddenly aware of his long legs, thin and gangly as a camel's. His too-big teeth. His clammy hands, which were as broad as bird traps. His dark skin, black as water on a moonless night.

He took a deep breath and turned right along the office wall, glanced through the doorway at Alex's back, passed more plants potted in rusty oil drums. He waved to Dina and Mustafa across the yard, but the turmoil in his chest was growing. By the time he reached the kitchen door his gait was stiff and his eyes were wide. His jaw was clenched in a manic smile. He walked in blindly and stepped to the orange water cooler, poured himself water and drank. His throat gurgled and the glass wobbled and his Adam's apple bobbed. Only when he dropped the empty cup on the counter with a clatter and looked around did he realize that Layla wasn't there.

How's the filming?' The question came abrupt and electric through the headphones, startling her.

She didn't answer, but felt his shadow lingering. Finally she pressed the stop button and pulled the headphones from her ears. She'd been following Mustafa around the compound all morning, and now they'd ended up near the two beds in the courtyard, he sitting on a stool with wet knees above a large metal basin full of bedsheets in bubbling water, she crouching opposite him.

'It's fine,' she said, looking up at Alex. There was an eagerness, an intrusive familiarity in the bold, dark eyes.

Mustafa stopped washing for a moment and flicked his hands into the dirt, drying them. Drops of water flew everywhere and Dina shielded the camera with her arm.

'What's it about, your documentary?' Alex asked. Small wild teeth winked in his stubble.

She glanced at the few scattered hairs on his chest, noticed a dark mole beneath a pale nipple. She looked away, more embarrassed by this physical intimacy than he seemed to be.

'I've just started filming,' she said.

'What's it for?'

'It's not for anything. It's for me.'

He paused, bewildered. 'But what are you going to do with it when it's finished?'

Again her eyes wandered down to his torso, to its easy nakedness.

'I don't know yet. Maybe nothing.'

He watched her fingers play on the knobs of the camera. Her short hair was hidden beneath a checkered red and yellow bandanna. The crisp colors of the expensive linen tunic that hung loosely on her shallow frame marked her as an outsider in this land of poor people's style—ragged T-shirts, ill-fitting dresses, and dusty, hole-ridden shoes. He had tried to strike up conversation with her on several occasions, but she was reticent, unfriendly almost, and he had managed to glean only the basic facts. Her family was from Khartoum. She had grown up in Seattle. She was staying in the compound for a few weeks while making a film— had made some kind of an arrangement with the organization in the capital.

'What's the point of making a film, if it will just sit there?'

The question vexed her. In this poor, troubled corner of the country there was room only for victims and saviors.

'And your map? What's the point?'

He registered the challenge in her question but his tone was casual when he answered. 'It's simple. Information. The more information we have the better, right?'

She smiled, not a friendly smile.

There was a sudden brightening, a glinting of the rim of the metal basin, and she realized that the clouds were thinning and the sunlight was getting stronger and she would have only a few more minutes of good morning light left to film.

'Do you mind?' She gestured toward Mustafa, who had been following the tense inflections of the conversation, though not the words, which he only half understood.

'Of course,' said Alex, spreading his hands. 'I'll let you get on with it.' He turned away and she watched as he ambled back to the office, his dark arms and neck seeming to belong to a different body from the ghostly torso that connected them.

Mustafa climbed up on one of the beds and unhooked the mosquito net from the bamboo poles reaching over the frame, dumping the material on the mattress. He went over to the other bed and did the same. It was almost noon. Dina had put away her camera and gone to the kitchen to prepare lunch for everyone. Layla had not shown up today, and no one had eaten anything all morning.

He heard the pop and fizz of hot oil and the smell of falafel drifted out of the kitchen doorway. The radio was still playing under the gazebo, though Dina had tuned in to the BBC station, and now the presenter's strange English speech drifted over the courtyard, staticky, sonorous, the words rippling over Mustafa mysteriously.

It was Thursday and the football championship final was tonight. There was only one place in all of Saraaya that was showing it: Omar's juice stall in the market, and it would cost him three hundred pounds to watch the game. But he had no money. Just last week he had spent all of his measly savings on buying merchandise for his underwear venture in the market. He had given his mother the rest of the fifteen thousand pounds a month he received for performing daily chores at the compound—cleaning and taking out rubbish and washing. His mother was widowed with four children and most of his wages went to help her.

His friends wouldn't have any to spare. His mother would think it a waste. And she had given him a thousand pounds last month as a present for his twelfth birthday, which he had spent already. He listed in his mind the things he remembered buying: three bottles of Coca-Cola, two sweet pastries at the market, a pair of battered sunglasses from his friend Ibrahim—eight hundred pounds in total. But he couldn't remember what he had spent the remainder on.

He picked up the nets in his arms and crossed over to the mudroom used for storage. The air was stuffy in here, dusty. Cartons were stacked against a wall all the way up to the wood-beamed ceiling. Piles of blue tarpaulin sat in one corner, on top of an old damaged generator with rusty gears. Cracked earthen pots were lined up underneath a wooden table by the door. Alex's belongings—a blue backpack and a small suitcase—were wedged in between them. On top of the table sat a rolled-up mattress and plastic bags full of bedclothes, pillows, and old newspapers. Mustafa stuffed the mosquito nets into one of the bags and went outside again, heading toward the beds.

On the way William hurried out of the office and caught up with him. 'Where's Layla today?' he asked in Arabic.

'I don't know,' said Mustafa. 'She didn't come in this morning.'

'Did she say anything yesterday?'

Mustafa shook his head. He had seen the way William's eyes followed her around the compound. How he tripped over his long legs when he noticed her watching him.

William drew closer. 'Can you find out where she lives?'

Mustafa considered, sensing an opportunity. 'Maybe. But.'

'But?'

'It's another chore.'

William stared at him. Then he smiled, understanding. He pulled some notes from his back pocket, counted them out.

'Here's two hundred pounds.'

'Four,' said Mustafa.

'Four? You're a thief.'

'It'll take up half my day finding out where she lives. I have to ask around, go looking, find the house . . . ' He tried to think of other ways to convey the magnitude of the errand.

'Fine, fine. Here's four,' said William, adding to the notes. 'Do it today. Tell me if she's coming tomorrow.'

Mustafa took the notes and folded them in half. The game. A bottle of Coca-Cola. He smiled. He stuffed the notes carefully in between his hipbone and the elastic strap of his underwear. He distrusted the pockets of his shorts, their gaping holes.

'I'll go after I finish here,' he said. William patted him on the shoulder and returned to the office.

He was dragging one of the beds toward the gazebo when there was a loud thumping at the gate. He continued pulling the bed until it was under the shade of the thatched roof, parallel to a hammock strung up between two poles made of tree trunks.

163

When he walked back into the light he saw William standing by the gate. There was the sound of voices, but he couldn't see who was outside the door. William opened the gate farther and three men walked in, struggling to carry a heavy bundle wrapped in sackcloth. Nilot men, tall and dark like William, wearing faded, dusty vests, T-shirts, and cutoff trousers.

William spoke to them in Nilot and directed them to the middle of the courtyard, by the bed. They laid the bundle down on the ground. Crouched over it. As one of them spoke he pointed to a location beyond the wall, his words visible in the excitement of his hands, fluttering up constantly, drawing a scene. The other two men sat quietly, listening and nodding occasionally.

When Alex stepped into the yard William called him over. One of the men drew open the top of the sackcloth. Mustafa couldn't see what was inside. Alex's eyes went wide and his face became suddenly paler. William covered his mouth and nose and drew his head back. Mustafa crossed over to the group. Something sweet and rotten in the air. Dina stepped out of the kitchen, drying her hands on a dishcloth.

'What is it?' she called, coming over. Mustafa wedged himself in between Alex and William.

One of the Nilot men was removing the sackcloth now, gingerly lifting the corners. The two men who stood on the other side of the bundle moved back as he threw the cloth open.

The stench rose, rancid and sweet and sulfurous, more a taste than a smell, filming their tongues. The skin—or what remained of it—was black and rutted in parts. It had melted onto the rib cage and flakes of it hung dryly on the bone; below it the scorched piping of the intestines spilled out. The arms stretched upward above the head, charred fingers coiling. Legs dry as wood were bent with the feet floating stiffly in the air. The lips had been burnt off, leaving the teeth protruding in a silent screech below the blackened stump of a nose and closed eyes.

The heat and stink concentrated around the grisly flesh were stifling. Dina stepped outside the circle. Alex covered his nose with his arm. William pulled his shirt over his face. Mustafa stood up and stepped back, breathing through his teeth. The three strangers were covering their noses now too, swatting away the fat, buzzing flies that spun above the corpse. The even drone of the BBC presenter's voice washed over them. In the brightening sunlight the rough outlines of the body were stark against the brown dust of the courtyard floor.

Alex spoke over Mustafa's head to William, his voice muffled by his arm. 'Where did they find it?'

William translated to the men, two of whom sat squatting along one side of the body. They were young and strong-muscled, their arms and faces splotched with dung ash. The same man who had spoken to William earlier—with high cheekbones and small, deep-set eyes—answered, the pitched syllables of the language moving fluidly back and forth between him and William.

'They were out grazing cattle upriver,' said William, turning to Alex. 'They found it in the grass, along the left bank.'

'Do they know who it is?' asked Alex.

'They say word's been put out that a body has been found but no one's claimed it yet.'

The space of the courtyard contracted into the tight circle of people around the corpse. There was a movement and when Mustafa looked up he saw Dina, back at the foot of the body, uncapping the lens of her camera and lifting it. The looming glass eye caressed the dead flesh, moving slowly, up and down, along the stiff curves of the legs and arms and torso. For a moment everyone's attention shifted to the thin woman with the camera.

One of the two strangers sitting along the left side of the body whispered something to his companion. They stared up at Dina. Then their eyes returned to the corpse.

William spoke again. 'They came to ask if we can drive them to the cemetery in the pickup truck. It's too far to walk and they want to bury it.'

'Did they go to the police?' asked Alex.

'They went there this morning. The police said the body's unidentifiable and there's nothing they can do about it unless someone comes forward. They will investigate, but they told them to bury it.'

They all looked on in silence. A donkey-cart rattled by in the street. A burst of music came from the radio, marking the end of the news program.

'I'll get the keys,' said Alex, and stood up and went into the office.

One of the men leaned across the body and pulled the sackcloth over it. Everyone rose. The sun suddenly disappeared behind a tufted cloud and the stark shadows of the walls, the gazebo, the colorful flags strung up along the periphery of the yard grew hazy as a dimness fell over the compound. A breeze drifted through the courtyard and the gate creaked languidly but insistently. The sack-cloth covering the body quivered, rising up, and William stretched forward and pulled it down again. Dina switched off her camera and held it dangling by the handgrip. Two of the cattle herders knelt and pulled the cloth taut around the corpse, then gripped the outstretched arms and feet. They lifted the body, and when Alex came out of the office, now in a blue T-shirt, he and William followed the men out through the gate.

Outside, the street was quiet in the midday heat. A stray dog trotting by slowed, then paused at a wary distance and tilted its

head, scenting the flesh. Three women walked past on the opposite side of the road balancing plastic tubs of water on top of small
padded cushions on their heads. They turned carefully, keeping
their long necks steady, to watch the group of men maneuvering
the brown bundle into the bed of the battered truck parked outside
the compound. Standing just inside the gate, Dina and Mustafa
suddenly felt a cold, wet pattering against their skin. They looked
up at the sky, which was low and heavy with rain, the sun that was
glaring only minutes ago nowhere to be seen.

William, outwardly calm, kept telling himself that he was
imagining things. He stood—Alex fidgeting nervously to
one side with a shovel, the three herders opposite him leaning on
theirs—in a cemetery on the outskirts of town. It was not clearly
demarcated so much as a patch of brown land that blended into
a broader patch of brown land, the only indication that bodies
were buried here the slight mounds of dirt rising from the earth,
here and there the occasional misshapen headstone.

The shrouded corpse lay a few feet away, to the left of one of
the herders. It had been found kilometers out of town, surely
far from where Layla lived. Things were flaring up again with
the rebels, who were somewhere in the area, and probably the
corpse had some connection to those troubles. But there would
have been news from her family if she'd disappeared.

Still, from the corner of his eye William was aware of the corpse's
fingers straining against the fabric, as if wanting to tear through
the shroud. He looked away, past the herders and the corpse, to
the tracks of dirt road near where the truck was parked, and farther along to the line of homesteads hugging the earth in the far
distance, marking the southern periphery of the town. The drizzle
had stopped, but the sun was still hidden behind a layer of clouds.

'Should we bury it here?' asked one of the herders, the same one who had done most of the speaking at the compound. The other two looked at William—the question was addressed to him. This was one of those times when he wished he could escape the burden of his own authority. He was from here, but his work, its educated nature in a place where most people were farmers and cattle herders, separated him from the locals. He was just a translator, but in Saraaya that meant being a big man.

Yes, he had to live in this town whose strategic importance in the war was in inverse proportion to its provinciality, its cut-offness, located, as it was, in the middle of nowhere—desert to the north and endless swamp and grasslands to the south—but here, at least, he'd been able to make a decent living for himself. Anyway, that's what he told himself. He'd had a good start, getting this job. He had a way with people, a talent for making himself likable (only with Layla did his powers seem to fail him), and because of it he knew how to get on with the police, the security men, the nomads, the Nilotes, the expats, and NGO staff whom he had to look after on their visits.

Besides, at thirty-three, his desires were simple: He wanted a wife, children, his own home. He'd wanted more once, back when he was still a young man in Khartoum, where he'd turned up at the age of twenty, accounting diploma in hand, determined to make something of himself. He'd ended up in manual labor, working on construction sites in the city, on the extravagant, garish edifices that were rising up with the oil money spurting from wells all over the south.

In his first weeks in Khartoum—shaved, shoes polished, fake gold watch glinting on his wrist, accounting diploma carefully secreted in a plastic folder—he'd assaulted the offices in the central districts.

'We don't need an errand boy,' was the bewildered response of the secretary in the first office he stepped into. He still remembered her: eyes winged with eyeliner, round face wrapped tightly in a purple headscarf that cascaded elegantly on one side onto her shoulder. She was confused, he knew, by his nice clothes. They didn't fit the skin and the gangly frame that broadcast him as a southerner.

The plastic folder crinkled as he reached into it. 'I have a diploma.' He handed it to her. She skimmed it. 'I see . . .' She glanced left and right as if looking for a rubbish bin to throw it in. She leaned forward. 'I'm sorry. No one will hire you for office work. I'm telling you this to save you the trouble. If you're looking for errand work, you might find something.'

William stared. He replaced the diploma.

'Thank you,' he said, and walked out.

In the next office, and the next, it was the same. Wide-eyed secretaries confused by his perfumed, elegant presence. His polished shoes. His spotless white shirt. The confident air with which he strode forward for a handshake. 'Hello, my name is William Luol.' Like an executive. Not a southerner. Everywhere the same answer. No. We don't have anything. Nothing. Each defeat emboldened him rather than set him back. He swaggered more. Flourished his diploma. Boldly stared down the secretaries. Demanded to speak to their bosses. The more desperate he grew, savings quickly dwindling in his pocket, the more persistent he became.

Until one day he had no money left to pay rent for the house that he shared with his cousin and three other men from their hometown. So he joined his cousin on the construction sites. Every day from six a.m. to six p.m., then back to the two-room shanty. Fava beans for breakfast, lunch, and dinner. Washing out back with a hose attached to a tap that supplied them, in the summer, with water heated almost to boiling point by the sun in the large metal tank that sat atop the neighbor's house.

The cinema had been his only escape in those days. He went there once a week, to watch Bollywood films with the little money he managed to spare. Doe-eyed heroines with bare midriffs and pierced nostrils. Handsome heroes garlanded with necklaces of flowers. Green pastures and palaces and ornamented doorways, far removed from that ugly brown city with its brown roads and its brown telephone poles. In the darkness of the cinema, discarded plastic bottles and bags snapping and crinkling beneath his feet, clusters of young men holding their breath when a bare arm, a throat, flashed on the screen, the exhaustion of the week would drain out of his body, out into the open space of the valleys in front of him, the hills and mountains, wash away with the waterfalls gushing their torrents.

Those films had, more than he realized, shaped his idea of love. He'd been back in Saraaya for three years, there was no shortage of eligible women and he could have easily been married by now, as his relatives wanted him to be, but there was something about the way marriage was done here that put him off. Cattle exchanged for wife. That was it. It was a transaction, an exchange of goods, not love. And he wanted love (though he told himself that those depictions in the cinema were just fantasies of love). He'd given up on wealth, on success, and was disillusioned enough to understand that not everything was within his grasp. That life treated you differently based on where you were born and who you were born to, and there was nothing you could do about it. And so with age (he felt not exactly old, but too old and too young all at once), he had readjusted his expectations. He was intelligent, yes; educated, likable, handsome, even, but a southerner nonetheless. All he wanted, all he hoped for now, was a wife, children, a home.

For the first time since his return he had felt that he was really, truly in love. Why Layla? Perhaps because she was, on some level, inaccessible: After all, he was a Nilot and she was a nomad. Perhaps unconsciously he sought to reenact a complicated plot line from one of his Bollywood films, star-crossed love triumphing against the odds.

The appearance of the body that morning, and the coincidence of her absence, had left him stunned. Up to that point the worst that he had been preparing himself for was disappointment—it was possible that she would reject him. But was it possible that she was no more? It was a terrible thought, especially with the corpse's fingers straining there, still, against the fabric. So he kept telling himself that it wasn't her. It couldn't be.

He nodded at the ground, to the place the herder had indicated.

'Here's fine,' he said. He lifted his shovel, ready to dig.

'But what if it belongs to the nomads?' asked the second herder, a long piece of grass waving from his mouth. He was older than the others, quieter; he reminded William, for some reason, of his father.

William lowered the shovel. He hadn't even thought about which cemetery, actually, they were standing in.

'If no one's claimed the body it's better to bury it. Doesn't matter where. Anyway, the nomads bury their dead quickly, within twenty-four hours.'

The herder reached up and took the grass out of his mouth. 'But if it's in the wrong cemetery—'

The other one, hands dangling over the handle of the shovel planted in front of him, interrupted him.

'It's all burnt up. You saw it. We can't know which cemetery to bury it in if we don't know who it is,' he said.

'What are they saying?'

William turned to Alex, who was standing too close to him—
William was suddenly aware of being crowded, pressed upon;
there was nothing but empty space around them, and yet Alex
had somehow ended up only a few inches away from him, so that
William had to step to the side. He looked down now at the stub-
bled face, the raw lips, the dark anxious eyes. The baggy T-shirt
made him look thinner, even, than he was.

He wished now that he had left him back at the compound.
For the past two weeks Alex had been pushing William to speed
things up with the authorities so that he could start on the map.
William had resisted, not out of negligence, but because he had
no control over how long it would take for the paperwork to be
processed; the authorities took their time, and more than that,
because they were the authorities. His job, of course, was to help
Alex, serve him even, but there was something about Alex's per-
sistence, the way he followed him around with his quick steps,
head craning, eyes squinting against the light, asking, 'Why's it
taking so long?' and 'Can't you talk to them again?' and 'What
am I supposed to do in the meantime?,' question after question,
without pause, with William trying hard to be polite but firm,
not wanting to antagonize Alex, but also itching to put him in
his place, to make it clear that Alex just didn't understand how
things worked here and it would be best for both of them if he
left things up to William.

Now Alex's fear—he kept fussing with the shovel in his hands
and glancing over his shoulder at the wide-open land behind
them, as if they might be ambushed out of thin air—didn't move
William; it irritated him. Keeping his voice neutral, he explained
that they didn't know who the body belonged to, the Nilotes or the
nomads, and so they were debating which cemetery to bury it in.

Alex looked left and right—at the shallow mounds of graves on one side, and then the other.

'It all looks the same,' he said. 'How do you know which cemetery's which?'

William pointed to five large stones, each about two feet wide, set in a row, separating the Nilot cemetery from the nomad burial grounds. They were easy to miss. The burial grounds were littered with stones of all sizes, some used as headstones, but everyone knew the configuration of these.

'Does it really matter where it's buried?' asked Alex.

William gestured to the herders, who, though they couldn't understand a word, were engrossed in the exchange.

'They think it does,' he said. 'If it turns out the body belongs to the nomads, and it's buried in the Nilot cemetery, maybe it's a problem. And vice versa.'

Alex's lips came together.

'Can't we just bury it in between?' he said.

'In between?' asked William.

'Yes. In between the two cemeteries. Like, in the middle.'

William translated to the herders.

Two of them spoke at once.

'In the middle? Not possible.'

'It's one thing or the other.'

'But if we don't know . . .' It was the elder herder.

William looked at the corpse, then up at the surrounding flat land, sparse tufts of grass receding with the end of the rainy season, earth and sky two broad blanks reflecting one another. He felt overexposed in this place where there was nowhere to shelter. Where was she, where could she be? He looked at the corpse again. It wasn't her, it couldn't be.

'Let's just bury it here.' He wanted to be done. He stepped forward, his brown shoes sinking into the soft earth, and thrust the shovel into the dirt.

'Here?' asked Alex, wobbling along and dragging his shovel behind him. 'Are you sure?'

'Yes,' said William. 'Come on.'

Two of the herders began digging, and Alex joined them.

The handle of the shovel was hot in William's hands. He dug without pausing for breath, dirt plashing against dirt, dust rising and coating his white shirt, stinging his eyes, aches running up and down his arms as his muscles burned, but he didn't stop—the pain in his joints focused his attention, concentrated him so that for moments at a time he forgot about Layla.

Through the amber tint of his sunglasses Mustafa saw Jane sitting on a low stool in a bright orange dress with a kettle in her hand, at her usual spot by the butcher's. A plastic rose bloomed from a braid in her hair. Her fat bottom spilled over the edges of her tiny seat as she sprinkled pinches of cinnamon into the boiling water. A handful of men were gathered around her, sipping tea from small glass cups.

Jane pointed at his sunglasses. 'What are you, a fruit fly?'

'They're new,' said Mustafa, smiling. He fingered the sleek frame of the sunglasses, nudging them up the bridge of his nose. They slid back down. Jane laughed, her cheeks dimpling, tiny squares of teeth showing through her lips.

Behind her, just inside the entrance to the butcher's, giant cattle thighs teetered from hooks, swaying in the breeze. Wooden counters were strewn with chicken carcasses. Bits of rump meat, brisket, fore rib, shoulder. Pink and white flesh glistened bright against green tables. A sheep's head stared, tongue lolling, from a high shelf.

Jane replaced the lid on the kettle and leaned forward, her eyes serious suddenly. 'I heard they found a dead body by the river today?'

Mustafa set down his plastic bags and wedged the glasses on top of his head. 'Some herders found it,' he said. 'They brought it to the compound this afternoon.'

The men around Jane leaned in, full of questions. He stood, puffed up, an arm on Jane's shoulder, ashy knees peeking from beneath the hem of his shorts, eyebrows, nose, mouth bobbing in his narrow face as he told them about the corpse, about the terrible, sweet smell that rose from it, about how it was impossible to tell even if it was a man or a woman. Just a burnt pile of flesh, like a scorched tree trunk.

'God help us,' said Jane. 'It's not a good omen, a dead body out of nowhere.' She picked up a straw fan lying on the ground beside her and fanned briskly at the coal stove.

Mahmood, the butcher, spoke. 'There's trouble coming,' he said. 'They're arming again.'

Jane's eyes widened. She pressed the fan to her chest. 'Haven't we had enough already?'

Mustafa lingered, listening. A Nilot herder said that the rebels were south of the swamps. Another man said no, they were as far north as the River Kinu. Yet another person said that soldiers were being sent down, due to arrive any day now. They interrupted each other, disagreeing about when the fighting would erupt, whether the dead body had anything to do with it, and whether they would have to pack up and run once the clashes got going.

A shadow fell on the roped handle of the teakettle and Mustafa glanced up. It was getting late—he still had to set up shop, and look for Layla later. He picked up his bags and waved to Jane, *shib-shib* smacking against his heels as he hurried north, his eyes flitting over merchandise displayed on rickety tables and shelves—secondhand radios and woven baskets and guava and watermelon and glass jars full of beads like hundreds of tiny eyes.

It was the time of day when returning from the fields, or from grazing cattle, people gathered in the market to rest, to gossip, to buy supplies for the evening meal. Now half the crowd lounged lazily under the shade of a neem tree or a tattered canopy, sitting in chairs or on their haunches, clustered mostly around the tea ladies, and the other half was busy selling and buying, laying out wares, haggling over prices, exchanging money. Here and there he caught snatches of conversation, news already flitting from mouth to mouth about the body.

He walked by Riek's place—a clandestine shop fronting as a mechanic's that sold Kalashnikovs and other small arms to Nilot and nomad herders alike, doing brisk business during the tense time of year when the nomads arrived. At the stall next door, Issa—neck smeared with batter—stood over a huge pan full of bubbling oil, frying fish. Farther down John sat with a straw hat drooping on his head, behind a table piled with tomatoes, cucumbers, limes, carrots—flies buzzing and spinning, scaling the vegetable skins.

He arrived at the spot he'd staked out the day before with heavy stones, across the road from Hassan's clothes shop. Dresses, blouses, skirts dangled from hangers hooked to the shop doorway, bouncing in the breeze. To his left was a battered Toyota van, its axles propped up on bricks. Beyond the van, on the other side, was a market woman selling toasted watermelon seeds packed neatly in small clear plastic bags. To his right was Khalid, a boy a little older than himself, arranging hurricane lanterns into a pyramid on a low table.

His hands moved quickly and his eyes flitted up and down the road as he unpacked his things, already on the lookout for customers. He hauled flattened cardboard boxes from beneath the rocks, folded them into shape, arranged them side by side, so he had two makeshift tables next to the van. The van would provide shade, and privacy for more modest customers. From the rest of the bags he pulled out knickers, frilly undershirts, slips, bras, spreading out his merchandise on the surface of the cardboard.

He wanted to raise enough money for school fees. He had staked all of his savings, and hopes, on underwear to get him there. He had quit school three years before, when his father dropped dead while out tilling a field one morning, to help his mother. Without school he had no future. Just a lifetime of taking out rubbish. Washing other people's laundry. Sweeping court-yards. He had bigger plans: not just a school diploma but university, in the capital, a thousand kilometers away from this small, dingy, useless town. Now, out of school, he worked hard to learn whatever English he could from the foreigners who passed through the compound. He threw around the English phrases that he picked up, casually peppering his Arabic with them until now a whole gaggle of twelve-year-olds were going about the streets interjecting strange words into their sentences—'I swear on the prophet, *cheers*, I saw it with my own two eyes!'

His sister, Hanan, had given him the idea. Women needed nice underwear, she said, and it was hard to find. Hanan was sixteen and suitors were already knocking at the door. She and her friends spent long afternoons braiding each other's hair, rubbing bread dough into their skin to make it glow, restitching old trousers into skirts, scarves into blouses. Mustafa had spent his savings on wholesale polyester and cotton goods that he'd found with his sister's help in the large market in Hasaniya, a town two hundred kilometers away. It was cheap underwear—hems already fraying and stitches coming apart—but it was pretty, and there was nothing like it in Saraaya.

Before he had finished laying out the goods, women were already stopping to look.

'What are you up to now, you little imp?' said a grandmother, a basket piled high with wood on her head.

'You've turned into a little man before your time, haven't you!' said one of the tea ladies he was friendly with in the market, picking up a slip and laughing.

A friend of his sister's came up, her eyes taking in the feast of red and white and blue and yellow underwear, striped, flowered, plain, spotted, laced, silky.

'How much is this?' she asked. She held up a blue bra.

'Four hundred,' said Mustafa.

'Do you have something more . . . ' She made a lifting motion beneath her chest.

He ferreted through the garments on the cardboard and picked up a green bra with black polka dots.

'Here.' He held out the bra, squeezed the cups with his fingers, then pulled it around his skinny ribs. 'Wire cups. I'll give it to you for seven hundred. Look at how pretty it is.' He pulled the bra tighter around his chest.

'Seven hundred? Do you think I'm a millionaire? Three hundred.' But she took the bra from his hands, turning it in the light. Stepping behind the van so that she was hidden from the street, she adjusted it over her T-shirt. It was too big.

'It fits just right,' he said.

'Really?'

'Yes.'

'It feels big.'

'I'll give it to you for five.'

'Four,' she said.

'All right, four,' he said. He took the blue notes, ragged with sweat and dirt, and stuffed them into a bag.

Alice, the bootlegger, bought a shiny black polyester slip for six hundred pounds. Mary and Nadia, two prostitutes who lived in a house on the edges of the market district, paid him five hundred for a matching set of blue underwear. Jane came and sifted through the merchandise. The women joked with him, pinched his cheeks and ruffled his hair, picked up garments and haggled with him. An hour after he had set up shop the plastic bag in which he kept the money was already filling with notes.

During a lull he looked up, surveying the street for more customers, when he saw, beyond cars parked on the other side of the road, a familiar yellow *thoub*. The woman was speaking to someone who walked beside her, and the *thoub* was pulled over her hair, hiding her face, so he couldn't be sure if it was Layla; but he called out her name, cupping his mouth and shouting over the broad dirt road. She didn't turn. He called again, louder this time, but by now she and her friend were farther along the street, heading north toward the Baynabi district, and he could only see the back of her. He moved to cross the street and catch up with them, but, glancing back at the spread of underwear before him—his short life's savings—he changed his mind.

Two sisters, one plump and tall and one thin and short, came up, and soon he was busy showing them his things. When he searched the road again the yellow *thoub* was gone, and he turned back to the underwear, telling himself he'd go look for her after he was done.

He was in the middle of negotiating the price of a pair of pink knickers with black trimming, urging the sisters to feel the smoothness of the polyester, when he saw Hassan—folds of fat bulging along his middle, bald crown glowing like a bulb under the sunlight—marching toward him from his shop across the street.

The shopkeeper pushed the two sisters out of the way, standing wide as a barricade before Mustafa. 'What do you think you're doing?'

'Selling underwear,' said Mustafa, planting his hands on his hips. 'What's the problem?'

'You can't just set up shop anywhere,' said Hassan.

'Why—does your mother own the street?' said Mustafa.

He had set up his stall exactly in this corner of the market, of course, because it was across from Hassan's. Women going into or coming out of the clothes shop were bound to see his underwear table.

'You think you can steal my customers, you little brat?' said Hassan. 'Out of here. Now!' He swept garments toward the edge of the cardboard box. Mustafa dragged them back, hugging clumps of underwear to his chest.

A massive knee surged up, hairy calf exposed for a moment, leopard skin shoe floating in the air, angling, before the shoe crashed into the side of the cardboard. Both boxes crumpled. Knickers, bras, slips tumbled to the ground. Mustafa dropped to his knees, picking up the underwear before it was trampled.

'Leave him alone!' The two sisters pulled at Hassan's *jellabiya*.

He shoved them off and leaned down, panting, to pick up the cardboard.

180

Mustafa—bra straps and leg holes looped around his arms, the plastic bag full of money dangling from one hand—jumped up, trying to reach the flattened boxes that Hassan now held high above his head. 'Give it back!'

'Get out of here,' said Hassan, elbowing him away. 'If I see you again you'll be in trouble, understood?'

The folds of his chin flapped. Drops of sweat clung, dancing, to the tip of his carrot nose. Cardboard gripped under his arm, he turned and waddled across the street, vanishing into the shadow of his shop.

'Bastard,' said Mustafa, sunglasses lopsided on his head, sweating under the hot polyester.

'Don't mind him,' said the younger sister. 'Just set up somewhere else in the market tomorrow, away from him.'

They leaned down to help him pick up the rest of the underwear scattered on the ground.

'What about the underpants?' said Mustafa, straightening and digging through the mess of things dangling from his arms and shoulders to find the pink pair he had been showing the sisters before Hassan arrived. He pulled them off his arm, held them up again. The black lace trimming was chalky with dust. The rubber waistband had stretched so that now it sagged, gaping, from his hand. The knickers seemed twice as big as they had been fifteen minutes ago.

The older sister blinked, her nose wrinkling.

'I don't think so . . . ' she said.

'Why? What's the matter?' he said, glancing from one to the other.

'Look at them,' said the younger one.

'You can wash them.'

He dusted the knickers against his shorts, but stopped, afraid the waistband would stretch more.

'And they're too big now,' she said.

'I'll give them to you for three hundred.'

'Next time maybe.'

'One hundred then.'

They began walking away. 'Next time!'

'Fifty!' He trotted after them for a few steps, holding out the underpants. But they had already disappeared into an alleyway, lost in the crowd.

The first time he stepped out in the town it occurred to Alex that he had been transformed into some kind of fantastic beast. Feathers waving from his head. A black-rimmed beak spiking from his jaw. Scaly wings sprouting from his back. A long hairy tail lashing left and right behind him. He saw it in the faces around him. Chattering mouths fell silent as eyes fell on him. Necks craned and heads pivoted, following him down the road. People called friends from shops to come and look. Little girls tugged at their mother's skirts and pointed. A crowd gathered, thickening, along both sides of the street. It was a shock, the way everyone stared at him, unblinking, mouths agape. He had looked down at himself, checking his arms, his torso. Touched his blue Bermuda shorts. Peered at his long toes in the open-toe sandals.

It was his second day in Saraaya and William was taking him on a tour of the town. His arrival, William explained, was something of an event. The only other foreigners in the vicinity were the Chinese oil workers who lived in little encampments out in the plains, by the oil fields, having arrived all the way from villages in China stocked up with supplies of strange salty sauces and dried vegetables that looked like underwater creatures that had died in the sun. They kept to themselves, these workers, clusters of leather-visaged men in dirty clothes, only occasionally coming to town for a night of love in the unofficial brothel on the edges of the market district. One or two slant-eyed babies had already appeared among the stalls, crawling in the dirt.

'So you see, you're an attraction,' said William, floating on his long limbs high up above Alex. His feet didn't seem to touch the ground so much as tread on air. Each knee rose for half a minute, each hand wafted through the atmosphere in a long pendulous motion by his side.

Next to him Alex stumbled on rocks and depressions in the ground. Strange parts of his body tingled with sunburn. His lips. The skin around his toenails. The small circle of exposed scalp in the middle of his crown. Pebbles rolled into his sandals and pricked his heels. He felt especially clumsy when he found the whole market gathering to stare at him. As he walked he looked back boldly at those who stopped to stare: the water seller with the skullcap, who had halted a donkey with two giant barrels strapped to its side; a string of old men telling rosaries; a group of teenage girls, who said something to him as he stepped past.

'Hi,' he said. 'Hello.' He waved and smiled like a celebrity. He nodded. 'Good afternoon.' He threw in the Arabic and Nilot greetings William had taught him, sprinkling them like sacred offerings on everyone he passed. Some of the onlookers laughed at him. Others answered back, gesturing with their hands. Intrepid boys detached themselves from the crowd. One grabbed the hem of his T-shirt, trotting after him and giggling. Another, taking courage, reached for the giant black watch around his wrist. Small dry fingers dug into his flesh, boldly pressing and squeezing.

Here and there William pointed out important landmarks. There weren't many: a mosque, a church, a police station, the small, dusty market. Army barracks somewhere by the highway that led to Khartoum. Alleyways careening and twisting at random angles. Huts that didn't look like houses so much as giant mushrooms that had sprouted from the earth. Goats that liked to perch high up in trees, snipping at leaves. A brown-green landscape, interrupted by the women's bright-colored dresses in bursts of red and saffron yellow and rippling blue and orange.

'This is the local drinking establishment,' William said, leading him through a doorway in an alleyway off the main road.

It was more like a dungeon. Low dark walls, no windows. Benches along two sides of the room. A narrow passageway led between stools on which groups of men sat with their knees and elbows pointing. Glittering eyes, sweat-sheened shoulders, calves blended into shadow and light. People paused with their cups in midair. Spoons tinkled against plates. In the quiet, flies buzzed and zipped from one sticky teacup to another. It was close and hot, drops of sweat trickling down Alex's jaw and into the hollow at the base of his throat, the tip of his nose gleaming.

Over the course of those first two weeks he'd slowly begun to get used to the place, adjusting to its rugged edges, people becoming familiar with him, he with them. He learned names. When he walked through town fruit vendors pressed oranges and guavas into his hand. He'd gotten up the courage to go out on his own, without William, communicating in a mixture of sign language and English and the few words of Nilot and Arabic that he knew.

He had accustomed himself to using the pit latrines. They had terrified him at first, especially at night, when the roving beam of his flashlight exposed all the creeping scurrying buzzing creatures that had made a colony of the bathroom in the compound. Cockroach antennae poking up from the pit. Mosquitoes looping in the air, angling to dig proboscises into his exposed behind. Flies clustering on walls, gleefully rubbing their hands together. It had taken him days to perfect the precarious procedure of maneuvering himself over the pit, his feet—constrained by shorts at his ankles—propped on either side on two crumbling bricks, his butt hauled up in the air, his leg muscles trembling at the thought of cockroaches darting up his ankles.

Now he paced back and forth in the cramped office in the compound, restless. His stomach had been queasy since the burial the day before, his body tipping between hot and cold despite the heat. He remembered dirt piling up as they'd shoveled onto the flesh, teeth screeching through the grime even as the eyes, the cheekbones, the hollow of the nose disappeared. On the way back from the burial they had stopped in the market to drop off the herders. They had been accosted by a crowd, full of questions about the corpse. Bodies pressed in and suffocated him, hands reached for him, tongues jabbered. A fight had almost broken out over whether the corpse belonged to the nomads or the Nilotes. Burial rites, ablutions.

He'd grown too comfortable in the town, forgetting that he was a stranger here, alone. Up until the appearance of the corpse danger had been a distant idea, despite rumors of southern rebels converging beyond the swamps, men with guns demanding rights, resources, autonomy. The town and its oil fields had been captured by the government five years before; the rebels wanted it back. He'd heard, not long after he'd landed—just his luck. of course—that clashes might be erupting again.

He paused in front of the poster of the raised hands, the floating globe. What, really, was he doing here? It was a long way from the easy, stable life he had known as a child. His father was a tax lawyer—with a small practice in the suburbs of Cleveland, where the family lived—and his two older brothers had followed in his footsteps, but Alex had always known that a job in an office, and a suit, and a house in the suburbs somewhere, were not meant for him. Instead of going to law school like his brothers, he'd opted for graduate studies in geography, an outgrowth of a childhood love of maps, which he'd collected ever since his school days: geologic maps, antique maps, topographic maps, of places far and near. They had given him, those maps, a desire for the world beyond the suburbs, away from his family's house, identical to every other house on the street, in a planned development itself indistinguishable from a dozen other planned developments on the outskirts of Cleveland.

Music was the other love that had marked him out as different back at home. When he was still in school he went to N.W.A. and Public Enemy concerts—on the rare occasion when these, among others of his favorite bands, purveyors of a new music called "hip-hop," made an appearance in Cleveland. There, his father—who insisted on accompanying him to the concerts because he was still in middle school—would spend half the time trying to clap his damp palms to Alex's ears when the more explicit lyrics burst forth from the loudspeakers.

Rotund of belly, bespectacled, in starched khakis and shirt, and, of course, white and middle-aged, his father was an eyesore in that crowd—and it was often a tussle Alex went through, when one of the bands came to Cleveland, over whether the delight of seeing them in person outweighed the embarrassment of appearing at the concert with his dad, especially amongst that cool crowd of jelly-curled, flattopped kids, into which his three best friends, Steven, Daniel, and Nandan (black, Dominican, and Indian—an anomalous group of friends in a suburban school sea of white) melted with ease, keeping, in fact, a distance from him and his father when they too were in the audience.

186

After finishing graduate school he applied to jobs abroad—it was time, he'd decided, to escape his familiar life altogether. Among them was the job here: *Mapping and Surveying Field Officer, Saraaya, Sudan*. Except for summers in between his graduate studies spent volunteering in Central America, he'd had no exposure to working abroad. He was too innocent to wonder, when he was offered the job, why they were giving it to a twenty-seven-year-old with little experience either in development work or fieldwork—even if, technically, he had the surveying skills that the organization was looking for. He didn't know much about Sudan, and even less about the town where he would be stationed, but it was as distant and exotic a place as he could think to go. What drew him to the job was that he would be out and about. *Fieldwork*. He had a vision of himself running naked through a plain.

It was only after he had been plonked down in Saraaya, tumbling out of a tiny UN plane one morning, tripping down the narrow steps to the dirt runway, his legs unsteady after the turbulent flight, that it began to dawn on him: No expat was naïve enough to agree to be stationed in that remote region, in that blip of a town with no electricity, few roads, and crucially, no other expats (they only flitted by, he'd learned when he was doing his training in Khartoum, for a few days every couple of months, and during the rainy season, when the UN plane couldn't land on the muddy runway, they didn't come at all).

No one wanted to work in Saraaya. It was why he had been offered the job. Still it was an adventure, and a worthwhile one at that. He would make a map, and the map would be an imprint leading the way to better things for people who needed it: improved development planning, a more efficient distribution of aid and resources. It was rewarding work, meaningful work,

187

and it filled him with a sense of purpose and mission. He'd been exhilarated by the challenge, and had been looking forward to it all. Until the corpse had appeared and thrown everything out of balance, making him question, for the first time, what exactly he was doing here.

He blinked at the poster, suddenly weary of his own company, of the thoughts scuttling around his head. He felt caged in the tight office. William, who'd gone to the police station to find out if there was any more information about the body, wasn't back. Looking through the office door, he was relieved to see Dina, in a pair of jeans, the sleeves of her yellow shirt rolled up to the elbows, bent over a table in the courtyard packing her camera bag.

She glanced up at him as he approached.

'You're going out?' he asked.

'Yes,' she said. She zipped up the bag, then began wrestling the tripod into a side pocket.

'Where?'

'Outside of town, to shoot,' she said.

'Alone?'

She nodded.

'Is that a good idea?'

She stopped, the tripod half in its pocket.

'Why wouldn't it be?'

He gestured to the spot where the corpse had lain. 'The dead body that turned up yesterday,' he said. 'Doesn't it worry you?'

She shrugged. 'We don't know what it's about yet.'

'There might be fighting soon,' he said. 'William says so. Some kind of attack, maybe, on the police, or the security.'

'Until that happens—*if* it happens—I have to get on with filming,' she said. 'Anyway, there's always a chance that something might happen *here*.'

He looked away, scanning the courtyard. The office, at the front of the compound, faced out onto the main road that traversed the town from south to north. To his right was the kitchen, a long, low rectangular room with blue shutters. In front of it sat a greasy red generator on deflated wheels, which was switched on for four hours every evening, between seven and eleven p.m. The gazebo was at the back. To his left was the bedroom where Dina slept and, next to it, the storage room. All of this was hemmed in by a low brick wall. It would do nothing to keep danger out.

Dina lifted the bag onto her shoulders. A sign that the conversation was at an end.

'How come you always do that?' he asked.

'Do what?' she asked, thumbs hooked into the straps of the bag.

'Cut things short. Talking. With me.'

His mood, his fear, made him reckless.

'I was on my way out,' she said.

'You don't like me,' he said. 'Is that what it is?'

She stared at him, taken aback. Then, collecting herself, she shrugged again. 'We're here for different reasons, doing different things. Let's just try to get along. While we're living together, anyway.'

'But why *aren't* we getting along?' he said.

That was it: He felt, around her, that he was guilty of some offense he couldn't identify or name.

'Maybe if you weren't so eager, Alex,' she said.

He stared at her blankly.

'To be friends, to talk all the time,' she said.

'That bothers you?'

She didn't answer, just stood there, arms crossed.

'Fine.' He raised a hand to his forehead in a mock-salute. 'Good luck filming.'

189

She glared at him, then turned. He watched as she walked toward the gate, each step a rebuke silently delivered.

Dina closed the gate behind her and marched down the street, past more homesteads and compounds, past a boy leading two cows, past rubbish floated up by a dusty breeze, stepping quickly, impatiently, despite the camera bag—which in the afternoon heat felt twice as heavy as it normally did—pressing down on her shoulders and back. Yes, she didn't like Alex. Why did he insist on being friends? She frowned. They weren't.

If she had to put a finger on it, it was his righteousness that bothered her. He was smug about his map. And condescending toward her own work. He'd wanted her to affirm his fear, just now, about the corpse. He was afraid for himself, and he was ready to run, and he had wanted her to make him feel better about it. She wouldn't. Typical of people like Alex, she thought, those types that popped up here. Full of their own heroism, until the first whiff of danger. They were all over Khartoum, in their SUVs, in their "expat only" clubs and parties and their monthly "Rest & Recuperation" vacations to safaris in Kenya, because it was such a hardship, to work in such a country, so unbearable—the weather, the boredom, the landscape. He was one of them.

She slowed, suddenly breathless, blood pulsing in her temples. She'd been walking too fast, and it was too hot. She reached for a water bottle in the side pocket of the bag. The water was warm, unpleasant in her throat, with a plasticky taste to it—as if the bottle itself were melting in the heat.

Time to put him out of her mind. She looked around, focusing instead on the filming ahead. Children's voices, repeating something, filtered from nearby. She remembered that up the road was an elementary school, and walked, slower now, toward it. A large section of the wall had collapsed, and as she passed she could see twenty or thirty children in the yard, crowded in a circle around a teacher sitting on a chair. She stopped, drawn by the image.

One of the children looked up and saw her.

He pointed. 'Is it a boy or a girl?' he said.

The whole class—a crowd of heads and eyes and teeth, bare feet bundled close to their bodies in the squashed circle—turned to stare. Chalk-slabs sat idle on their laps. The teacher, a young man in dark trousers and a neat white shirt, lowered the open book in his hand.

A child rose. Then they all flooded, tumbling, elbowing one another, hurrying toward the gap in the wall.

How strange she must look to them. She forgot it sometimes. She'd shaved her hair down to the scalp back in Seattle. Now it had grown out into short, shiny curls around the dome of her head. Her short hair and trousers confused everyone. Some women wore their hair short in Saraaya, but usually in tightly plaited braids. Women never wore trousers. And Dina's narrowness and her prettiness had about it the angled quality of boyhood. Broad shoulders and spare bony hips, small breasts gone missing in the loose Nehru-collared shirts she liked to wear when she was filming. Something boyish, too, about the jutting triangle of her jaw. Her earrings—two flower-etched jade medallions dropping from each ear—confused matters more.

Not wanting to disrupt the lesson, she continued on her way, but a small group of unzipped and unbuttoned children clambered over the rubbled wall and trailed behind her down the road, deliberating.

'But he's wearing trousers!' called out one child.

'What about the earrings? A boy doesn't wear earrings!'

'But his hair's short!'

They went back and forth as if discussing a strange animal that had materialized out of the heat-mirage of the midday sun. She smiled to herself, listening to the conversation. Occasionally glanced back at the group of boys and girls who took the chance to peer at her face more closely. They weren't interested in her own opinion. They walked on for a few minutes more beyond the schoolhouse when she stopped. The children came to a halt behind her.

'Don't you have to get back to your lesson?' she asked in Arabic.

'She sounds like a girl!' a tiny boy with two missing front teeth said.

'I am a girl,' said Dina. Those who had insisted she was a boy gasped in disbelief. An excited rumble went through the group.

'Why's your hair so short then?' asked a girl in a dirty yellow dress with puffy sleeves.

'Because I don't want to bother with brushing it all the time,' said Dina. She'd walked into a barbershop in Seattle two years earlier, determined never to comb or braid or blow-dry her hair again, and asked the barber to shave it all off. A group of teenage boys across the street watched the whole scene through the glass window, their movements miming shock and disbelief as the long strands of thick, wavy hair fell to the floor, collecting in a lifeless mass at the barber's feet.

'But you're a girl, you *have* to brush your hair!' a boy called out.

'Not if I've cut it all off,' she said, running her hand over the short glossy curls. The children stared, stupefied.

'You won't find a husband if you look like that,' said a girl, bigger than the rest, with two pigtails bent outward and suspended in the air as if with their own stubborn willfulness.

'That's fine by me. Who needs a husband?' said Dina.

'Every woman needs a husband,' countered another boy. 'Otherwise, you'll end up a . . . a *spinster*.'

Giggles rose up in the crowd.

'That's good. It means I won't have to cook and clean and look after some ugly old man.'

The children didn't know whether to approve or disapprove of this blasphemy, but it thrilled them. They pressed closer around her.

'What's your name?' one of them asked.

'Dina,' she said, crouching down. 'And what are yours?'

They went around the circle telling her their names, shy and excited.

'Where are you going?' asked Daoud, a boy of about eight or nine who wore the child version of the long robes that the nomads wore.

'I'm going to take pictures,' she said.

'Can we come with you?'

She saw the teacher hurrying toward them. 'I think you should get back to school,' she said.

Before the children could scatter the teacher bore down on them, shouting, his white shirt flapping from his trousers. They swept around him and ran back toward the schoolhouse. He trotted after them heavily. Daoud waved to Dina as he fled. 'We'll find you later!' he called, and she waved back.

Treading on her lengthening shadow, she walked on down the street. Thatched roofs peeked up above the mud walls of the homesteads. Every now and again a cattle byre—much larger than the tiny huts in which the townspeople lived—loomed over the houses. The chatter of chickens clucking in a hidden courtyard mingled with the wind echoing dryly in her ears. Toward the end

193

of the road there were fewer homesteads, and then the track spilled suddenly into a dusty clearing with two large stones—makeshift goalposts—set wide apart at either end. In the stillness, she remembered the corpse. Maybe Alex was right. Was it wise to be going out on her own? She hesitated, glancing around. It was quiet, empty. Annoyed at herself for thinking of Alex, she walked on, resolute, and crossed the dirt road that marked the end of the town's living quarters.

It was late afternoon. Sunlight cast a warm glow over the scene in front of her: the sprawling clay plain north of town, grass already fading into patches of brown and pale green and yellow, stretching for miles and miles on end, flat, open, broken only at the horizon by a line of trees and shrubs that seemed black in the distance, behind which was the river, hidden from view. Above the trees cumulus clouds rose up into the sky, their soft spreading bulk casting huge pools of shadow on the grass. It was what she'd come for: to capture this broad sweep of the land that lay around her, around the town. She forgot about the corpse, swept up by the scene. She pulled the tripod out of the bag and loosened its locks. The legs lengthened with a heavy jerk. Peering down at the green water bubble set in the tripod head, she shifted the legs carefully, lengthening one and shortening another until the bubble settled where it should and the tripod head was balanced, then locked the camera on top.

She leaned forward and pressed her face against the eyecup, flicking on the power button. The camera whirred beneath her fingers. The picture blurred and sharpened and blurred again as she adjusted the lens and focused on the view in front of her.

Refracting the light, the lens miniaturized the landscape, flattening the soft upsurge of white clouds, the trees undulating in the distance, the rough bristle of grass. When she honed in with the zoom lens the silhouette of trees grew clearer, the tendrils of grass sharper, but then she lost the openness of the sky. For half an hour she played with the toggle control, zoomed in and out, moved forward and backward, readjusting the tripod each time, but still the image fell flat.

She looked up and rubbed the back of her neck, watching cloud shadows shift slowly over the plain. Frustrated by the smallness of her body. The meagerness of the device latched to the tripod. She didn't know how to approach this landscape with the lens of a camera. There was nothing to focus on, nothing to draw the eye to a point. It was all planes and lines and blocks of pale color extending outward and upward, defying containment.

Looking through the lens again, she tilted the tripod head higher so that there was only a strip of grass at the bottom of the frame, then trees, then clouds above. An image floated up from the recesses of her memory, a panning shot of a savannah in a David MacDougall film she'd seen in film class in college. Now her hands traced the outline of the shot as she remembered it, slowly moving the tripod arm in a 180-degree angle beginning to her right and unfurling in a steady sweep to the left. Halfway through the glide her arm muscle slackened and the camera jerked, slowing, then lurched forward. She tried again. Her arm was steadier this time, but in her rush to avoid another lurch she moved too fast. The lens zipped recklessly, impatiently, across the landscape.

She straightened and rubbed her damp palms against her trousers. She clenched her jaw muscles, whether in despair or determination even she didn't know. How had MacDougall done it? It had seemed so easy, so effortless. There had been something of it the morning before, when she had filmed Mustafa sweeping the courtyard. An alchemy of light, luck, perspective, and positioning. She'd filmed him for hours at the compound, striving and straining day after day, taking up one position, then another, hand-holding the camera, balancing it on the tripod, capturing him under the shade, in the sun, washing, sweeping, resting, talking, laughing—and yet yesterday was the first time that that mysterious conjunction had materialized out of nowhere and there was magic in the moving picture of the boy.

Still, she put her hope in effort. In her mind she had a dim vision of the film she wanted to make, and the promise of it made her push on. What drew her was the possibility of lacing together the pieces of this place into something whole. It would be a mosaic, made up of shards of images arranged to create a wider portrait, each fragment deriving meaning from its neighbors to give a picture of the land and its people.

Her fingers stroked the buttons on the right side of the camera. Moved along the exposure lever. The ND filter switch. Roamed over the gain and the audio level dials. The f-stops, she knew, controlled aperture, and the ND filter wavelengths of light. The gain button adjusted image brightness. The white balance toggle calibrated color. She'd learned all the nooks and crannies of the device, an obsession that had taken hold when she'd stumbled into a documentary film class during her third year of university in Seattle. After graduating she took out a loan to buy a camera, tapes, microphones, and—to the dismay of her parents, who didn't understand why she wanted to go back to the country they'd fled fifteen years before—a one-way ticket to Sudan.

All she had known of the country until then was Khartoum, glimpsed on summer vacations she'd spent there as a child. Full of so many relatives she couldn't keep track of names. Fat aunts and chain-smoking uncles. Cousins and second cousins who multiplied in number every year. Weddings, funerals, naming ceremonies. She had avoided Khartoum. It was her parents' city. And her parents refused to understand anything about her filmmaking, or her lack of interest in boys. So she had gone as far away from them, and from Khartoum, as she could.

Looking up, she saw that the sun had descended into the trees and the light was softening. A day moon hung above the horizon. Faint sounds filled the air. The distant croak of frogs calling for mates in pools of warm water, cricket trills, and then the rise and fall of the muezzin's voice announcing the call to prayer from the minaret, wafting over the town and the plain and the hidden river. The camera stared blindly at the horizon. She capped it finally and packed up her things, telling herself that she would try again tomorrow.

L ayla?'
Dina turned. William's shadow hurried ahead of him across the doorway, then he himself appeared, and halted just inside the kitchen. His face dropped. Lips came together, frustrated.

'Oh. I thought you were Layla,' he said in English.

'Sorry,' she said in Arabic.

His gaze darted to the corners of the kitchen, as if Layla might step out of the refrigerator or unfold herself from the onion basket by the stove, and then he looked at Dina again. She saw herself, the Not-Layla, her thin frame so different from Layla's voluptuous one. An absence of long, thick plaits that refused to hide coyly under the hood of her *thoub*, as they were supposed to do, preferring, instead, to parade their loveliness for all to see. And none of Layla's finesse in the kitchen. Dina stood clutching a carrot in her hand like a microphone. Everything turned into some variation of camera equipment in her hands. She set the carrot down on the countertop.

'She didn't show up today,' she said.

'Where is Mustafa?'

It frustrated her, William's tendency to address her in English.

'Haven't seen him,' she said in Arabic. 'Any news about the body?'

He shook his head. He stood there, filling the kitchen with his long floating presence, and she found herself absorbing the details of his appearance. Rectangular jaw framing soft plump lips. Scraped planes of cheekbones interrupted by a boldly sprawling nose. Severe brow bones set against the gentle, friendly flicker of curious eyes. Narrow khakis tunneled the long length of legs down to the sandals. The sleeves of his blue shirt were buttoned just above his wrist bones. She could see the silhouette of his white undershirt beneath the blue shirt, which pointed to another William, a less formal, more intimate William. She searched in herself, casting about like some exploratory fisherman, for some romantic response—a reflex from the days when she'd still hoped, for her mother's sake, if not for her own, that she was attracted to the opposite sex—but found none. Her appreciation was visual: She wanted to film him.

More than that, she wanted William's friendship. But there was this strange awkwardness between them. For instance, this English thing. He always spoke to Mustafa in Arabic, but, for some reason, never to her.

'How was the burial?' she asked, 'Did it go all right?'

'It's done,' he said. 'The police have to investigate now.'

'Why do you always speak to me in English, William?' she asked.

He looked at her, surprised. He was anxious, hectic today. His face was shinier than usual, a glint of sweat high on his cheeks.

His shoulders hiccuped. 'I thought—' He stopped and began again in Arabic. 'I just thought maybe it was easier for you.' He paused. 'Your Arabic is a little—' A hand floated up, palm downward, fingers spread, and wavered in the air like a rickety Sudan Airways craft on the brink of crash-landing.

She blinked at him. 'My Arabic is good,' she said. 'Not bad, anyway.'

'You're right. Sorry,' he said. His eyes kept darting around the kitchen. 'I really need to find Mustafa.'

Dina's professional relationship to William was unclear. She was in the compound as a guest, had made the arrangement through a family friend who worked for the organization in Khartoum. He wasn't obligated toward her in any way, but when she arrived she'd discovered that he had an interest in film—Bollywood films—and because of it he was enthusiastic about her work, though at first he couldn't grasp what there was to film in the dusty, sleepy town that was Saraaya. But he'd been helpful, suggesting places she could shoot, introducing her to people in the town, and always curious about her progress.

The front door squeaked open and shut. William turned and stepped out of the kitchen.

'Mustafa!' He disappeared toward the gate.

A minute later Mustafa came in, stick arms struggling with the weight of two large plastic sacks, followed by William. Mustafa's sunglasses, low on his nose, gave him the allure of a cool mosquito. He said hello to Dina and dropped the bags on the floor, then, standing in the middle of the kitchen, rotated his shoulders like an athlete warming up. He clasped his hands behind his back and stretched his arms.

'You *saw* Layla?' asked William. He leaned down, hands propped on his knees, to stare Mustafa in the face as he stretched.

'Yes,' he said.

'Where?'

199

'In the market. Or I *thought* I saw her. It looked like her. But I couldn't see her properly. She was across the street—'

'So you *didn't* see her,' said William.

'I did.'

'But you just said—'

'I saw her again later.'

'You mean, after the market?'

'Yes.'

Mustafa went to the water cooler, reaching on tiptoes for a cup on the shelf above.

William went up to him, breathless. He put a hand on his shoulder. 'Look at me.' Mustafa turned. 'You *found* her?'

'Yes.'

'Where? Tell me everything.'

'I went to her house. I had to ask a million people in the market before anyone could tell me where she lived, then it took me an hour to walk there. I got to one village but I couldn't find the house, and then someone told me I was in the wrong village. So then I had to walk another four kilometers to the *right* village. The one by the wadi, the new one where all the nomads have settled. Then it turned out her house wasn't exactly in the village—'

'Cut it short. Did you *speak* to her?'

'You want to hear everything. I'm telling you everything.'

Watching this back-and-forth between William and Mustafa, Dina tried, once again, to pin down the quality of their relationship, which was something like a father and a son, but more or less than that, she wasn't quite sure which. Mustafa, whose head just reached William's elbow, was about a third of William's age, and his livelihood depended on William. But he seemed to think that he was his equal. He wasn't afraid of him, knew William went out of his way to look after him. Mustafa had told her he'd been working at the compound for three years, since he was nine. In the first week, Alex had huffed about this, lecturing William under the gazebo. How could a humanitarian organization working to lift people out of poverty employ an underage child? Shouldn't Mustafa be in school? Did the office in Khartoum know about this?

William had rolled his eyes at Alex and turned to Mustafa, who was busy slopping the courtyard with water.

'He says you're too young to be working here,' William said in Arabic.

Mustafa had looked pointedly at Alex. 'No,' he said in English. He turned to William. 'Tell him: I need the money.' He continued to slop water. That was the end of it. Alex didn't bring it up again.

Now Mustafa, displeased with William's questioning, had turned his back and was calmly rummaging through his bags.

'Just tell me,' said William, in a softer voice. 'You found her house?'

'Yes,' said Mustafa.

'And she was there?'

'Yes,' said Mustafa.

'When is she coming back?'

'In a few days' time. Her father's sick—she's looking after him.'

'You saw her?' said William. 'You spoke to her?'

Mustafa peered up at him like he was crazy. '*Yes*. I *spoke* to her.'

'She's fine?'

'*Yes*.'

William was silent. He looked at the ground, watching this news anchor there, solid. He closed his eyes. A shudder went through his body, a ripple of tensing and loosening muscle, so that his hands and his arms and his shoulders clenched and unclenched, and when he opened his eyes again it was as though his body were longer somehow, freer. Dina understood: the gruff-ness, the distraction. He'd connected the corpse with Layla's absence, and he had been worried.

When he looked up, he was suddenly interested in their affairs. 'What's in the bags?' he asked Mustafa. Mustafa told him about the underwear, and his run-in with Hassan the day before. 'Avoid trouble with Hassan,' said William. 'He has a cousin with the police. Just move to another spot in the market.'

He asked Dina what she was making. Could he try a little bit of salad? He picked up a slice of carrot from the chopping board and crunched it, jaw muscles rippling. He stepped about the kitchen—tall, relaxed, friendly, the room suddenly suffused with his energy. He inquired about the film. Where did she go today? What did she shoot? She answered; she couldn't help feeling happy, too, telling him about her day.

'Where's Alex?' he asked.

'In the office,' said Dina. He had kept to the office ever since she'd returned from filming. It was their conversation earlier, she knew. He was avoiding her. For the best, probably. She squeezed half a lime into the bowl of chopped salad. 'Is it true,' she said, 'that there are rebels in the area? Alex was worried earlier.'

William waved him away. 'Alex is worried about everything,' he said, as though he himself hadn't been fretting only minutes ago. 'Who knows? It's just rumors.'

Mustafa, broom in hand, straightened. 'Everyone was talking about it in the market. They're saying the corpse has something to do with it.'

'Maybe. Maybe not,' said William. His face suddenly grew seri-ous. 'When did you say Layla is coming back exactly?'

'She said Sunday, or Monday,' said Mustafa.

'For sure?'

Mustafa blew out a breath. 'How am I supposed to know? That's what she told me.'

'Well.' William paused. 'She will be back.' He smiled. 'That's the important thing.'

He surged forward and, hooking one arm under Mustafa's knees and the other under his shoulders, swept him off his feet and went circling and dipping with him around the kitchen. Mustafa, squealing, legs flailing, dropped the broom, clinging to William's shirt.

Dina felt laughter bubbling up. She liked these two. She liked watching them together. Suddenly she missed her camera. It was in her room. She moved to get it, then stopped. Sometimes, she scolded herself, you just have to enjoy the moment. Forget the camera. It was the first time she'd seen them laugh since the corpse. She leaned back against the counter as William swung Mustafa in the air.

Michael Salu

is a creative director, artist, and writer.
His fiction, nonfiction, and art have
appeared in a range of publications,
including *The Short Anthology*, *Grey*,
Under the Influence, granta.com, and
Tales of Two Cities, published by OR Books.
He runs the multidisciplinary creative
agency salu.io and is part of the
American Suburb X team.

The Nod

MICHAEL SALU

WELCOME TO S.O.U.L.

Your Dreams, remembered.

User010 sat up, bleary-eyed and alone. Alone in the way you can only be when faced with the specter of your own S.O.U.L. He wondered aloud whether he was awake or not, having already resigned himself to the numbing addiction of this new experience. He could not bring himself to EXIT, particularly as he has yet to reach LEVEL 9. "It's when S.O.U.L. gets fucking badass mate," he's been told repeatedly by a smug elite User with far too much time on his hands and has now long since moved on from this realm. He leaned forward blinking, which in turn expanded the main menu. Recent history and countless forums bloated with griping ex-Users suggest that while S.O.U.L. is insanely addictive, it has always been an awkward environment to navigate, so User010 looked around for HELP. He hastily scanned the list of FAQs, which were even for him (a highly proficient LEVEL 8 user) intimidatingly dense with information, and halted the scrolling mass with a double blink.

10. How do I change my face?

Your face can be changed through the disruption of a set of variables that we have provided on your behalf. Simply select a number of the aforementioned predetermined parameters and choose "randomize." You'll be offered infinite variations on how you might like S.O.U.L. to perceive you.

> *INFORMATION ALERT*
> *Systemic Obfuscation of User Liberalism, or S.O.U.L. for short, was what everyone who was anyone was doing right now. Dive right in or quickly slide into an irreversible obsolescence.*
>
> *S.O.U.L. is a self-generated behavioral and dream experience predetermined by its own highly valued members.*

User010 blinked twice again and found himself moving through a narrow hallway lined on both sides with seemingly endless symmetrical rows of equidistantly positioned glass-walled plinths. More closely inspected, they weren't glass at all, but particularly granular three-dimensional projections of plinths. He squinted at the refracted light bleeding through the narrow rectangular columns, drifting languidly like globules of weightless liquid. Curiosity aroused, he moved tentatively through the hallway, making extra effort to remain within the narrow red carpet running through the center. He could see no end to the symmetry.

The dismembered heads floating within each plinth were motionless, except for their backlit eyes, which blinked occasionally and most disturbingly, following the exact cadence of his steps as he moved through the hallway. The eyes tracked him unflinchingly, every head scanning his movement, their eyes remaining fixed on him even when he was past their immediate view. As though they would forever. He avoided eye contact as much as was possible, but the hallway was tight and the heads were in such close proximity that he could not avoid holding heavy their relentless gaze in his peripheral vision. They stared, but, he thought, without malevolence. They stared curiously and somewhat mournfully, as though they were not quite ready to plead but maybe soon they'd ask for help to escape their prisons of light.

The silence began to unsettle User010, but the quicker he walked, the quicker the collective gaze moved to track him. Picking up the pace, the plinths began to blend into a wall of light and the eyes from each head folded into a solitary blur of unrelenting attention that sent a throbbing pulse of anxiety through User010's temples. He tried in vain to find an exit.

The claustrophobia of this collective gaze and the narrowness of the hallway continued to accelerate User010's anxiety. Exasperated, he stopped abruptly in front of one of the plinths, plucking up the courage to stare back. He and a dismembered head held a direct gaze whilst the others looked on in silence. The head didn't flinch, fidget, or look away, so User010 did his best to sustain the stare. The head would blink only periodically, just like all the others. Its eyes were saying much. They were asking questions of him. Questions he didn't know but could already feel he didn't care for. Those eyes were homing in on something that drew them together, whatever that might have been. He was disturbed.

Floating beneath the heads were the words "SELECT ME" along with a HEX color code. User010 looked up and down the hallway at the other heads staring at him, and only now he noticed they all had the same word suspended beneath them.

The heads were arranged in HEX color order, each a slightly different variant of the previous, resulting in a spectrum of color codes right through from #000000 to #FFFFFF. The head facing User010 was a tepid, sort of noncommittal brown—a #BCAF9F, if you will. Desperate to escape this space, User010 reached forward, touching "SELECT ME" and upon doing so realizing he had done exactly what he had been told he would do.

To begin LEVEL 9, I must tell you about *The Nod*, but I am guessing you may not be interested in the formalities. The LEVEL 9 experience has been much discussed, analyzed, and retold, but it is of paramount importance for our participants to be prepped for the actual experience. In fact your eyes might glaze over and your brow may even furrow in condescension, but I will try anyway. Maybe I can hold your attention for just a moment?"
"Where am I and who are you?
"You're in the Grooming Bay. This is where we brief our volunteers to prep them for entry into LEVEL 9. Think of it as a kind of green room."
"You could be me for a moment and understand how lost I am right now."
"Just listen. The first and most crucial lesson for a truly sustainable and even progressive S.O.U.L. experience is reaching a level of competence in the practices of *The Nod*."
"Er, OK."
"I'll go through the LEVEL 9 prerequisites and you may follow after with any questions. Got that?"
"I guess so."

"*The Nod* offers the opportunity for Users playing LEVEL 9 within the #BCAF9F HEX color range to become proficient with a code, or a language if you will. This language will benefit you hugely in navigating the inevitable obstacles of LEVEL 9. To those outside this range, the language will seem irrelevant, or often even invisible, but you must focus on its potential and solace. You might be strolling a busy high street, it'll be cluttered with crates of fruit pungently maturing in the sun. The fruit will be sold, as will the recent carcasses of animals hung in their own stupor and drained of life. Held out into your path will be a leaflet, garishly colored and illustrated with airbrushed faces from another HEX range, carrying with them benign expressions. From its cover arms will be outstretched toward you in an invitation to a better path. The smiles will be flat, numb, and smeared with the print of cheap gloss. The leaflet will be held by a lady. She'll likely be middle-aged, positioned very close to your #BCAF9F selection, and she will look up to your eyes. A weariness will betray her systematic ethereality, fatigued as she is by the very trust she has had in her singular path. She will look at you closely, as a grandmother does her rapidly growing children's children, while she contemplates the nearing of her own last breaths. Her gaze will hold in an attempt to peel away your preset defenses, but you must not pause to allow for the gaze to grip. As you move on through the growing crowds you could even meet another of this range. His gender selection will be male, like your own. His hair might be very similar to yours too. Yet, he'll be set apart from you by something and you might see flecks of a secret, or an ideology, worn colorfully upon his body and you will not ignore him and his smile will be sturdy and brief. His head will nod curtly but gracefully and you might focus on the graying point of his narrow beard and his hand may even reach where his heart beats and tap

209

it lightly in a fist and you will nod accordingly and you needn't know why and that will be OK. So you might move on from here and continue down the main street of LEVEL 9 and you should do your best to avoid the stumble, the lurch, and the call out to you through the missing front teeth of another from toward the failing, pale end of your HEX range as he relays to you a story. He'll have your S.O.U.L. age or maybe be a little newer. The story will be about his own exasperation. About how S.O.U.L. has not given him a chance, or his inability to see how to whittle out that chance, and you might nod in solidarity and your eyes might meet firmly and he might prod further as he'll see you have a sense of what he is talking about and he'll tell you how difficult LEVEL 9 is and how he keeps walking into cul-de-sacs, repeatedly blighted by every attempt to beat it or even just to leave it, and you'll nod again. He'll ask you for a few LEVEL 9 credits to help find the next exit and on this one occasion you'll relent from your usual stance (at this point it's useful to remember how to use the MENU to transfer those credits from your inventory, remembering that LEVEL 9 offers only a limited number of charitable transfers), because the whole time you talked, your eyes were fixed on the face of his fading HEX code, upon which the salty residue of trauma drew a tributary to some kind of oblivion. On this high street you'll see the entrance to The Artery. The Artery is a twenty-four-hour nighttime establishment and you'll enter and you'll pass the staggering hoards and find yourself in the bathroom, peeing alongside a few others from another HEX range, and they will sway in an inebriated silence, concentrating on keeping their penises straight and that silence will be too suffocating for them so they'll try to hold a conversation with you mid-pee and you'll ignore this and sometimes they'll glance over and down and you might shift your angle to hide your own penis from their opportunistic curiosity. Then you will begin to leave the narrow bathroom, but before this you will wash your hands under the previously disinterested but now curious gaze of one from your HEX code, who will be guarding a sink littered with cheap fragrances and sweets that refract into each other harshly through the rust-mottled mirror and you will look at him and he will nod before taking out his phone, which will be wallpapered with a photograph of his three young children back home. Somewhere. He will ask you where you're from and your route from the previous LEVEL might be similar to his and this will raise a smile and a nod. An odd deferent nod that you will think about later. Maybe a respect for how you made your way through the previous LEVEL. Here you will transfer another credit and he'll offer a sheepish thank you and you will head back out to the din of The Artery. Yet within the locale of The Artery and its surrounds, you'll need to beware of the erroneous Users from your HEX code range intent on concealing their own difficulties with the tasks of LEVEL 9 by hindering your progress. You'll notice them, the HEX code is clear, but the eye contact they hold shudders inwardly with loss. There will be no nod here, but they will examine you closely and you will keep moving. Then LEVEL 9 comes into its own, as you will have passed enough checkpoints to travel beyond the first realm, but the dangers also lie beyond and you will see less and less of your range, but you must keep going, as the challenge will be greater but so will your arsenal. These greater challenges will require completing certain tasks before you proceed farther, which may or may not top up your credits and you could even find yourself entering a credit repository and as you do so you place a mask from a lightly colored HEX code and you might even deploy a weapon from your arsenal at this point utilizing what you've learnt to make a withdrawal and then you can move on. These newer lands will come with more space, but also isolation, and you may enter a taxi and there is a slim chance your driver will be of exactly the same HEX code and he'll notice this only once you're inside the car and you will see his shoulders loosen and you will ride along to the sounds of his merriment as he takes you only to another checkpoint he can reach but not pass. When you arrive you might move through wide alien boulevards and you may see another User playing as a female from the one of those other HEX ranges and she'll be walking toward you and in her hand will be the small hand of a small child stumbling in an attempt to keep pace with limbs not yet able and the child's HEX will be much nearer to your own and the child will stare in that way only children can and this may unnerve you, as her eyes will be asking questions of you as she blinks and the female User will be smiling with fondness as maybe she has found a replacement but it isn't you so you must press on and keep moving as the next checkpoint beckons and somewhere beyond that maybe even LEVEL 10.

"Any questions?"

Honor Moore

Honor Moore's most recent collection of poems is Red Shoes and her most recent book, *The Bishop's Daughter*, a memoir, was shortlisted for the National Book Critics Circle Award and was a *Los Angeles Times* Favorite Book of the Year. She edited *Amy Lowell: Selected Poems* and *Poems from the Women's Movement* for the Library of America and lives in New York City, where she is on the MFA writing faculty at The New School.

The Mogul Gardens Near Mah, 1962

HONOR MOORE

It was the place where five rivers begin, the five rivers which mark the
     subcontinent
as lines mark the palm of a hand.

In the language spoken there, Punjab means "land of five rivers."

I was sixteen, we were all sixteen, American, the year of the twist, the
     year of the young
president, of the young president's beautiful wife.

Men and women were separated there, and

once when we danced a tea dance in the Himalayas, a soldier said to me,
     or to one of us,
I've never danced with a girl before.

At the movies, the young men downstairs, in the balcony the women in
     shalwar kameez or sari,
Doris Day and Rock Hudson, a shock rising in the dark when they almost
     kiss.

Kisses were censored.

A road down the center of the city called the Mall, the boy Kim sitting
on a gun, on a cannon,
a boy invented by a writer. All we cared about were boys.

The water was the clearest I had ever seen, and on a table nearby, small
glasses of what was called
"cold coffee" and also "cheese toasts" (for weeks we had eaten just curry
and roti).

We had walked ruins of a city built by Alexander the Great, a place where
the Buddha taught,
and climbed foothills, in the letter home: *all jagged green with goats
and men in turbans.*

A small clear lake, *the stones on the bottom were blue* and *there were
great big fish.*

We were driving up the Swat Valley in a van, nine of us, three or four
of them, young Pakistanis,
the women, secular enough to travel with the men, wore shalwar kameez,
dupatta.

At the edge of Afghanistan, the men taller and carrying Kalashnikovs, some
had pale blue eyes—"descended from Alexander."

and near them, a little girl in a sapphire dress, bits of mirror sewn in
with saffron thread.
We were meeting a dignitary, she was welcoming Ohio, Milwaukee,
California,

the young Americans. We were barely sixteen, all girls but one, still
children really,
our desire stronger than any will to diplomacy.

The water was the clearest I have ever seen, and soft. It was as if this
were
the source of all water, this pool at the beginning of five rivers.

216

There were nine of us, and all at once, we leapt into it, the water, the
     education secretary in her sari
and the quiet formal men trying to laugh with us.

In that water everything came pure and clear. What I remember is
     even though there was no sun
and even though it was not hot, our clothes dried, so that quickly

we became ourselves again, drinking cold coffee and eating cheese toasts.

Nightfall at the edge of Afghanistan, a bazaar, glass bangles of every color
     and fur hats, fumes
of incense, and also a marketplace for guns.

I think of that water, no water ever again like that clarity, as if at the
     beginning of the world.

Dave Eggers

is the author of many books, including *The Circle* and *A Hologram for the King*. He is the cofounder of 826 National, a network of writing and tutoring centers. He is also the cofounder of Voice of Witness and ScholarMatch, a college access organization serving low-income students around the United States.

The Fork

DAVE EGGERS

Edward Henri, seventy-two years old and wearing a tuxedo, has long been a gentle and happy man, but now he has a fork in his pocket. Blessed by good health and vast family, married forty years, with five children, eleven grandchildren, two great-grandchildren on the way, Edward has considered himself lucky to be enjoying his retirement and twilight years without care or controversy. But now he is at a wedding reception, and he has a fork in his pocket, and this is threatening to undo everything. He first noticed it a second ago, when he put his hands in his pants, looking for a mint, and instead found the sharp prongs of the fork. He quickly pulled his hand away, smarting from the pain. And then it dawned on him: There was a fork in his pocket. Had he stolen it from the silverware at dinner? He'd never done anything like that in his life, and didn't need to. He has his own silverware at home. But what if he had taken it, bowing to some long-latent subterranean kleptomaniacal urges? And what if someone had seen him? What would become of this wedding and Edward if it was known that a seventy-two-year-old guest was stealing flat-ware? Edward knows he must first do some research, so while pretending to be watching the dance floor, he sneaks a peek into his pocket, and notes, with great relief, that the fork is not from the wedding. With its pattern-etched handle, it's clearly one of his own, from the set he and his wife were given at their own wedding. So he didn't steal it. He is relieved for a moment but then, Edward realizes, this new truth is no less troubling. Having a fork from home in his pocket means he brought a fork from home. He is standing at the wedding, near the dance floor, watching the bride and groom's first dance, and is now greatly concerned. He had no reason to have brought a fork along to this event, a wedding that he could have been reasonably sure would be providing its own silverware. So what could this mean, that he left the house with a fork from his own kitchen? The implications are many, and all are problematic. He cannot remember thinking about forks that morning, and cannot remember taking the fork from a drawer and putting in his pocket. And thus memory loss could be at play. Could it be that finally he's succumbing to Alzheimer's or some equivalent? He was so proud to have retained into his sixties and seventies a well-organized and seldom-failing memory, and now, just when he would hope to think back on his life with total recall, it's slipping away. Could this be the beginning of an irreversible slide? Not now, no. His wife is trying to pull him to the dance floor. But he can't. If he tries to dance, he will be discovered. Who can dance effectively with a fork in his pocket? She will see it. She will pull him close and feel it. And then she will know about the fork, and she will ask about the fork, and because he will have no answers, she will want him to go in for tests. She will begin planning for a life with a husband on the decline mentally and otherwise. They will see more doctors. They will look at assisted-living centers. Could he tell her he brought it on purpose? "Everything tastes better with this fork! I love this fork!" he could say. No, that's worse. She'd have him committed. He plumbs his brain for options. Options, options. Could he stab her with it? Hm. That way the only one who would know he'd brought a fork from home would be dead. Not bad . . . But surely that would attract some attention at a wedding. Would it? Of course it would. And besides, he loves his wife, and does not want to stab her, no matter how tidy the solution her death would provide. He waves her off. No, he can't dance with her now (she goes off to dance with the father of the groom, an enormous man with a woman's hips). Maybe later, but not until he gets rid of the fork. But how? Anyone who spots him removing a fork from his pocket—a fork from home!—will consider him nuts. Can he go to the bathroom and throw it away? No, there were attendants in the restrooms when he went there earlier, and anyway, the fork is part of a beloved set, and his wife would be troubled if it went missing. Finally he acknowledges the only solution: He must find a way to hide the fork for the duration of the wedding, and somehow get it home afterward. And then, once it's home and he's safely home too, he can examine just how the fork got into his pocket, and how he made it all the way to the wedding without noticing he had a kitchen utensil—a heavy one, at that—in his right front pocket. Jesus. He is losing his mind. Only a madman would have brought a fork here. Maybe he is crazy. Yes. He is. It's happened. He's senile, he's gone. So what does he have to lose? Maybe the fork is an opportunity. Maybe this is God's way of showing him the door to a new life. Yes. That's it. That's the only answer. It was divine intervention that brought the fork to the lining of his pants, and now he must seize the opportunity. With the fork, he will break free of the bonds of all this family, all this happiness and contentment—and all that is staid and complacent! Yes, he will free himself, and fly into a world of excitement and chaos, really the only way to leave this world. He will stand on a chair, fork raised high, and declare himself King Trident! King Small Trident! Lord of Utensils! Yes! Or not. Maybe there's a more immediate problem. Maybe suddenly there are a hundred or so wedding guests staring at him. Maybe there are a hundred or so wedding guests staring at him, and the band, which is no longer playing, is also staring at him, at this septuagenarian named Edward, the father of the bride, standing on the edge of the dance floor as his daughter and her new husband dance, one hand in his pocket, furiously exploring the contents of that pocket. Maybe this man Edward has been furiously exploring his pocket for many minutes now, his eyes fixed in concentration, ostensibly watching two young people dance, and maybe for those minutes, as he has been forging deeper into concentration, more and more guests have begun to notice this man, standing stock-still but for his very active right hand. And maybe by the time Edward notices this, that he has been so noticed, the problem of the fork is the least of his problems.

Lydia Davis

is the author, most recently, of the story collection *Can't and Won't* (Farrar, Straus and Giroux, 2014) and a new version of the 1898 children's classic *Bob, Son of Battle: The Last Gray Dog of Kenmuir*, by Alfred Ollivant (NYRB, 2014). She is also a translator of French and other languages; her most recent translations include a new version of Gustave Flaubert's *Madame Bovary* (Viking Penguin, 2010) and the very short stories of the Dutch writer A. L. Snijders. She lives in upstate New York.

On Learning Norwegian

LYDIA DAVIS

In late spring last year, I began reading Dag Solstad's "Telemark novel," as this family saga is called for short, even in Norway, since the full title is formidably long. It is a book described by some dissatisfied critics in its native land as "tedious" and "unreadable." This thick tome calls itself a novel, but, say the critics, how can it be a novel? It has been compared by some of them, in both size and dramatic interest, to a telephone directory, though it also received much admiring praise. And indeed it is something like a catalogue, a catalogue of ancestors, though it is far more than that.

It is a long book—426 pages, not counting the appendix. It is entirely factual, and its plot consists for the most part of detailed accounts of the births, marriages, deaths, and property transactions of Solstad's ancestors in Telemark from 1691 to 1896, with little incident, almost no real drama, much authorial speculation, and the occasional memorable character, such as the pipe-smoking widow Torhild; the spendthrift Margit; Halvor Johannesson, who marries a woman forty years his senior; and the power-hungry Halvor Steinulvson Borgja (b. 1625). When, after a while, I looked ahead, sure that the action would become more various as we approached our own times, I saw only more of the same.

I have finished it now. I don't often read very long books. In fact, I don't often finish even a much shorter book, even in English. I usually put it aside, however good it may be, after, sometimes, eighty or a hundred pages, or less, having in some sense not only absorbed its nature but saturated myself with it. But I have read this one right through to the end. What made me go on? Certainly a kind of suspense, but hardly one that involved the "plot" of the novel, if it can be called that. It was a complex, multifaceted kind of suspense, involving not only the stories within the book, but also suspense over the author's investigation, curiosity about how the book would evolve, and, probably most of all, the suspense of learning a language I did not know before.

That was what made this reading project even more unlikely when I began it—the fact that the book is written in Norwegian, and I did not know Norwegian, beyond a few words, like the strange *ikke* for "not," the strange *og* for "and," the grandmotherly *gammel* for "old," the not-quite-right *til* for "to" (as well as for "until"), and the fact that—what seemed even stranger, and was not true of any other language I knew—in Norwegian the definite article "the" is often tacked onto the end of a word, appearing only as a suffix.

I was reading the book for the most basic of reasons: It did not exist in English, and would, I thought, perhaps never be translated into English, so if I wanted to read it—and I did, and right away—I would simply have to start in and do my best to understand it. Soon after beginning, I decided to continue as long as I could, making my way word by word, regardless of how much

I understood, through the whole of the book. I would also do it "cold"—without looking anything up in a dictionary and without seeking help (*hjelp*) by turning to a native Norwegian.

first Norwegian lessons

The seeds for this adventure in learning Norwegian were planted more than a year ago, when I was visiting Oslo for a literary festival. By now I know that if I am in a foreign place, I will be intrigued by the language and, though I may vow not to, will begin trying to figure it out from reading billboards, bilingual menus, signs in restrooms, train stations, hotel rooms. So this time, in advance, I asked the organizer if he could arrange a few Norwegian lessons for me. He found me a teacher, and she turned out to be my own Norwegian translator.

Each day for three days, as long as I stayed in the city, we had an hour-long lesson in the hotel lounge, on a comfortable sofa. Johanne decided on the method, and it suited me very well. She produced from her bag an old-fashioned children's picture book with family scenes in bright colors. Speaking only Norwegian, she pointed to the pictures and described what was happening: Mother was standing in the garden, the children were playing with the dog, Father was picking apples from a tree. Johanne, though far younger than me, has a nice, motherly manner—she is in fact the mother of a five-year-old—and I felt a little like a child as I watched and listened, tried to understand, and occasionally spoke.

I did pick up a few words. Take the middle letters out of "mother" and you have the Norwegian word for her, *mor*. Do the same to "father" and you have *far*. As for "child," the Norwegian *barn* is close to the Scottish *bairn*. And then, logically, but pleasingly, the odd-looking *mormor* (nothing to do with "murmur" or "marmoreal") is "mother's mother," or maternal grandmother, while *farfar* is paternal grandfather, and *barne-barn* is grandchild.

the first word lists

After our language lessons were over, I went on studying a little on my own. Johanne had given me a children's picture book called *Mo i mørket*, by Sara Li Stensrud, about a little girl, Mo, who wonders if she still exists and is the same person, *i mørket*, when the lights are off. We had looked at the first page together, and with some rereading and stopping to think, I could understand some of it. It took me a while, though, to see that *mørket* had nothing to do with "market," for example, but meant "the dark," *Mo in the Dark*—that -*et* was the pesky tacked-on "the." An English cognate would be "murky." ("Cognate" = "born together," and means that the words come from the same original word or root.) I began to make lists, on small pieces of paper, of the words I was learning from this book.

I had not made my way through all of it before the time came to leave on a side trip to Bergen. The next stage in my learning of the language began in the train station at Bergen as I prepared to return to Oslo. Someone had suggested that another good way to start a foreign language was to read comic books. So before I boarded the train heading back over the mountains, I browsed the shop in the station and found the adventures of *Mikke Mus i grenseland* (in frontier country). (The front cover incited kids to buy it with the words *Ny!* (New!) and *Kul!* (Cool!)) So my next vocabulary lists were from the comic book and included words like: mystery rangers, gang of robbers, "Right!," jail (*fengsel*), "We're freezing!," supernatural, gold, black magic (*svartekunster*), "We're alive!," "Just as I thought!" ("*Som jeg trodde!*"), and "Out with it now!" ("*Ut med det nå!*").

Reading the comic book was interesting, but not easy. I misunderstood things. I did not at first see the relationship between *spøkelse* (ghosts) and our "spook." I had to readjust my expectations to exclamatory comic book style dialogue: "Quick—after him!" ("*Fort—etter ham!*") And to the one-word responses: "Wrong!" ("*Feil!*")

The train trip was seven hours long, and during that time I managed to read very slowly through only one story. "Read" meant put my eye on a word, hear it in my head, try to figure out what it was, reread it, try again, go on to the next word. Of course, a great deal of the time I was also staring out the window at the mountain peaks, lakes, snow, hiking trails, cycling families, lonesome huts, railway stations, snow tunnels, roads, clouds.

The small population of Norway is thinly spread over the land, so there is a lot of unpopulated scenery. The vastness of the mountains and fjords makes the people seem tiny, dark figures against the expanses of land and water, both the people of now, at least from a train window, and also those in photographs from earlier times. In Bergen, I had found the photos of the nineteenth-century Bergen photographer Knud Knudsen in a museum gift shop. His black-and-white images of the dramatic and wild landscape, and the families in that landscape, and also on the city streets, exist as individual cards in shops, and also in great numbers online, but, strangely, are not collected in any obtainable book.

acquiring the Solstad novel
When I returned to the United States, I did not go on with my Norwegian studies. But some months later, Johanne came on

a visit, and in the course of a conversation I described to her the difficulties I was having with a project of my own involving several generations of my ancestors, one that promised to be long, complex, and confusing. She recommended a new book she admired by the writer who is considered by many to be Norway's preeminent contemporary novelist, Dag Solstad (pronounced "Soolstad"), now in his early seventies. I had already dipped into two paperbacks of his which I had in English translation. Johanne told me this new one was highly unusual, and quite controversial: How could it be called a novel? She said that although I would not be able to read it, I might find it interesting "just to browse." I could at least look through it and get an idea of what he was doing.

In late May last year, I wrote to the Norwegian publishers, hoping to buy the book directly from them. They offered to send me a copy, commenting that in their opinion Solstad was truly one of the great authors in not only Norway but the whole of Scandinavia. I was anticipating a colorful mix of contents: photographs, drawings, charts, family trees, maps. I looked forward to leafing through it, studying the decorative loops of the old handwriting and the somber nineteenth-century portraits, picking up helpful ideas for an approach to at least organizing my own problematical family saga.

The book arrived in June. It was a fat hardback with a strikingly austere and handsome white dust jacket. The letters are in black and red; the words of the title are all in capitals and are run together with no spaces between the words, as in Classical Greek and Latin inscriptions, so that *Det Uoppløselige Episke Element i Telemark i Perioden 1591–1896* becomes: *DETUOPPLØSELIGEEPISKEELEMENTITELEMARKIPERIODEN1591–1896*, except that it is laid out on the jacket like this, forming a column of strange nonwords:

DAGSOLSTAD
DETUOPPLØS
ELIGEEPISKE
ELEMENTITE
LEMARKIPER
IODEN1591–1896

Nothing interferes with this block of text on the white space, because the only other words present, *ROMAN* (novel) and the name of the publisher, *FORLAGET OKTOBER*, are in minuscule point size; thus:

ROMAN | FORLAGET OKTOBER

directly under the last part of the title, so much smaller that from a distance you don't see them at all, thus (more or less):

IODEN1591–1896
ROMAN | FORLAGET OKTOBER

The design seemed to me brilliant, so striking that I asked about it. I was told that the designer responsible for it was one of the most distinguished book designers in Norway, Egil Haraldsen. Credited along with him in the book is Ellen Lindeberg.

I don't yet understand the whole of the title. It is something like "The un-*oppløselige* epic element in Telemark in the period 1591–1896." I might have been able to figure out the unknown word when I encountered a form of it again near the end of the book, but I could not, and now I can't find it again.

This design is not only handsome in itself, but is of course appropriate for the form this novel takes: the run-together words reflect the choice Solstad has made, to present his text in almost unbroken blocks, with no chapters and few paragraph breaks. (The running together of the words also, oddly, seems to contradict the directive with which the book opens, which asks us to read the book one word at a time.) The cover design also later came to seem to me symbolic, in two ways, of my confrontation with the unfamiliar language: The letters formed an almost impenetrable wall; and the words were almost all strange to me.

I opened the book and was surprised. Yes, the endpapers front and back were maps of the towns, rivers, and mountains of Telemark, and an appendix gave the genealogy of each line of Solstad's family that he discusses in the book. But no charts, photographs, drawings. The book consisted, for page after page, 426 pages, of solid blocks of text, margin to margin, with rarely any sort of break. I wondered what to do with it.

I had been all set to examine it carefully, live with it a while, pick up some useful ideas. I also wanted to read it, now that I had it. I was frustrated: This was a book I wanted to read, and it did not exist in English. I wondered if I could simply start reading, one word after another, and find out if I would begin to understand. I had done something like this before, with two other languages, though in both cases I had had much more of a head start than I did this time. Having as a teenager acquired the rudiments of Spanish on my own, decades later I read *Las Aventuras de Tom Sawyer*, which turned out to be a good choice, since I knew the story so well. Years and years after that, by now interested in Dutch, I read several detective novels in that language. As the police figured out the crime, its details were repeated over and over, which helped me to understand. I was carried along by both the drama of the story and the revelations of the language.

I resolve to read it

If I wanted to know at first hand what Solstad was doing in this book, the only way to find out was to try and read it. I was intrigued by what Johanne had told me about it. I thought it might be useful for my own project. So, seeing no alternative, I opened the Dag Solstad "Telemark novel" to the first page and read the first part of the opening sentence: *Les langsomt, ord for ord.* I was encouraged by the fact that I understood the first two words, and not because Johanne had taught them to me, but because I guessed them from their German cognates, *lesen* and *langsam*: "Read slowly." That was good advice, and I would have to follow it in any case.

It took me a few more minutes and several rereadings to realize that *ord* had nothing to do with "order" or G. *Ort*, "place," but meant "word": "Read slowly, word for word." I went on: *hvis man vil forstå hva jeg sier.* This was more difficult, but I understood some of it: "Read slowly, word for word, *hvis* one will (or wants to) understand (G. *verstehen*) *hva jeg sier.*" I thought *jeg* could mean "I" (Fr. *je*). By now I knew that the whole contained a surprisingly apt directive: "Read slowly, word for word, if you want to understand what I am saying." Having got this far, I then made up my mind that I would simply keep reading. Even if at first I understood almost nothing, I thought, I would in time understand more and more, and perhaps actually learn to read Norwegian.

why I found the book so entrancing

It is hard to explain why the book became so entrancing. It is hard to predict what is going to excite us. On the face of it, I would not have said that to read, laboriously, word by word, in a language I did not know, understanding only a little, a book with very little

233

plot and a multitude of three-named Norwegians of centuries past would be such an inviting prospect that I was eager to wake up in the morning and go read, read for several hours, often, and reluctant to put the book down and turn to other things.

One part of the pleasure, I know, was that through this reading I journeyed so far away, both geographically and in time. I journeyed into a landscape thinly populated even now, necessarily more so in centuries past, and characterized by dramatic scenery that stretched away into the distance or loomed over the people who lived there.

In the photographs of Knud Knudsen, in the rural scenes, the people, dwarfed by the landscape, gather by the shores of a lake or river or fjord, preparing to embark for a wedding celebration across the water, or trail along a winding dirt road on foot alongside a cart and ox or horse. These photographs would sometimes come to mind as I read Solstad's novel, though of course we enter the nineteenth century only well along in the book.

It was therefore partly the attraction of the foreign that drew me, foreign in place and time. There were multiple layers of a figurative mist in front of me as I read (with some breaks in the mist, more and more as I went along): the mist of my incomprehension, the mist of the past stretching back, the mist I imagined over the landscape of Norway, even wilder then than now, and the mist of the telling—the intervention of the narrator between us and the people or the documents. Reading it in a language unfamiliar to me removed it even farther in time and space. And perhaps I absorbed this landscape and these characters more deeply because I dwelled on each sentence so long, long enough to figure some of it out, and then also returned to it, dwelling on it again.

The past was mysterious in part just because so much of it was missing, so much was unknown. The novel goes far back in time, and there is very little information about each character. There was a real, though quiet, suspense in wondering what would happen next to these people of Telemark so many years ago: who married whom; which children survived to grow up; whether they lived on a *stor* farm or a more modest one; if widowed, whether they remarried; what the children thought of their new stepmother, the extravagant Margit, with her chests of linens; what was inside the lunch bag packed by the lonely widow and opened by the itinerant carpenter in a clearing in the woods; and why old Erik Sakeson hanged himself.

There are dramatic stories in the book, and they are a welcome burst of color when they come along. They come without warning, told in the same even tone as what came before and what will come after. They are usually brief. A man gets into a fight at a wedding feast, after drinking too much *øl* (which I mistook, in an earlier passage—where it appeared in a list of household food and drink—for "oil"), and kills another guest, then goes into hiding for two years before being found, brought to trial, sentenced, and beheaded.

For me, the fact that these events actually took place heightens the interest. Because the plot turns were not invented by the author, but were determined by chance, character, genes, environment, they are often abrupt and surprising: not only the births and deaths, but also the wildly mismatched marriages, the thefts and murders, the evictions of poor widows, the accumulation of wealth, the descent into destitution.

Solstad does not just give us the answers, but takes us along with him in the process of finding out. He speculates in detail about one possibility, it is plausible, and we believe he is right. Then he shows us, as though working it out for himself, why that possibility is unlikely. And then why another possibility is more likely, or must in fact be the case. And some of his speculations are frustrated and we are left, with Solstad, simply not knowing. So this is another kind of suspense: Solstad's historical investigation.

Certainly Dag Solstad is very present in the book, regularly commenting, sometimes exclaiming (*Hva??*—What??), as though spontaneously. On the very first page, he explains that originally he had intended to write a completely different kind of novel (*Jeg skulle opprinnelig ha skrevet en helt annen roman*) but that he found this family material so compelling, when it was collected and sent to him by a younger relative, the *sønn* of his *kusine Birgit*, that he changed his plan.

Occasionally he bursts out with an opinion, sometimes quite emotional. So, for a struggling reader, the author's own emotional involvement in the book is a part of its power.

But of course for me one of the most exciting aspects of the experience, adding to the suspense, was the adventure of gradually learning the language, beginning the book without knowing it and gradually acquiring it as I went along, seeing more and more mysterious words become familiar. In the beginning, as I made my way into this partly incomprehensible Telemark of the 1600s and 1700s, I felt, pleasantly, all the farther away from home in both time and culture for not knowing half of what I was reading. Then the mists began clearing, and each page offered another reward: not only the unfolding story, but also a linguistic revelation—again and again came the little burst of understanding, like a little light coming on, as a word that looked so mysterious—*miljø*—abruptly revealed itself: "milieu."

This confrontation with the densely printed text in the unknown language turned out to be oddly exhilarating. It was like diving, or jumping, into the deep, cold, and mysterious waters of a mountain lake. Or, to change the metaphor—I'm searching for a way to express just what this project was like—it was like confronting a rock face, or a mountain which I had to climb. The fact of doing it by myself, independently, without help, was part of what made it exhilarating. No one was going to lift me up that mountain. I would have to find the handholds and footholds by myself.

As I went along, I understood more and more—one bit of understanding helped me to another; the more words I under-stood in a sentence, or the more clearly I understood its construc-tion, the easier it was for me to guess or figure out the rest. The mists were clearing a little, or the mountain was leveling off a bit, or offering more small passes; or the forest that had been almost impenetrable was revealing some small paths and clearings.

And so, in fact, the experience of reading the book kept chang-ing for me as my understanding improved; it was never quite the same experience one day as it had been the day before.

The activity also became something of an addiction. I became very dedicated to my daily immersions in the tales of Solstad's ancestors in distant Telemark. Every part of the reading was a pleasure: the clean, white page, the sharp pencil for making notes, the comfortable armchair, the bright light, the complete erasure when I erased a misspelling or an awkwardly written letter, and most of all, of course, the progress word by word through the narrative, with an occasional touch of frustration, but, far more often, with a feeling of satisfaction.

my method of reading and learning: no dictionary
I read without a dictionary, understood some of each sentence, did not understand quite a bit of it, and was willing to read on ahead without understanding everything I had read.

There were several reasons why I did not want to use a dictionary. First, it was more comfortable not to be constantly picking one up, or sitting in front of a computer. Since, at first, there would be a quantity of words on any given page that I would not know, I would have been looking words up constantly, which would have been a cumbersome chore. I wanted to sit with this heavy book in a comfortable chair, with nothing more, besides the book, than a sharp pencil and a piece of paper.

Second, though, and more important, the work of trying to figure out what the words meant was stimulating and completely absorbing. I realized, after a while, that using my brain for something as difficult as this made thinking a very physical act, much more so than the easier, almost unconscious use we make of our brains most of the time.

Third, I remembered the words much better when I figured them out myself. I even remembered words that I couldn't figure out, so that when I met them again later in the book, I recognized them (without knowing what they meant). I saw that finding the unknown word in another context might give me the answer.

I remembered the words better, too, because I encountered them in an interesting context. I learned *respekt* (though that word was clearly not a difficult one) on page 303, in December, in the context of *respekt* for the *døde*, particularly for the *døde fedrene* (forefathers), *respekt* which ought to make one hesitate before disturbing an old burial mound (*gravhaug*). But that did not stop one of the foremost theologians (*teologer*) of the time, a bishop (*biskop*) keen on archeology (*arkeologi*).

The story is longer than this, but the short version is: He obtained permission from the owner of the property to hire some workers to excavate an ancient burial mound. The work was still going on when he had to return home (*måtte reise hjem*).

The workers, however, had noticed something (I did not understand exactly what) that made them believe there was a money chest deep in the hole. The owner of the land ordered them to cover over what they had dug. But later, after some underhand activity that, again, I could not understand, a chance passerby (if that is what *tilfeldig mann* means) discovered a chest full of silver coins (*sølv-penger*) below the bathhouse (*bad-stue*). He told no one, but took them to an old woman (*gammel kona*) to be washed.

There is more. But I will skip to a related story, about what the landowner himself found in another mound on the same property: a large sword, a heavy iron key, a silver plate with engraved circles and spirals, and a heavy gold cross (*gullkors*). The owner of the property, not realizing the cross was gold, sold it to a certain sergeant (*sersjant*) who was well aware of its value and became suddenly wealthy (*plutselig rik*) (G. *plötzlich*, Eng. rich).

But now, I must add—since it reveals something about his narrative technique—that Solstad denies this last part of the story, and tells us the sergeant's sudden wealth was only *folks fantasi*.

Words occur in Solstad's book that occurred earlier in the only previous reading I had done in Norwegian: In *Mo*, people look down from the windows (*vinduene*) and see Mo in the street below with her orange ball—"There goes Mo," they say. In the Solstad novel, the wealthy and pitiless Halvor Borgja, who is known to drive his workers like slaves (*som slaver*), hangs his red hat in the *vindu* of his room so that a hired man toiling in the field, stopping work for a moment to catch his breath, will look up at the windows of the main house and believe that the boss is there watching from under the brim of his hat, and will bend down to work again. And so, as a language does when one learns it this way, *vindu* is beginning to gather associations for me.

Similarly, a character in the *Mikke Mus* comic uses the word *trodde*, "believed," in his exclamation: "Just as I thought!" ("*Som jeg trodde!*") At one point in his narrative, Solstad, as he speculates about his grandmother's childhood, also uses the word: He mistakenly *trodde* something about her foster parents that turned out not to be true. So for me, now the word *trodde* is gathering associations that it wouldn't have if I had learned it off a list of vocabulary to be memorized.

Another reason I did not want to use a dictionary or ask anyone for the answer was that, almost right away, this experiment interested me *qua* experiment, and I wanted to keep it quite pure. I was trying to learn a language the way we learn our own native language from babyhood on up. Words are repeated in certain contexts, some the same and some different, and eventually, over time, with much repetition, we learn what they mean.

blind immersion

This experience with Norwegian was not my first experience of learning a language more or less from zero and with very little help, but mainly through immersion. There was, to begin with, my original acquisition of my native language, English, as baby and child—with quite a lot of active coaching, I'm sure, from parents interested in language. Then came a second experience. When I was seven years old, my family moved to Austria for the year, and I began the fall term of first grade at the Ursulinenkloster Schule (Ursuline Cloister School) in Graz. I was repeating first grade; I had already begun learning to read in English the year before. Now I was going to continue learning to read, this time in German. It was my first experience of a foreign language, if I don't count the snatches of French I had been so surprised to hear in Paris, where we stopped for a few days on our way to Austria, and where I went out to play every day in the Tuileries Gardens with my hoop and stick.

I had been given no prior preparation or coaching in German, and the first-grade teacher spoke only a little pidgin English. But she was a kind woman, and my classmates were friendly. Every day I sat in the schoolroom, dressed like the other girls in long woolen stockings, sturdy buckled shoes, dress, and smock, my hair cut short, and listened and watched and stared down at the attractive pages of the grammar book, with its pretty illustrations and its words printed very large in the beginning of the book and progressively smaller as the book went on. After about a month, when the teacher called on me to read aloud, I was able to, and during the rest of that year I continued to learn more and more rudiments of German, not only how to read it and speak it, but also how to form the letters of my script in the Austrian way, with tiny loops in the upper parts of the *o*'s and *a*'s and *d*'s and *g*'s. By the time my family left to return to the U.S., I had a well-ingrained and "natural" understanding of the basic syntax of German and a good pronunciation, and could talk fluently within a child's limited range of vocabulary and syntax. Back in the U.S., I missed the German language.

In the present case, true, I had had those three lessons with Johanne, and some preliminary vocabulary gained from two other texts, and I also brought to this language my previous experiences of other languages, so this experiment is far less "pure" than the experience in the Graz classroom, which was in turn less pure than my original acquisition of English.

marks on the page
On the first page of the novel, which was page 5, I learned these words: read, slowly, word, for, will, I, material, a, must, also, begin, with, not, shall, written, whole, other, from, my, cousin,

was, gathered, son, and, me, use, over, time, work, equally, it, we, after, ago, understand, then, in, copy, four, years, eight, months, so, strong, basis, as, long, that, mother's father, goes, back, us, are, many, no, idea. I know this because I wrote them in pencil in the white spaces at the top of the page and on the blank facing page. Some of the words I wrote down on that first page have question marks after them, though none of them was in fact wrong.

Then I saw that because so many words were going to be new to me as I read on, I could not continue writing them in the margins, because there would not be room for them all. So I started keeping lists on separate pieces of paper.

longer word lists

The reward of figuring out a word was to write it down in a running list and see how my vocabulary grew and grew. Some words were followed by a question mark. Some words recurred many times, still with a question mark. Some I had wrong.

The reason to keep a list was in part acquisitive: I *had* this word now, I had acquired it. Then I had another. I was collecting them.

But there were other reasons: The act of writing out the Norwegian word made me pay close attention to what it was, how it was spelled. Writing out the English helped me to remember it. Having the word there on paper allowed me to review it.

After a while, becoming impatient with myself that I could not remember certain basic and important words, I would write them in capitals, or put asterisks next to them.

On June 15, I noted on the back of a vocabulary list that I was not writing down some new words because I would always recognize them, such as *reagerte*, "reacted." Other words easy to recognize were *motivet*, "the motive"; *resultatet*: "the result"; *insolvente*, "insolvent"; *pekuniær*, "pecuniary"; *introduserer*, "introduces"; *instinktivt*, "instinctively." Later, I did write down obvious or easy words too, because, as part of my experiment, I wanted to see how many new words I was learning in all.

From *instinktivt* and other easy words, such as *sarkastike*, "sarcastic," I learned that Norwegian did not seem to use a *c*—"no *c*'s?" I noted. Where we in English had a hard *c*, their equivalent word had a *k*.

Learning that their *k* might be our *c* gave me another clue to deciphering a word that looked strange. Easier words early in the book were *kusine*, "cousin," and *kom*, "come." Later in the book, *kalkulene*, "calculations." But a stranger-looking *k*-word was *auksjon*. When I substituted our *c* for their *k* and tried to say it, I saw what it was: "auction." Figuring out this word gave me another possible spelling hint: *sj* might always be pronounced "sh." I had first suspected this reading the *Mikke Mus* comic, when, among the vivid words for sounds that sprawled in fat letters across the frames, I encountered *splæsj* (splash) and *krasj* (crash), along with others: *splooosj*, *svooosj*, *flasj* (cameras popping), *svisj* (pursued and pursuers racing past), and the sound of a sneeze—*atsjoo*—from a character concealed among some burlap sacks of soap powder. Knowing how to pronounce *sj* might help me with other strange-looking words.

There are certainly words that look strange as written in Norwegian but that are not difficult once you give them a moment of attention, or try saying them out loud. For example, *miljø* (milieu)—which also tells you how to pronounce the *j* and that odd (to me) letter *ø*, whose name I don't yet know.

creating a grammar for myself

Fairly early on, I realized it would be helpful to devote one page of the word list to the main verbs and their principal parts as I learned them: do, make, have, see, say, know, etc. Some were quite confusing, and I still have to look at that page sometimes. For instance, "see" is *se* (pronounced "seh," I think), past tense *så* (pronounced "so"), while "say" is *si* (pronounced "see"), past tense *sa* (pronounced "sah"). See, *se*, saw, *så*; say, *si*, said, *sa*. "Give" and "go" are also confusing.

On the same page, I grouped all the *hv*-words together in an irregular box that became more and more crowded as I found more of them: *hvor, hva, hvis, hvordan, hvem, hver, hverandre, hvortil, hvilke, hvorav, hvorfor*, etc. These words that begin with *hv* are, many of them, equivalent to our English words that begin with "wh": where, what, whom, which, etc. The English and Norwegian words were closer in the past: in Old English, our "wh"-words were "hw"-words: "what" was "hwaet," etc. "Wherefore" was "hwarfore" and meant, as the Norwegian *hvorfor* means, "why." "Wherefore (why) art thou Romeo?" (when you could belong to some other family with whom my family is not feuding).

I also made a list of *d*-words: *de, dem, den, der*, etc. They mostly corresponded to our "th"-words: the, them, that, there, etc.

I learned from its function in a sentence that when a word that looked to me like an adjective had a *t* added to the end of it, as in the case of *instinktivt* , it became an adverb. Other examples would be *generelt*, "generally," and *formelt*, "formally." I made a note of that. And when I began noting how adverbs were formed, I realized that I was not only accumulating vocabulary in this new language, but also creating my own grammar.

Another piece of grammar I learned was that -*es* added onto the root of a word seemed to indicate the passive voice. *Vites* = "is known."

Once I realized I was creating my own grammar of the language, I saw the similarity between what I was doing and what an anthropological linguist does (and what some Christian missionaries used to do, and may still do) when attempting to record the language of a people whose language has not previously been studied: Living with the people, they learn the language through day-to-day immersion, devising symbols for the sounds and deriving syntactical rules.

Figuring out a grammar for yourself is an adventure. When you stumble onto the answer to a question that has been plaguing you, a problem that you haven't been able to solve, it is a satisfaction, and a relief. (Either you find it out inadvertently, by reading a book of poetry with facing translations, or you allow yourself to ask a single question of a Norwegian friend: What does *hos* mean??) It is far more satisfying to have one's own urgent question answered by learning a point of grammar than to have to memorize that point of grammar before you actively want to know it, as in conventional language instruction.

marks on the page (cont.)

When I started keeping lists on separate pieces of paper, at first I did not underline the words on the page. Maybe, out of respect for the handsome book, I wanted to keep it relatively clean of marks. That lasted only for a while, because my system of marking changed through the course of reading the book. After that first page, the only marks, for a while, were little straight lines dividing the different parts of the word to help me figure it out. And sometimes the names of some of the characters.

On June 19, at about page 80, I noted that in half an hour I wrote down fourteen words. Some of those words were repeats. When I had trouble remembering a word, and was learning it over again, I would write it down again. Sometimes the same word occurred only many pages after I had first read it, so that I had more or less forgotten it. Writing it down again also helped me remember it.

This is one of the reasons that reading without a dictionary, and writing down the words I learn, is most effective for me as a way to learn to read a language I don't know. Rereading the sentence once or more, taking the time to think about it, coming to an answer myself, and then taking the time to write it down all help me remember the new word better than if I were to look the word up and find the answer right away. More generally, I like doing things myself rather than having them done for me (by the dictionary).

I also liked using the pencil. I liked sharpening it to a fine point, and I liked being able to erase a mark cleanly and rewrite correctly on the page with the sharp point. I sharpened the pencil often, with a little rose-colored plastic "portable" sharpener. Later I used, instead, a sharpener that looked like a glass inkwell.

Sometimes, then, my penciling was a notation of how long it had taken me to read (which at that time still meant: decipher) a passage. Often, it seemed, one page took half an hour. I became so absorbed in reading this book that one, two, even three hours would go by before I could drag myself away from it. I would read it with my first cup of coffee—it became a motivation for getting up in the morning. Then I would read it while I ate my breakfast, which I would eat very slowly. At last I would have to get on with the rest of my day. But for quite a few weeks in the beginning, I also read it again in bed before going to sleep, until I decided that it was too stimulating to my brain and did not help me get a calm and deep night's sleep. So there were some days on which I read as much as ten pages, others on which I had time only for two, three, or four.

my method of figuring out the words: breaking the word into its component parts

Solstad, or the book designer, had elided all the words of the book's title on the cover. One of my strategies in trying to understand a word was to break it into its component parts, which were, in fact, its root, prefixes, and suffixes. Often, especially in the beginning, I marked only the suffix, which was the tacked-on article: *fjord\en*, the fjord; *kong\en*, the king; *provins\en*, the province; *barn\et*, the child; *munk\ene i klostr\ene*, the monks in the cloisters.

Although I knew long ago, before I began this, that in Norwegian and other Scandinavian languages the definite article (the) is usually tacked onto the end of the noun, it is still one of the hardest things for me to grasp "instinctively" or automatically. As I read along, I had to keep reminding myself, and saying "the" aloud in my head where it didn't seem to appear with the word.

I learned early on that *u* at the beginning of an adjective would probably mean "un-" or some other negating prefix, an example being: *u-tro-lige*, "un-believ-able." Once I learned what *u* meant, I could separate it with that line: *u\lykka*, "mis-fortune" (cognate, Eng. "luck); *u\tallige barn og barnebarn*, "countless [un-countable] children and grandchildren" (cognate, Eng. "tally").

Here is a good example of learning the word by separating it into its root and prefixes and suffixes: *uavhengighet = u-av-heng-ig-het* = un-from-hang-ing-ness = independence (page 325). In fact, come to think of it, you can separate the English word, "independence," into almost exactly the same elements. But because it's derived from the Latin, we don't see the root "hang" quite as clearly: in (un)- de (from) -pend (hang) -ence (-ness). Another example: *mektig* means "powerful." *Allmektighet = all-mekt-ig-het* = "all-might-i-ness" = omni-pot-ence.

mistaking the component parts

Breaking the word into its component parts was usually helpful, though occasionally I would break it the wrong way, into
parts that didn't mean anything. For instance, I looked at the
phrase *opparbeidet seg* (page 290), about the activities of one
Jørund; first I saw *op-par-beid*—even though I should have
known that since *opp* is a word ("up") it should remain intact;
par and *beid* meant nothing to me. Then I looked again and
saw it divided the right way: *opp* and *arbeidet*. The German
cognate (*Arbeit*) gave me the clue that this word had something to do with work, even though I did not fully understand
it (up-worked himself?; worked his way up in the world?;
improved his position?).

Another word that I more recently separated the wrong way
was a word in a poem by Olav H. Hauge: *snøkvelden*, which
I separated into *snøk* and *velden*. *Velden*, I thought vaguely,
could be "world" or "field," but what was a *snøk*? Then the
correct division came to me: *snø* and *kvelden*—"snow" and
"(the) evening"—an evening of snow; a snowy evening. (The
word *kveld* figures also in Solstad's novel, in a story about a
resurrected Swede.)

Another misunderstanding, late in the book, in a passage about
crossing a lake, was *sjøormen*, which I separated into *sjø-or-
men*. I knew that *sjø* was "lake," and because of the water, I
carelessly, reflexively (for the brain will sometimes be lazy and
reflexive unless one directs it firmly) interpreted *or-men* to be
"oar-men"—i.e., men employed to row people across the lake.
Not at all, of course. The correct division was *orm-en*: The noun
was *orm*, with the suffix "the." Since *orm* is worm, or snake, the
sjø-orm-en was probably some kind of water creature, no doubt
mythical.

248

the book's elusive title

Then there is that word in the title of the book that I still don't know: *uoppløselige*. I break it into its parts: *u-opp-løse-lige*, "un-*oppløselige*," "un-up-*løse*-able." I keep returning to it, but I haven't been able to figure it out yet. I have a feeling its root has something to do with solving, but that may just be because I am so occupied with trying to solve the problem of this word.

marks on the page (cont.)

Soon, I began marking something interesting Solstad was doing in the writing of the book, often with an asterisk. On page 83, for instance, I marked a spot where a paragraph break would very naturally go, but where Solstad had chosen not to make one:

"But [now let's get] back to the will left by Aslak Veinungson Fossheim."

At page 92, I started making more marks on the clean pages. First, I began putting a long diagonal line in the side margin where I had begun reading for the day, with the date below it. That day was June 20. On that day, I also noted in the margin, "description of house," since I was interested in what a house would have been like in those long-ago days of Solstad's earliest documented ancestors. Of course, I could read only part of the description:

"The main house was an old *stue* [farmhouse? house?] with a *tilbygd* [built-on?] *bu* [building, structure?] with a loft over it, and a *spon*-roof. There is reason to believe that this *tilbygget* [built-on addition?] was added when Kittil Jonson from Baugerud in Hitterdal came and moved to the farm and the farm had two families. Then one family, Ingerid Tweitan and her husband Ole Samundson, lived in the old farmhouse, while Anne Eivindsdatter and her husband and later her large flock of children lived in the added-on section w/ loft." (Here I am also translating Solstad's abbreviation of "with": *med* becomes "*m.*" Part of the charm of the book is his occasional casualness.)

At about this point, although I was not yet writing new words in the margins of the book, I began underlining the new words I was acquiring.

a break from Norwegian

On June 24, I had to suspend my reading. I was going off on a trip that would take me into July, with another, complicated trip on the horizon that would begin in late August and go into September. I would then be teaching a short course, and I had other work to catch up on. I did not resume my reading until mid-October—a break of four months. I had reached only page 120. I wondered if I would have the same interest and dedication when I returned to it. (I did.)

Berlitz: bending the rule a little

During the month of teaching, however, I had tried adding something to the project: I acquired a Berlitz language learning booklet plus CD—designed, of course, for the casual tourist in Norway, not necessarily the reader of Solstad. I did not intend to study the booklet, not at first anyway. I had bought the CD because I wanted to know more about how Norwegian sounded.

Since, however silently I read, I always hear in my head whatever I am reading, I had been hearing my own version of the Norwegian words in my head for some time now. I had become impatient with not really knowing how they were meant to sound. I therefore did not particularly mind if the sentences on the Berlitz CD all had to do with such things as airplane flights, hotel reservations, and ordering a drink, as long as I could learn to pronounce the words. And so, for the month of October, driving back from the class late in the evening, I would listen to the CD in the car. It was rather a relief, after three hours of discussing plot, character development, and sentence structure, to say over and over again in the dark, as correctly as possible: *Kan du anbefale en bra restaurant?*"—"Can you recommend a good restaurant?"

And, as I was bending my rule a little, I did learn a few words that had mystified me in Solstad's novel.

my method of figuring out the words: cognates

After separating a word into its parts, if it's a long one, I can usually figure out the prefixes and suffixes easily enough: un-, or up-, or out-, or to-; -ly, or -able, or -ness, etc. I search my mind for what may be the possible cognates of its root—the essential, core part of the word: e.g., "pend" in "independence." A cognate may give me the answer to what the word means, or at least a hint.

Here is an example of a short word and its cognate: If a *bekk* runs through a farm, a handy source of water, and if one remembers the Northern English word "beck," then one can assume this is a little stream.

Here is an example of a large sentence fragment that can be understood entirely via cognates: One of Solstad's regular "connecting" statements in his narrative is: "*Vi skal komme tilbakke til . . .* "—"We shall come to-back to . . . " (All English cognates.)

Sometimes I was able to find the cognate by removing that strange (to me) *j* that seemed to creep into certain words: remove the *j* from *kjop* and I would nearly have the Dutch *koop*, meaning "buy." Remove the *j* from *gjerne* and I would be closer to the German *gern*, "gladly."

mistaking the cognates

The word *flyttet* occurs again and again in the Telemark novel, right from the beginning of the book. A character often *flyttet* away from the place he lived, often *flyttet* from one farm to another. The word has resemblances to the English words fleet, flit, flight. So I thought *flyttet* had to mean "flew," or "fled"—the character was running away in fear of something like an enemy, or from debt. But no. I knew after a while this couldn't be right, because Solstad's characters were so constantly doing this. It simply meant "moved."

I thought the Norwegian *ferd* was related to the G. *Pferd*, "horse," but it is not: The Norwegian for "horse" is *hest*.

When I first encountered it, I thought *giftet seg* (literally "married oneself," got married)—a phrase which occurs over and over in this book, since it so much about one person marrying another—must have something to do with poison because of the G. *Gift*. But it wasn't possible, of course, that his characters kept poisoning themselves and then having children. So I realized what it meant. I later learned that the Norw. *gift* by itself also does, like the German, mean "poison." Solstad's great-grandmother, the clever little Aaste, though she is so good at her catechism, grows up to have a tongue that is rather *giftig*.

I was easily misled by some Norwegian words having to do with time. The word "time" itself, *tid*, I understood fairly soon, though its cognate in English is "tide," so the relationship is not direct. But then, to confuse things, their word for "hour" is *tim*, cognate with our "time." And their word for "while," as in "a while," is *stund*, cognate with German *Stunde*, "hour." So *to timer* is "two hours," not "two times" (or "two-timer"). And what about our "hour"? The only word resembling it that I could think of right away was *houri*, Persian for a beautiful young girl.

Then, two days after I had puzzled over "hour" and *houri*, I learned the Norwegian *ur*, meaning "watch" (as in wristwatch), which I had not known before, and of course that reminded me of a word I should have remembered, the German *Uhr*, also meaning "watch." These are both cognates of "hour."

Solstad imagines the fearsome and powerful Borgja, in his afterlife, watching his descendants from where he sits up in the heavens, in the *skyer*. *Sky,* with the indefinite plural suffix *-er*, must be "skies," or "sky," of course. Of course! But no, it is "clouds."

marks on the page (cont.)

Around page 140, soon after resuming my reading, I began occasionally writing, in the top or bottom or side margins, words I was having trouble with that were repeated regularly, like *enda*, "still," as in *enda tidligere*, "still earlier." This way, I could compare instances. For most of the book—324 pages—I had trouble with *i tillegg til*. Then at last (why after so long?) I understood it: "in addition to."

On October 25, on page 161, I changed the approach yet again: I abandoned my system of writing new words on those folded sheets of typing paper—which had been a bit of a bother, after all—and went back to what I had done the first day: I wrote my newly acquired words directly on the page. I could have done this long before, because by now I was learning fewer new words on each page—I knew a lot of the basic vocabulary, and a lot of it repeated. Writing the words directly on the page was not only easier, but much better for reviewing the new words in context and comparing them with earlier instances. There might be as few as six words on a page, or even just one, or, sometimes, as many as fifteen. Recording just one new word on a page could be good or

253

bad. It could mean I understood almost everything on the page, or it could mean any combination at all of knowing the words already and not being able to figure out any of the ones I did not know.

I loved the way the book looked, its handsome production, not only the front cover design, but the inside: the solidity of it, the quality of the paper, the blocks of text on the pages. Each time I turned a page, what I saw were two fresh, clean pages—large in format, with good heavy paper, clear, large, dark type. Then I would begin reading, and by the time I left the page, it was covered with thin, faint pencil marks—words and lines, the occasional box and the rare circle, not always neatly done. I was reading the page in an active way. I wrote as I read. The fresh, unread page was beautiful, the page once I had read it was not.

my method of figuring out the words: contexts
I learned the words from cognates and also from their context. Cognates allowed me to guess (sometimes wrongly, but usually correctly) what the word might mean. The context would confirm this, or further limit the word, narrow the possibilities of what it could be.

I realized at a certain point that this, too, followed a model from science. When I was not certain of a word, I made a guess, based on cognates, context, etc. That was my hypothesis. Finding the word again, in another context, was a test of my hypothesis. It might confirm that I was right, or disprove my hypothesis, in which case I would have to form a new hypothesis; or it might do neither, simply leave me in doubt. Eventually, another context (and maybe a little more thinking it through) would allow me to form a hypothesis that could finally be proven to be correct.

Here are two examples of how a context teaches a word, the first one easy and immediate:

1) I learned the word for "tower" as soon as I read it, from the association with Babel. Since I knew already that an s on the end of a noun, with no apostrophe, most often indicated the possessive, *Babels tarn* had to be "Babel's tower," or "Tower of Babel."

2) In one passage, Solstad lists animals a couple of times—I know these are animals because he is talking about what things are on two different farms and I recognize *hest* (horse), and (I think) *sauer* (sheep). In one of the lists he includes *gris*, which I don't recognize—it doesn't resemble any likely word I can think of—and then he remarks that the new owners of that farm will have a *gris* for Christmas (*jul*, pronounced more or less like "Yule"). I assume that the animal they will want to slaughter for Christmas is a pig, or hog, so *gris* must be pig, or hog. But I realize now that it could also be a goose. In this case, I'm not sure, but the possibilities are at least limited by the context: either hog or goose. (Not *lam*, in any case, also on one of the lists, which would probably be for Easter.)

3) Just one more example, which combines both cognate and context: *spelemann* is probably "play-man," if I choose to trust the German cognate *spiel*, meaning "play," and therefore could be a gambler, actor, or musician. But the context here decides it: this *spelemann* is in demand at weddings—so he isn't likely to be an actor or a gambler, and must be a musician.

4) I'll add a fourth example, because it shows how the scientific experimental model works, how one context leads me to a first, tentative hypothesis which is then disproven by the next context.

It is a continuation of the story of the bishop and his desecration of the ancient burial mound. The family is now plagued by misfortune and the people believe it is because of this desecration. They say: Those who dwell underground, the *underjordiske*—the *døde*, or dead— do not like to be *vanaeret*. I thought—and I knew it was a little odd—that *vanaeret* might have something to do with "exposed to the air" because of the root *aer* and its resemblance to our "aerate." I let that hypothesis stand and went on reading the story. A few pages later came another word with *aer* in it, characterizing a certain lineage as *aerverdige*—*aer*-worthy. Well, then, *aer* could not have anything to do with "air," after all. Thinking more about it, and considering the context, as well as the lineage and its worthiness, my memory was jogged enough for the German *Ehre*, "honor," to come back to me. *Aer* most probably meant "honor." Farther down the page, Solstad confirms this new hypothesis quite explicitly by saying the same thing two ways: *De underjordiske . . . skal aeres, og ikke vanaeres.* The underground-dwellers [i.e., the dead] . . . shall be honored, and not dishonored."

Sometimes a mysterious word appears in a context in which it is the only missing part in the drama of the sentence—and the story. For instance, well on in the book, one character always wanders the roads carrying a *ljå*. Solstad tells the reader this more than once. Each time he repeats it, I don't know what a *ljå* is. I imagine, and imagine, this character on the roads with a *ljå*, but can't figure out what. How much did it change the experience of reading those passages not to know what he was carrying?

Much later, I find the missing piece of the image in a poem I am reading, with facing translations in English. I am cheating a little, or, rather, changing the rules. The change in the rules is that if a helpful book comes my way *by chance* (in this case, the book of poems was a gift from a Norwegian friend), I am allowed to look at it and be helped by it. The book was by the very well-known (in Norway) and much-quoted twentieth-century poet Olav H. Hauge, who lived all his life in the same place, tending an orchard on his small farm. A *ljå* is a scythe. This surprises me, since to me the word "scythe" looks almost Norwegian—the word for it should be almost the same, I think (somewhat indignantly). But in any case, because of my earlier struggle, and because of the vividly described character who is carrying it, I won't forget what a *ljå* is.

my method: rereading

I also discovered how important rereading was. It was a rule from the very beginning that I couldn't simply skip over a sentence and go on, but had to work on it until I either understood or saw that I could not. So unless I did understand it right away, which happened more often as I continued to read the book, I would have to reread the sentence. The first reading of a word or sentence might reveal nothing at all, and leave me mystified. But with just the small increase in familiarity that came from reading it a second time, the words would begin to suggest themselves. I wondered what happened in the brain between the first and the second reading.

marks on the page (cont.)

Eventually I added a little box around the date so that I could quickly find the days as I leafed through the pages.

I would occasionally write the word's meaning directly above the word, and continued to do this to the end of the book, especially when the word was one that could mean several things. One of the tricky ones was *som*, which could mean "who" or "which," but also "as." This was not meant to be a note that I would return to later, but was an active way of reading, an aid to comprehending as I went along.

I sometimes underlined a phrase of two or more words so that I would read it as such. Later I began collecting phrases, such as

257

mer enn nok, "more than enough," writing them on a blank page in the back of the book.

In the top and bottom margins, I'd sometimes write the names of ancestors who were being talked about, if they were important or if theirs was an interesting continuing story, and sometimes also the topic of a story (e.g. "extravagant Margit" or "Erik Sakeson kills himself" or "murder at a wedding feast" or "Ole Halvejord and his two artificial hands"). In the side margin, sometimes, with the name of an ancestor, I added birth dates, and children, if I wanted to keep track. But I'm not sure I wanted to keep track—maybe this was simply a reflexive response to feeling overwhelmed by the enormous cast of characters.

(One of the interesting stories: Ole Hovdejord, alone and unarmed, comes unexpectedly face-to-face with a bitter enemy, one Kaptein Nägler, and loses his right hand to the sword of the captain's bodyguard. Ole runs to the nearest smithy (*smid*), which lies in the valley next to Hitterdal Church, and sticks his arm stump into the glowing embers to stanch the blood. Long afterward, he has two artificial hands made for himself, one of silver (*sølv*), for Sundays and holy days, and one of iron (*jern*), for everyday use.)

(We will never know anything more about Ole Hovdejord, because that is the way it is with stories that come from public records, from a limited collection of primary documents, and that are not supplemented, or not much, by the writer's imagination.)

what I did not do enough of
I simply didn't review my word lists enough, or copy them often enough into my "master" word list—the alphabetical "Norwegian Word List" that I at some point began compiling in a computer

file. Regular reviewing—rereading and reviewing—would have helped my comprehension. I was too impatient.

Also, I could have compiled a list of problem words and where they could be found, so that I could regularly compare contexts and figure them out.

(For instance, I see that on page 293 I have figured out that *ledd* means "generation," but not even ten pages later, on page 302, I seem to have forgotten all about that, and think that *ledd* means "layer." Of course, on some days I must have been tired or for some other reason not been thinking clearly.)

I should have copied new words into my Norwegian Word List at the end of every day's session of reading, so that I did not have to learn them all over again.

some of the words, phrases, and expressions I encountered
Og, which means "and," is a strange word. It is not unlike the Dutch *ook*, or the German *auch*, both of which mean "also." But how did it come to mean "and," whereas the Germans have *und*, so much closer to our word?

What about the dropped *w* in their *ord*, "word"—or is it that we added the *w*? There is another case of it: *orm* for "snake," like our "worm" but without the *w*. I look up both etymologies: Back in the proto-Germanic, where both have their source, the *w* was present.

Some words I became quite fond of, without knowing why: *tvil*, for "doubt." The sound, the modesty? Did it remind me of the material twill?

Another pair I liked, so short, so economical, so cheerful: *hit*, *dit*—meaning hither, thither. This pair made me think again about the h-, th-, wh- sets in English, something I always like to think about: The most common set is here, there, where—these words we use all the time. Another is hence, thence, whence—of this set, we use "hence" quite often, but less often the other two; and all three have a slightly precious sound to them now. And the last (or is there another?): hither, thither, whither. These we never, or very rarely, use, except in "hitherto"—even more precious. Oh, there is a fourth, or part of a fourth: therefore, wherefore. *That* and *what* are probably part of another set, the third member of which is not *hat*. Now that I go on thinking about them, I remember some combined forms: thereupon, whereupon; whereof (the Norwegian equivalent of which is *hvorav*); heretofore; thereafter, hereafter; herein, therein, wherein.

The Norwegian for "throw" is *kaste*, which of course is cognate with our "cast." And our "cast" was once more commonly used than it is now. "Cast" has declined in use, certainly in casual use to mean "throw." Although *kaste* and "cast" share a very early source, "throw" looks to me like a very old word, too. I look up the answers—"cast" comes from Old Norse *kasta*, to throw; "throw" comes from Old English *thrawan*, to twist, or turn. That's a surprise—early on, then, the idea of "throw" had, it seems, an element of twisting in it; to throw was to cast with a twist.

Sometimes a Norwegian expression that is the same as one in English will yield a few new words: For instance, on page 115, in a passage describing the extreme poverty of one Johannes who marries above his station (a priest's daughter), I was pleased to come upon *blakk som en kirkerotte*. I knew *kirke* (Sc. kirk), so it wasn't hard to guess "poor as a churchmouse"—or maybe *rotte* is "rat," and their expression is slightly different. On page 134, reading the story of Torhild, the hardworking widow who is so fond of her pipeful of tobacco, I encounter the same expression as ours: she *røyker som en skorstein*—"smokes like a chimney."

Abbreviations: These can be a challenge. Again, context helps. If Solstad is about to give some examples of something, and precedes his remarks by *f.eks.*, I can guess that this is short for *for eksempel*. I tend to pronounce it, in my head, with a certain pleasure: "fecks." Others, harder, are *dvs.* = *det vil si* = "that will say" = "in other words"; and *bl.a.* = *blant annen* = "among others." And there were two that I think he made up. Two men he was discussing had the same names. Tired of writing out "the older" and "the younger," he abbreviated them to "*d.e.*" and "*d.y.*"

Sometimes—on page 356, for instance— he describes what he means by a word and thus defines it for me. I was in doubt about the word *venner*, though I had some guesses. These *venner* acted as godparents to the child of a young couple. Then he went on to describe who they might have been: "not relatives, either on Anlaug's or on Anders's side, but *venner*, people they could *stole* on [count on?], without being in the same family, we must assume . . . people they had met, often married couples in the same generation, through the fact that they were, like them, *leilendinger* [occupiers of rented property?] and *husmenn* [farm managers?]." *Venner* = friends.

In other cases, he will say the same thing two ways, and thus allow me to learn a new word. A clear and simple example of this is his introduction of the word *oldemor* on page 130: *min mormor Birgithe Andersdatters mor, min oldemor*—"my grandmother Birgithe Andersdatter's mother, my great-grandmother." Farther along in the same sentence, when this *oldemor* marries, I learn the word *oldefar*. Later in the book, in the same way, I learn the perky-sounding term for yet one further generation back: *tippoldemor* for great-great-grandmother.

Another example of this is the word *eneste,* or "only one," which is clearly "taught" in the following sentence, the second part of which in effect repeats or enlarges upon the first: "Halvor Johannesson did not marry again; his marriage as a young man, aged twenty, to a widow who was more than forty years older than he, remained his *eneste*."

speaking of Halvor Johannesson: a digression about the names in the book

The ancestors, or characters, in Solstad's book are always at some point identified by their full names, and they always have three—quite rarely, they have four, some people having two "first" names. There is the given name, for example Halvor, the choice of which is ruled by several principles which I won't go into, except to say two things: Solstad was sometimes able to use those rules to make useful deductions about relationships and lineage from studying a first name; and in keeping with a curious custom, the first son born to a widow who remarried would generally be named after her previous husband.

The middle name is always "son of" or "daughter of" plus the father's name. This allows a genealogist to make a good guess as to who the male parent was.

The last name was the name of the place where the person was born or where he or she now lived. So, interestingly, though the first and middle names usually did not change during a lifetime, the last name might change if the person moved, and might even change more than once if a person moved several times. This gives the genealogist clues as to where the person was living at the time of a baptism or marriage, or, in some cases, with which place a person chose to identify him- or herself.

Thus, these three-part names identified individuals quite thoroughly, in three different ways.

Last names became fixed in at least one family line, Solstad says, in the second half of the nineteenth century. Why then? Why not before, and why not after? What also changed at about that time was that middle names might be given for no other reason than that the parents liked them, as happens nowadays in our country.

difficulties

Certain phrases I stumbled over every time, because they were "counterintuitive": one was *en eller annen*. I figured out that it meant "one or another," but the fact that *en* meant "one" or "a" and *eller* was a longer word meant that I kept thinking, first, that it meant "an *eller*," an *eller* being some kind of thing. Or I thought *eller* was an adjective modifying *annen*: "an *eller* sort of *annen*." Right up to the end of the book, I stumbled over that, even though I knew it.

In June, I thought *skiftet* meant "funeral." But in November, I decided it meant something like "will," though by the end of the book I still wasn't sure what it meant, because there were contexts in which both "funeral" and "will" made sense, but others in which neither of them did. Maybe the word had more than one meaning. In one story, for instance, "*skiftet ut*" was a fate about to be suffered by a couple of horses that were included in the farm bought by the hardworking Peder, or Per, Håkonsson Moen, and were probably too old to continue pulling the plow and the carriage; they would probably be "traded out"—in other words, gotten rid of. Later still, I decided that one meaning of *skifte* had to be "change."

I tended to keep mixing up pairs of words that looked somewhat alike, such as, at first, *også* and *altså*, later *enda* and *ennå*, *våre* and *være*, *enke* and *ekte*, *vist* and *visst*, *skjedde* and *skjebne*, *jul* (Christmas) and *juli* (July), *nettopp* and *neppe*, and *må, mål, måle, mat, måte, måten, måtte*. To a Norwegian, these words are miles apart in meaning, perhaps, and it's laughable to mix them up. But I mix them up because, after all, the first thing you encounter, looking at a page of unfamiliar language, is not the meaning but the appearance of the words, the way they look.

Trying to learn, or to be sure of, the word *mat*, which I think means "meal"—or "food"—as I read my way into the beginning of another book of Solstad's, an earlier novel called *Armand V.: fotnoter til en uutgravd roman* (*Armand V.: Footnotes to an Unexcavated Novel*), I compare the *mat* in a student cafeteria with the *mat* in the Telemark novel's story of the wandering (and fugitive) Swede—the *kvelds-mat(en)* at which he dropped dead—to make sure I'm not mixing this word up with another of those *m*-words. (There is also, in another story, *mat* and *drikke* flowing freely at a wedding feast in the year 1684 that ends in a fatal stabbing.)

The story of the fugitive comes late in the novel: A Swedish miner who is on the run because of a murder he has committed is in the home of strangers, eating his evening meal (*kvelds-maten*), when he drops dead. They lay him out in the *koven* (I'm not sure what that is). The next day, his wife finds her way to the house, asks if they have seen a wandering Swede, hears the news, and shrieks. At the sound of her cry, her husband comes back to life and appears in the doorway.

264

As you struggle to learn something difficult, you are constantly aware of the limits of your brain's strength, agility, alertness, etc. You look at a word—*ser*, for instance— and you know you know it, but you can't recall it. Where is its meaning in your brain, and where are you in your brain, as you try to find that meaning? It comes to you after a while, or you come to it, somewhere traveling through your brain. In fact, it means "see."

Sometimes I "get" the word, I know what it means, but a perceptible few seconds go by before the equivalent English word comes to me (in the latest case, the word happened to be "confirm"). I experience this as quite physical when it happens: The understanding is there, somewhere nearby in my brain, I am in touch with it, but it is still unarticulated, still formless or inchoate; then a connection is made, and the English word appears.

It took me quite a long time to realize that *andre* meant more than just "other" or "another" (G. *andere*), as in *ene etter den andre*, "one after another." It could not mean "other" in the sentence "She was his other wife"—since the early Norwegians were not polygamous. Eventually, I understood that it could also mean "second." Another example:

Hun var 47 år. Hun ventet på sin andre ektemann. På mannen.

Translation: She was forty-seven years old. She was waiting for her second husband. For a husband.

This was a nice little story about a widow and a carpenter. A widow hires an itinerant carpenter, Ole Olson, to build something for her on her farm. He's there several days, does good work, and she evidently takes a liking to him. When the job is done and the time comes for him to leave, she packs him a substantial lunch to take with him. He goes on his way. When, after an hour or so, he is hungry and stops in a clearing in the woods to see what she has packed for him, he finds, gleaming behind the sausages and other food, the key to the *stabbur* (which I first thought meant "cupboard," then "storeroom"). He understands the message, turns around and rides back, and she is standing there waiting for him. They marry, etc. This was in the year 1678.

But, says Solstad, the real sensation (*sensasjonen*) happens two years later, when the hitherto childless forty-nine-year-old gives birth for the first time. Almost a virgin birth, he nearly said—he says—but kept it to himself (he says). (And this is another interesting moment in his approach to the form of the narrative: Solstad denies saying something that he has in fact just said.)

I am sometimes slowed down by the French words in my head, like *vide*, "empty," when I try to understand *utvidt*, *ut-vidt*. It is not "emptied out," but "extended" (out + widened).

It is hard for me not to read *det* as always meaning "that"—and often enough it does. Many of Solstad's sentences begin with *Det er*. *Er* means (conveniently) both "is" and "are." So I would like to read, always, *det er* as "That is," or "It is." But *det* also means "there," and often enough Solstad is saying "There are." As in English, one word can have several meanings, and one phrase can have several meanings. But whereas I take this for granted in English and am completely used to it, it surprises and frustrates me when I am trying to learn a new language.

For means "for," which is easy enough. But it also—when it wants to—means "too." *Få* means "have," but it can also mean "few."

Something I learn from a movie subtitle about the word *penger*: In the Telemark novel, since so many of the historical records concern financial transactions, I encounter the word *penger* (*peng* + the suffix *-er*, the indefinite plural) over and over, and I always understand it as "coins" rather than what it also is: "money." I.e., in the contexts in which it appears—sales of property, wills, etc.—I read it as something concrete, whereas the more usual translation would be something I see as more abstract—"money."

I do not know this until I am watching a Norwegian movie with subtitles. A character says "*penger*" and the subtitle reads "money." (Here, by watching this movie and reading the subtitles, I am again bending or modifying just a little my "no-help" rules.)

In all this reading and studying, I am also watching how the brain works— or, sometimes, doesn't work. My brain opted for the concrete, coins, over the abstract, money.

what the words I learned told me about English

The revelations were not only about Norwegian, but also about the roots it shares with English. From reading this book, and from learning some Norwegian, my English words became at once stranger and richer.

When I learned *svar*, I glimpsed the source of our "an-swer." I knew "neighbor" was related to "nigh," or "near"; when I learned that the Norwegian *bor* meant "dwell," I could see "neigh-bor" for what it is: one who (for better or worse) lives nearby.

I learn the Norwegian word for "bells": *klokker*. I say to myself: That looks so much like the English "clock"! And the German for "bells" is rather similar—*Glocken*. Did our English "clock" once upon a time mean "bell"? And could that have been because we told the time from listening to the church bells? And what about the nautical way of identifying the time: eight bells, etc.? I haven't yet put it all together.

I learned, or relearned, *klokker* in the story of Erik Sakeson's suicide, since the church bells (*kirkeklokker*) rang loudly at his funeral, and were heard by a woman imprisoned on the other side of a mountain, and the sound of the church bells gave her hope, though I am not sure why (since some words were missing for me) or why she was imprisoned.

progress
page 78

I noted on June 15 that as I read on in the book, I would turn back to the first page now and then, to see if I understood more. By about page 78, I could read the whole of that first page, missing only a few words.

page 226
By page 226, I could sometimes read two pages in half an hour.

page 346
By page 346 (eighty pages from the end), I could read many sentences "fluently" without stumbling. True enough (*riktig nok*), there were almost always a few words I could not figure out. But more and more rarely did I find myself caught for a moment in a small thicket of impenetrable language.

page 426
On January 12, 2015, I finished the book.

(But in late January, unable to break my habit, I began another novel by Solstad called *Armand V.*, this one consisting of footnotes to a nonexistent novel. I had not planned to read it, but one morning I simply opened it out of curiosity and read the first page. Then I went on.)

marks on the page (cont.): characteristics of Solstad's writing
In addition to marking names of characters (from the beginning), dates of events (starting halfway through the book), words I learned (starting on page 161), material that interested me (now and then, from the beginning), along with, starting on page 92, the date of that day's reading, I also noted the following:

p. 129, a particular sentence rhythm of Solstad's;

p. 132, how he tells a story;

p. 142, an exclamation of his;

p. 145, a comment about what we know about the characters' lives versus what they themselves know;

p. 151, a shift in his narrative mode as he explains something in a different way;

and, on succeeding pages, to the end of the book: his changes of pace; variation of short, very short, long, and very long sentences; use of refrains; inclusion of the reader with the word "our"; occasional English words; specificity; speculations; invitations down false trails; rare information about the larger historical context; frustration that he can't write something if he does not know for certain that it is true; a single account of visiting an ancestral site for his research; his resolve not to investigate something, a thing which he decided "shall," like so much else, "remain lying untold in darkness."

One recurring feature of his style was his use of repetition—of facts, epithets, opening phrases purely for the rhythm of the sentence ("Fortunate were those . . . Fortunate were those . . . "). For me, this repetition became a truly lyrical sort of drill of the words and phrases I was learning, but I was also more and more aware, as I struggled less with the language, of its rhetorical beauty.

thinking as I was reading

I realized, now and then, that because my attention was mostly on learning the language, I was not reading the book with the wider, and deeper, and more thoughtful attention with which I would have read it in English: I was not absorbing it effortlessly while at the same time thinking about it, as I would have been doing in English. Because my brain was so busy trying to understand it in the most basic way, I did not tend to remember much from page to page.

I was not trying to keep track of the family lines, or the relationships. I was not trying to remember the characters, especially since, usually, we would be moving on and leaving them behind quite soon. Although I was very interested in it, and planned to think about it later, I was only occasionally thinking about the form of Solstad's novel: what he was doing, why he was doing it, what effect it had.

But, increasingly, I did stop to think about it, and now that I've read it, I can think more.

some ways in which his book is different from a conventional novel

From the beginning, I was curious about whether this book would change as it went on, and also whether it would eventually feel to me like a novel. But what interested me most, at first, was the ways in which it was not like a conventional novel.

For one thing, it was not the author, but fate, that determined the plot lines. Solstad then decided in what order to organize and narrate them, and how to present them. Solstad refused to fictionalize, tempted though he sometimes was. (Page 392: "I burn to tell about that . . . ") The principal material in the book seems to have been the information collected by his cousin's son. Solstad set himself the challenge of writing a "novel" which was entirely nonfiction.

So, then, all the premises shift concerning what is dramatically or narratively interesting or important: Because so much is unknown to Solstad himself, or to anyone, because the plot turns may happen quite unexpectedly, with no forewarning, we learn to have no expectations. And these sudden turns of event can't be seen as artistically arbitrary or gratuitous, because we know they did happen.

Solstad is able to conjure up a character's life working only with the traces left behind: If a child was five when his mother remarried, and seven when his mother died, Solstad can imagine that these were difficult years for the child. He can state this plainly, and the child comes to life dramatically. Reading this book confirmed for me that it is possible to create dramatic interest using just the few "dry" facts at hand, combined with the author's distinct voice and style.

I find it very affecting to be given a fragment of a story and know it is true. At the same time as the meanings of the words I am reading become clear, or remain obscure, the characters in the book appear suddenly, and disappear just as suddenly. But while they are here, they are fully present, and all the more striking because the rest of their lives "must remain lying untold hidden in darkness," as Solstad says.

There was something eerie about the events of the book, because they seemed to have been fated to happen just as they did happen—but fated only in retrospect. For instance, there is the case of the German ancestor who enters on page 367. We meet him as he is crossing a lake on his way to church on the Sunday following Trinity Sunday. But no sooner do we welcome him into the story, prepare to remember him, to see him developed, to witness the ups and downs of his life, than, in the next sentence, he falls overboard (the words are hard to mistake: *faller over bord*), drowns, and disappears forever—from his own life, from future historical records, and, quite soon, from this story.

Because this man, Lauritz Türninger, drowned, and because the officials recorded this, we know his name and what he was doing on that particular day. And when he died, he left behind a son, so that—not at the moment he drowned, but in time, after his children had children, and after those children in turn produced further generations—he came to be an ancestor of Solstad's.

Or, because a boundary was revised in 1887, and because this boundary change was recorded, and certain families were living in the vicinity of the change, and their names were recorded, we know what we otherwise would not have known—where the little foster child Bergit, eleven years old, was living in the year 1887, this child who was not yet, in that year, but would grow up to become, Solstad's grandmother.

a recurring theme: these are his ancestors; and the chance events that result in a person's becoming his ancestor

I sometimes forget for a while that these are his ancestors. Then he reminds me not only of that, but of the strangeness of how haphazard it all is: for instance, at the top of page 142, how a financial calculation on the part of one man—a father choosing a suitable husband for each of his daughters—causes another man (and thus, with him, a whole widely branching line of previous generations) to become part of Solstad's own lineage.

272

the plot of Solstad's own investigations: how he discovers what he knows

There are the story lines of the various characters he tells us about; but there is also another story line that appears and disappears—the story of his own investigations, what he is able to find out and what he is not able to find out, what he guesses or assumes or doubts.

What I learn from this is something I had already suspected: how interesting the tale of the investigation itself can be. It solves another problem I had been facing in my own project: that the investigation which I would carry out, with all the drama of its puzzles and solutions, hints and discoveries, would be more engrossing than any neat presentation of the results in the eventual book. Now I see that the investigation itself should be written into the book.

another story line, one that doesn't appear very often: the shaping of this book

Another story line consists of Solstad's thoughts and plans about how to shape the novel itself, what to include when and where—it arises every so often, and when it does, it brings me as reader actively into partnership with him. I witness him deliberate on how he will shape this novel I am reading.

bare facts relieved not only by exclamations and observations, but by brief dramatic stories

Solstad offers detailed facts about births, deaths, marriages, and property transactions for many pages at a time, unrelieved by any drama, but I tolerate it, partly because of the ongoing excitement of learning the language, but also because I sense the animating spark of Solstad's strong emotion and personality, and because I am moved by the very style of the writing, which I can perceive even from the beginning, when I do not understand many words.

Can I, too, be exact and factual, detailed and meticulous, about fairly dry data throughout certain passages of the book I have in mind, and will a reader tolerate that? (Can I, come to think of it, be a little too detailed at certain points in this present essay, about words that were exciting for me to learn but are perhaps not exciting for a reader to hear about, and can I perhaps go on for too long and yet rescue myself with certain other passages?)

Because so much of the text is in this sense "dry," the moments in which there is imagery or a sustained dramatic narrative come like bursts of color into the novel. There is, for instance, the story of "Pipe-Torhild," who at the age of twenty-seven was left a widow with a two-year-old son, and who was remembered in later years for two things—her industry and the fact that she smoked a pipe. She managed two farms on her own, and according to the stories people told, she would wake up in the morning on one farm and milk the *dyra* (animals) there before walking the long distance to the other, where she went out into the fields and scythed the day's portion of grain before walking back to the first farm and doing the evening chores. This was in 1680.

Or the story of "the great (or fearsome)" Halvor Borgja hanging his red hat in the window to deceive his workers, and the decline in the fortunes of his family in later years, down upon which Solstad wishes Borgja could have gazed from up among the *skyer*.

the end of Solstad's book—and the reaching back over the generations

Close to the end of the book, on page 401, Solstad recounts the one memory his mother had of her grandfather. And this single vivid memory—the only memory she has of him—is enough to bring him to life, for Solstad and thus, in turn, for me as reader. Of his great-grandfather, he says, he has this one "wholly concrete picture," the oldest he has of any of his ancestors.

"My mother sees her old grandfather go *målbevisst* away to a barrel with *sild* that stands *gjemt* under a roof of *skrot* in the *fjøset*, or some such. She sees the old man lift the barrel, with a strength-*anstrengelse*, and drink from it. She sees him set it down and turn his face directly towards her, the little nine-year-old granddaughter. She sees that the *silde*-fat is running down his face. Just that. That is what she remembers. And that is the picture of the ancestors. Of my great-grandfather, and all his ancestors."

the end of the book—and the importance of detail

The memory that Solstad's mother had of her grandfather is the sort of ordinary memory we have in great numbers in our minds—of small incidents and encounters, odd and inconsequential. It doesn't matter that the moment was undramatic, even completely inconsequential. In fact, that may make it all the more effective, because the memory is taken from ordinary, everyday life and thus makes that everyday life seem very present, very close. What matters is that it is concrete, and detailed, and thus vivid—that one moment seems to prove that Solstad's great-grandfather existed, in flesh and blood.

the end of the book—flesh and blood

Solstad, after starting with the remote ancestors in 1591, at the end of the book comes all the way down to his grandmother (married in 1896), with whom he spends time when he is a child. He sees her in person, and listens to her talk, and watches her. It is satisfying to us, the readers, after having witnessed so many of his ancestors from afar, in little fragments, to be in the presence of a flesh-and-blood forebear of his. The little girl who emerged from the mists of the past through her birth date and the facts of the place where she lived, just as so many other ancestors of Solstad's emerged for a moment, then slipped back into obscurity, now stays in the present, remains visible, sits by the window and watches the highway.

is the book a novel?

In my effort simply to read it and find out what was in it, for a long time I put aside the larger question of whether I would consider this book a novel. Or rather, I did ask the question now and then, but did not concentrate very hard on it. Actually, I did sometimes concentrate hard on it, but I could not arrive at a definition of a novel that would include this one, until I did arrive at such a definition but was left a little unsatisfied by it.

It is already an unusual book. For a novel, it is even more unusual.

The fact that Dag Solstad chose to call this a novel has been much discussed in Norway. About half the critics admired the book and its unique project, and the book was nominated for several important prizes. The other half were provoked or bored, and could not see how this could be called a novel—along came that comparison to a telephone directory. It also added fuel to the larger debate in Norway about what a novel is or can be.

The debate must already have been well under way after the publication of Karl Ove Knausgaard's long autobiographical novel. That novel is not as purely factual as Solstad's. But it does claim not to have invented anything—all of its content, making allowances for undependable memory, is taken from Knausgaard's own life. If we think a novel needs to include stories, that one certainly does, and it is also one larger continuous story—as, really, the Solstad Telemark novel is, too.

Apparently Solstad and his editor did not talk about the question of genre. Nor, apparently, did those in the publishing house discuss it among themselves. They simply saw the book as truly original and groundbreaking. It has its many devoted fans. One Norwegian friend said she was completely obsessed by it last winter—she read it all and was sad to finish it. Readers in Norway feel that the book is written in Solstad's characteristic style, even if the material is unusual. My Norwegian friend feels that the way Solstad sequences the facts and the way he handles them, along with his interjections and the rhythms of his prose, make it very much a novel of his.

I mentioned the novel to an editor here (American), and he said he had heard Solstad read from it last fall and there was something mesmerizing about the language. About the question of whether it is a novel, he said that the project itself seemed like an interesting challenge: how to narrate factually and yet get "the lift of fiction." After he said this, I thought about the word "lift," since it seemed he was pointing out something that fiction might give and that nonfiction might not give. I would interpret "lift" to mean a sort of transcendence: we are lifted out of our lives, imaginatively, into another realm, perhaps a realm full of surprises, either factual surprises, or stylistic ones, or emotional ones. Perhaps Solstad's "novelistic" treatment of his material, and his characteristic stylistic turns, and his injection of his own passion, give it, in the end, the "lift" of fiction.

I've been told that Solstad does not see himself as a historian, but a novelist. And this leads, as several paths lead, to what I feel, for now anyway, is one definition by which this book could be seen as a novel. It is that if an author feels, and declares, that his or her book is a novel, then that is enough to define it as a novel—of some sort. To qualify that a little: If an author truly sees and intends his or her book as a novel, then it is some variety of novel, and it is up to the reader, or critic, to figure out in what way it can be seen as a novel. I believe this, for the time being anyway.

other thoughts as I read

Was my Solstad-Norwegian language project a misguided one? Should I not have been doing it? Did I not have other things I had planned to do? What things will I now never do because I did this? But, on the other hand: Which projects are a "waste of time" anyway? The projects one had not planned to do? But does such a thing as a waste of one's time even exist? Or, in a larger sense: In the end, is not everything in one's life equal—whether washing a floor, figuring out a page of Norwegian, writing something one had promised to write, or talking to a neighbor for an hour on a winter afternoon about the risks involved in continuing to take certain medications?

The homeliest thought: I see, as I do this, how doing a little each day, if it is done regularly, adds up to a lot. (There are many mottoes to this effect.)

I am still trying to figure out whether a beginner in a language understands a surprising amount, considering she knew so little a year ago, or whether she understands vastly little. Or maybe, contradictorily, the answer must be: both. In other words, I'm surprised that with an accumulation of a quantity of fairly basic vocabulary, including those so-important, so-revealing prefixes and suffixes, I can read and understand so much of not only the Telemark novel by now, but also the other Solstad novel I am reading, *Armand V.* But on the other hand, I'm aware of how much I am missing, on every level, and must necessarily miss, without years of study and a wide range of reading, and, preferably, some time living in Norway and conversing with Norwegians.

Now that I've read the Telemark novel, if I were to try to have a conversation in Norwegian, my vocabulary and idioms, and my syntax too, would be almost entirely limited to what I know from this one book. Aside from whatever few scraps have remained in my head from last year's *Mikke Mus* and *Mo i mørket,* I wouldn't know anything beyond this material and this way of speaking about it, or this way of speaking, period. Conversing with a Norwegian, I could say that my son has the strength of a bear—*har krefter som en bjørn*—as Solstad says of the hardworking Peder Moen, *hammermester* and farmer, or that my husband had plowed a field with his grandfather behind two horses (which he did, as a child). But I could not talk about the Internet, or airplane travel, high-rise buildings, streetcars, or many other things.

It also occurred to me, as I bent over my thin pencil scratches on the handsome pages of the book, that we read selfishly—and we read in whatever way we choose. The author has no say in how we approach the book and what we do with it. He controls his creation while he creates it, but then, when it is published, he must abandon control of it. In this case, for example, Solstad might object to my reading his book without understanding all of it. He might also object to my marking every page with my own discoveries and ideas. He might object to my being just as interested in learning the language as I am in the book itself and how he has conceived and written it. He might object to my telling some of the most dramatic stories here in this essay, out of context. And more.

A somewhat desolate thought, though a familiar one, and inflected by resignation: Because most publishers these days are usually reluctant to publish a book that may not sell in great numbers, the most innovative and adventurous—and therefore "difficult" to read and difficult to sell—contemporary literature, including Solstad's Telemark novel, may never appear in English. So the fiction writers of the world who read only English, or only English as their second language, but no other foreign language, such as Norwegian (or Icelandic, or Faroese), will be denied the vital stimulation of reading the most avant-garde work of many, many other cultures. And there are only so many languages we will have the time to try to learn in order to read the books that will not be translated into our own language.

I'm thinking about words all the time as I continue this project. Words on their own. Words in sentences. The histories and changing meanings of words. I occasionally return to some very basic, mathematical thoughts: There are only so many letters in our Roman alphabet. It is then by the power of the math—the infinite (or not strictly infinite, but huge) number of combinations of letters—that we have so many words. But then, further expanding the number of possibilities, truly to infinity, one word (one combination of letters) can have multiple meanings. Further multiplying the number of meanings, even within one given dictionary definition of a word, is the effect of its context, both immediate and larger, which can endow it with, again, an infinite number of subtly differing shades of meaning. Further enriching the single word, within and beyond its contexts, is one's own personal associations with it, either from one's reading or from one's life experiences.

And even in one's own native language, there are a great many words, meanings, and shades of meaning that one simply doesn't know and may never encounter. I copied out these two words recently, which I did not know and still have not looked up, from an American novel of the twentieth century: "temulent" and "succedaneum."

Contributor Notes

FATIN ABBAS was born in Khartoum, Sudan, and attended university in the United Kingdom and the United States. She is a graduate of the Hunter College MFA Program in Creative Writing.

TAHMIMA ANAM is the author of two novels: *A Golden Age*, which was awarded the Commonwealth Writers' Prize for Best First Book, and *The Good Muslim*. In 2013 she was selected as one of Granta's Best of Young British Novelists. She lives in London with her family.

RAHUL BERY, a secondary school teacher and translator of Spanish and Portuguese, is based in Cardiff, Wales. He has translated essays and stories by Daniel Galera, César Aira, and Enrique Vila-Matas.

GARNETTE CADOGAN has written about culture and the arts for various publications. He is currently at work on a book on walking and is slowly at work on a book on rock-reggae musician Bob Marley. He lives in New York City.

ANNE CARSON was born in Canada and teaches ancient Greek for a living.

LYDIA DAVIS is the author, most recently, of the story collection *Can't and Won't* (Farrar, Straus and Giroux, 2014) and a new version of the

1898 children's classic *Bob, Son of Battle: The Last Gray Dog of Kenmuir*, by Alfred Ollivant (NYRB, 2014). She is also a translator of French and other languages; her most recent translations include a new version of Gustave Flaubert's *Madame Bovary* (Viking Penguin, 2010) and the very short stories of the Dutch writer A. L. Snijders. She lives in upstate New York.

DAVE EGGERS is the author of many books, including *The Circle* and *A Hologram for the King*. He is the cofounder of 826 National, a network of writing and tutoring centers. He is also the cofounder of Voice of Witness and ScholarMatch, a college access organization serving low-income students around the United States.

LOUISE ERDRICH is the author of fourteen novels as well as volumes of poetry, short stories, children's books, and a memoir of early motherhood. Her novel *Love Medicine* won the National Book Critics Circle Award. *The Last Report on the Miracles at Little No Horse* was a finalist for the National Book Award, and *The Plague of Doves* won the Anisfield-Wolf Book Award and was a finalist for the Pulitzer Prize. In 2012, *The Round House* won the National Book Award for Fiction. Louise Erdrich lives in Minnesota and is the owner of Birchbark Books, an independent bookstore.

DANIEL GALERA is a Brazilian writer and translator. He was born in Sao Paolo, but lives in Porto Alegre, where he has spent most of his life. He has published four highly acclaimed novels in Brazil, the latest of which, *Blood-Drenched Beard*, was released in the United States in 2015. In 2012, *Granta* named Galera one of the Best Young Brazilian Novelists.

TED GOOSSEN is a professor at York University in Toronto, Canada, specializing in modern and contemporary Japanese literature. He has translated a number of Japanese writers, including Naoya Shiga, Masuji Ibuse, and Haruki Murakami.

ALEKSANDAR HEMON was born in 1964, in Sarajevo, Bosnia and Herzegovina. He began writing fiction in English in 1995 and was awarded a "genius grant" from the MacArthur Foundation in 2004. He is the author of *The Question of Bruno*, *Nowhere Man*, *The Lazarus Project*, and *Love and Obstacles*. His collection of autobiographical essays, *The Book of My Lives*, was published by Farrar, Straus and Giroux in March 2013. His latest novel is *The Making of Zombie Wars*, and this fall he will publish *Behind the Glass Wall*, a nonfiction chronicle of the United Nations. He lives in Chicago with his wife and two daughters.

BEN HUFF is an Alaska-based portrait and landscape photographer.

ISHION HUTCHINSON was born in Port Antonio, Jamaica. His poetry collection, *Far District: Poems*, won the PEN/Joyce Osterweil Award. Other honors include a Whiting Writers' Award and the Academy of American Poets' Larry Levis Prize. He teaches at Cornell University.

FADY JOUDAH is a poet, translator, and physician, in Houston, Texas. His poetry has received the Yale Series prize and a Guggenheim fellowship. *Textu* is his most recent poetry collection, from Copper Canyon Press.

ETGAR KERET was born in Ramat Gan and lives in Tel Aviv. A recipient of France's Chevalier de l'Ordre des Arts et des Lettres, he is a lecturer at Ben-Gurion University of the Negev and author of five short story collections and, most recently, *The Seven Good Years: A Memoir*. His work has been translated into thirty-seven languages and has appeared in the *New Yorker*, *Paris Review*, and *New York Times*, among many other publications, and on the NPR radio program This American Life, where he is a regular contributor.

BARRY LOPEZ, a winner of the National Book Award, is the author *Arctic Dreams* as well as nine works of fiction and six other works of nonfiction. His stories and essays appear regularly in *Harper's*, the *Paris Review*, *Orion*, and the *Georgia Review*. He is the recipient of an Award in Literature from the American Academy of Arts and Letters, as well as fellowships from the Guggenheim, Lannan, and National Science Foundations. His new book, *Horizon*, will be published by Knopf. He lives in western Oregon.

COLUM McCANN is the internationally bestselling author of the novels *TransAtlantic*, *Let the Great World Spin*, *Zoli*, *Dancer*, *This Side of Brightness*, and *Songdogs*, as well as two critically acclaimed story collections. His fiction has been published in thirty-five languages. He has received many honors, including the National Book Award, the International IMPAC Dublin Literary Award, and a Chevalier d l'Ordre des Arts et des Lettres award from the French government. He teaches in the Hunter College MFA Creative Writing Program and lives in New York City with his wife and their three children. His new book, *The Thirteen Ways of Looking*, was published in October 2015.

DAVID MITCHELL is the award-winning and bestselling author of *The Bone Clocks*, *The Thousand Autumns of Jacob de Zoet*, *Black Swan Green*, *Cloud Atlas*, *Number9Dream*, and *Ghostwritten*. Twice shortlisted for the Man Booker Prize, Mitchell was named one of the hundred most influential people in the world by *Time* in 2007. With his wife, KA Yoshida, Mitchell cotranslated from the Japanese the international bestselling memoir *The Reason I Jump*. His latest novel, *Blade* House, was published in October 2015. He lives in Ireland with his wife and two children.

HONOR MOORE's most recent collection of poems is *Red Shoes* and her most recent book, *The Bishop's Daughter*, a memoir, was shortlisted for the National Book Critics Circle Award and a Los Angeles Times Favorite Book of the Year. She edited *Amy Lowell: Selected Poems* and *Poems from the Women's Movement* for the Library of America and lives in New York City, where she is on the MFA writing faculty at The New School.

HARUKI MURAKAMI was born in Kyoto in 1949 and lives near Tokyo. His work has been translated into more than fifty languages, and the most recent of his many international honors is the Jerusalem Prize, whose previous recipients include J. M. Coetzee, Milan Kundera, and V. S. Naipaul. His debut short novels *Wind* and *Pinball*—nearly thirty years out of print, newly translated, and in one English language volume for the first time—were published by Knopf in August 2015.

MICHAEL SALU is a creative director, artist, and writer. His fiction, nonfiction, and art have appeared in a range of publications, including *The Short Anthology*, *Grey*, *Under the Influence*, granta.com, and *Tales of Two Cities*, published by OR Books. He runs the multidisciplinary creative agency salu.io and is part of the American Suburb X team.

KAMILA SHAMSIE has written six novels, including *Burnt Shadows* (shortlisted for the Orange Prize) and *A God in Every Stone*. In 2013 she was one of Granta's Best of Young British Novelists. She is a Fellow of the Royal Society of Literature and former deputy president of English PEN. She grew up in Karachi, attended university in America, and lives in London.

SONDRA SILVERSTON, a native New Yorker, has been living in Israel since 1970. She has translated works by leading Israel writers, including Amos Oz, Etgar Keret, Eshkol Nevo, and Savyon Liebrecht. Her translation of Amos Oz's *Between Friends* won the 2013 National Jewish Book Award for fiction.

HELEN SIMPSON is the author of five short story collections, including *Getting a Life and In-Flight Entertainment*. She was the first *Sunday Times* Young Writer of the Year and has also received the Hawthornden Prize and the American Academy of Arts and Letters' E. M. Forster Award. Her next short story collection, *Cockfosters*, will be published later this year. She lives in London.

SJÓN is a celebrated Icelandic novelist born in Reykjavik in 1962. He won the Nordic Council's Literary Prize (the equivalent of the Man Booker Prize) for his novel *The Blue Fox*, and the novel *From The Mouth of the Whale* was shortlisted for both the International IMPAC Dublin Literary Award and the Independent Foreign Fiction Prize. His latest novel, *Moonstone—The Boy Who Never Was*, was awarded the 2013 Icelandic Literary Prize. Also a poet, librettist, and lyricist, he has frequently collaborated with his countrywoman Björk, including writing songs for her recent musical project *Biophilia* and contributing to her controversial retrospective at New York's Museum of Modern Art. Sjón is the president of the Icelandic PEN Centre and former chairman of the board of Reykjavík, UNESCO City of Literature. His novels have been translated into thirty languages.

LAURA VAN DEN BERG was raised in Florida. Her first collection of stories, *What the World Will Look Like When All the Water Leaves Us*, was a Barnes & Noble Discover Great New Writers selection and a finalist for the Frank O'Connor International Short Story Award. Her second collection of stories, *The Isle of Youth* (published by FSG Originals in 2013), received the Rosenthal Family Foundation Award for Fiction from the American Academy of Arts and Letters. *Find Me* is her first novel. She lives in the Boston area.

GHASSAN ZAQTAN, a Palestinian living in Ramallah, is one of the most prominent poets writing in Arabic. His poetry and prose have been translated into several languages. A translation of his poetry into English, *Like a Straw Bird It Follows Me*, won the Griffin Poetry Prize in 2013.

About the Editor

JOHN FREEMAN is the author of *How to Read a Novelist* and *The Tyranny of E-mail*. The former president of the National Book Critics Circle, he edited *Granta* until 2013. In 2014, he published *Tales of Two Cities: The Best of Times and Worst of Times in Today's New York*, an anthology about income inequality in benefit for Housing Works. His essays and poetry have appeared in the *New Yorker*, the *Paris Review*, and the *New York Times*. He lives in New York City and teaches writing at The New School University.